The
Pacific
Princesses

PRINCESS VICTORIA

HARLAN
HINEY

The Pacific Princesses

AN ILLUSTRATED HISTORY OF
CANADIAN PACIFIC RAILWAY'S
PRINCESS FLEET ON THE
NORTHWEST COAST
BY ROBERT D. TURNER

SONO NIS PRESS
Victoria, British Columbia

1977

Canadian Cataloguing in Publication Data

Turner, Robert D., 1947-
    The Pacific Princesses

    Includes bibliography and index.
    ISBN 0-919462-04-9

    1. Coastwise shipping — British Columbia —
History. 2. Steamboat lines — British
Columbia — History. 3. British Columbia
Coast Service. I. Title.
    HE770.T87   387.5'24'09711   C77-002010-0

Published by
SONO NIS PRESS
1745 Blanshard Street, Victoria, B.C., Canada

JACKET ILLUSTRATION AND FRONTISPIECE: The *Princess Victoria* is
depicted in 1908 crossing the Strait of Juan de Fuca with a backdrop of
the Olympic Mountains. The painting is by artist Harlan Hiney.

Designed and printed in Canada by
MORRISS PRINTING COMPANY LTD.
Victoria, British Columbia

TO MY MOTHER AND
THE MEMORY OF MY FATHER

PREFACE

THE NORTHWEST COAST of North America from Puget Sound in Washington to the Lynn Canal in Alaska, including all of coastal British Columbia, was home to the ships of the Canadian Pacific Railway's Princess fleet. For over one hundred years, the Princesses and their predecessors provided the communication links, the routes to market and often the only means of travel along the rugged, glacier-carved Pacific coast.

In the south are the sheltered waters of Puget Sound and the Strait of Georgia, protected from the Pacific Ocean by the Olympic Peninsula and Vancouver Island. Here, the climate is mild, almost Mediterranean, with dry, hot summers and relatively warm, wet winters. The surrounding islands and coastal lands are rolling and forested, flanked by mountains a few miles inland. Oak, arbutus and Douglas fir characterize the drier exposed areas where rainfall averages about 30 inches a year.

On the west coast of Vancouver Island and farther up the coast, from Quadra Island at the northern end of the Strait of Georgia, all the way to Skagway on the Lynn Canal, the land is more rugged and the water more exposed to winter storms. This portion of the coast is distinguished by many deep, narrow fjords surrounded by the high, glaciated mountains of the Coast Range. The forests of the lower windward slopes are dominated by Sitka spruce, hemlock and cedar, which thrive in the 200 inches of rain that may fall annually.

Even in winter the seas can be calm, but the frequent unpredictable storms and squalls can quickly turn the most tranquil inlets into foaming, windswept deathtraps for ships. Fog is common along all of the coastline, obscuring the land and making navigation hazardous. The fate of many ships has been determined by the thick, impenetrable mists that will close in on the coast for days without warning.

In summer the north coast presents a different picture. The weather is warm and more moderate, with clear skies and cooling winds off the ocean. The spectacular mountains and fjords then become an attraction for tourists and cruise ships.

All along this coast, isolated communities developed as white settlers came in search of furs, gold, fish and timber. Such settlements as Victoria, Vancouver, Seattle and Prince Rupert, grew and became the cities of today. Others languished and were forgotten, and some continued as remote outposts. Before the widespread use of the aircraft and the proliferation of highways the isolated coastal settlements were totally dependent on the steamer for food and mail and for transporting their products to the outside world. The steamers became, along with the railroads, the key links of business, family travel and tourism. Virtually everyone living on the coast, at least until the late 1940's, depended in some way on the steamships, and often those ships carried the name "Princess."

The Princess fleet traced its ancestry to the ships of the Hudson's Bay Company and the sternwheelers of the Fraser River gold rush of the late 1850's. As British Columbia developed, the steamers became more sophisticated and the shipping lines more permanent. In 1883, the Canadian Pacific Navigation Company was formed and more modern steel-hulled vessels were acquired. In 1901, this company was taken over by the Canadian Pacific Railway, and many fast inter-city and coastal liners were added. These were the fine Princesses that were to establish a reputation for speed, service and elegance matched by few other steamship fleets.

While the Princesses ruled the Coast the latest technologies were used in their designs. The early steamers, with single or perhaps double expansion (compound) engines, were replaced with more modern vessels having triple or even quadruple expansion engines, which made use of steam three or four times for improved power and efficiency. The later fast ships used turbines and eventually turbo-electric drives, where steam turbines drove generators to power motors, producing high speed, efficient operation. As early as 1923, a diesel-powered ferry was built and belatedly, after the mid-1950's, diesel electric propulsion systems were used in new additions to the fleet.

The Princess fleet was at its peak of development and service about 1930, but thereafter fell victim to changing economics, patterns of living and transportation requirements. By the 1950's, the fleet was in decline, bypassed and left behind by a society that was too fast-moving for the relatively leisurely pace of the 1920's on which the CPR's Coast Service was based.

The passing of the rakish, elegant Princesses was inevitable, when society found it could no longer afford the time to enjoy the luxury of their presence. Those who remember the Princesses or other steamships of their era have every right to look back on them with affection and admiration, for they represented many of the best and most striking attributes of a way of life that was ours. Yet, society as it is known today on the Pacific coast could not have evolved if the Princesses of past years still dominated the Coast.

ROBERT D. TURNER
Victoria, British Columbia
December 1975

ACKNOWLEDGEMENTS

MANY INDIVIDUALS have graciously contributed their time and effort to this book and it is with real pleasure that their help is acknowledged. I would like to thank the following for their assistance in providing photographs, documents, advice and criticism: Harry Atterton, the late Bob Brown, Colin Browne, Ron D'Altroy, F. L. Chappell, Elvid Davies, Captain Brian Donnelly, Tom Goodlake, Ed Lewis, Mark Horne, Richard Horne, John Newman, Leonard McCann, Ed MacPherson, Basil Richards, the late Ted Robson, Jack Shave, Gerry Wellburn and Joe D. Williamson. In addition, the following companies and public institutions have been most helpful: British Columbia Legislative Library, British Columbia Provincial Archives, British Columbia Provincial Museum (Modern History Division), British Columbia Department of Travel Industry (Photographic Branch), Canadian Forces Photo Unit, Ottawa, CP Rail (Public Relations and Advertising), Leonard Frank Photos, Maritime Museum of British Columbia, National Film Board, Seattle Historical Society, Suzzallo Library, University of Washington, University of British Columbia Library, University of Victoria Library, Vancouver Maritime Museum, and the Vancouver Public Library (Historic Photo Section). Their staffs were always co-operative, helpful and encouraging.

A special word of thanks is due Harlan Hiney, who painstakingly produced the beautiful painting of the *Princess Victoria* which is reproduced on the cover and as the frontispiece for this book. Better than any artist I know, he is able to bring to life long vanished scenes from the Age of Steam.

I am also deeply indebted to David Parker, Maritime History Curator at the British Columbia Provincial Museum for the many evenings and weekends he spent critically reviewing the manuscript.

My wife Nancy took many hours from her own research to type the manuscript and provided continued enthusiasm, support and advice throughout the years this book has been in preparation. Bill Turner, my brother, was always a willing listener to ideas about this project and gave most helpful advice.

Finally, my sincere thanks to Dick Morriss of Morriss Printing Company Ltd. for taking on this project and for transforming my collection of illustrations and text into book form. The staff of Morriss Printing was enthusiastic and co-operative. Their efforts are sincerely appreciated and made the completion of this book very enjoyable.

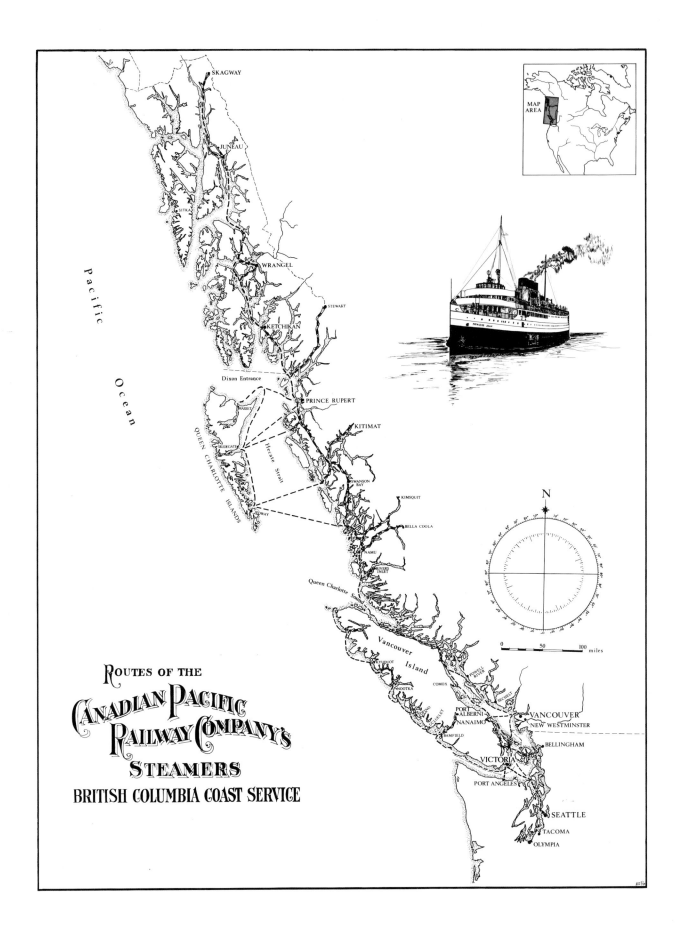

SKAGWAY

JUNEAU

SITKA

WRANGEL

STEWART

KETCHIKAN

Pacific

Ocean

Dixon Entrance

PRINCE RUPERT

MASSET

KITIMAT

SKIDEGATE

QUEEN CHARLOTTE ISLANDS

Hecate Strait

SWANSON BAY

KIMSQUIT

JEDWAY

BELLA COOLA

NAMU

RIVERS INLET

Queen Charlotte Sound

N

Vancouver Island

KYUQUOT

POWELL RIVER

COMOX

SECHELT

NOOTKA

TOFINO

UCLUELET

PORT ALBERNI

VANCOUVER

NEW WESTMINSTER

NANAIMO

BAMFIELD

BELLINGHAM

VICTORIA

PORT ANGELES

SEATTLE

TACOMA

OLYMPIA

MAP AREA

0   50   100 miles

ROUTES OF THE

CANADIAN PACIFIC RAILWAY COMPANY'S STEAMERS

BRITISH COLUMBIA COAST SERVICE

CONTENTS

LIST OF M APS

David Murdoch's hand carved relief map of the British Columbia coast and adjacent parts of Washington and Alaska vividly illustrates the rugged nature of the country served by the CPR's Pacific Princesses. — ROBERT D. TURNER

Wrangell, an isolated community on the Alaska Panhandle, was
typical of the many coastal settlements for which the steamship
became the only means of communication with the rest of the
world. In this tranquil scene from the 1890's, the Canadian Pacific
Navigation Company's *Islander* is tied up at the town's wharf
exchanging cargo and passengers before resuming its journey
along the rugged and frequently stormy coast.
— SUZZALLO LIBRARY, UNIVERSITY OF WASHINGTON

The *Otter* was the second steam powered vessel to
operate along the coast of British Columbia and
Washington. She is shown here loading cargo at
Victoria probably about 1880.
— PROVINCIAL ARCHIVES

CHAPTER I

THE EARLY YEARS
AND THE
CANADIAN PACIFIC
NAVIGATION COMPANY

*Early Transportation
on the Northwest Coast*

THE NORTHWEST COAST of North America was in the 1840's and 1850's an isolated, remote part of the world. The first white settlements developing at that time around Puget Sound, on southern Vancouver Island, and along the Fraser River were outposts in a rugged land, still largely unexplored. Communications and transport between these communities, when they existed at all, were sporadic and dangerous. Often, the only means of travel was to charter a native dug-out canoe for passage along the coast.

Gradually, as the trading economies of the settlements expanded and some local farming and milling developed, improvements were made in transportation. The Hudson's Bay Company, whose forts at Victoria and Langley were the main centres of settlement in the British territories on the Coast, had operated the pioneer sidewheeled steamer *Beaver* since 1836. This vessel was used by the HBC as a mobile trading post and as a means of transporting furs, merchandise, passengers and mail between Fort Simpson on Chatham Sound, Fort Victoria on southern Vancouver Island, and Fort Nisqually on Puget Sound. The *Beaver* was the first steam-powered ship on the north Pacific coast. She demonstrated the necessity of steam propulsion if vessels were to be operated safely and efficiently in the confined waters of the Northwest Coast.

The *Beaver* was followed by the screw-driven steamer *Otter*, which reached the coast in 1853. Particularly before the arrival of the *Otter* and even with two steamers in operation, many small ports of call could not be served adequately, even on the south coastal waters of Georgia Strait and Puget Sound.

While the Hudson's Bay Company could operate its steamers economically in conjunction with its trading enterprises, would-be private ventures based solely on transporting people and merchandise between the scattered settlements were faced with a frustrating situation. Despite the growth of population occurring in the region, the number of people was insufficient for many years to support a large seaworthy steamer over the long distances separating the communities. To begin an operation,

The Otter *was* . . .

1

an investor in the early days could justify the purchase of only a small vessel which would be cheap to operate, even if safety and reliability were sacrificed.

In the mid-1850's an American named John J. Scranton brought a small steamer, the *Major Tompkins*, to Puget Sound to operate between Olympia, Port Townsend, Bellingham Bay and Victoria. Unfortunately, the *Major Tompkins'* life was short for the little steamer was wrecked on Macaulay Point just outside of Victoria Harbour in February 1855. Other small steamers appeared on the scene during the decade, but it was a long time before a really reliable service was established between either the Fraser River or Puget Sound and Vancouver Island.

In April 1857, Scranton was granted a mail contract for the routes on Puget Sound and to Vancouver Island and, as a result, he acquired the 530 ton steamer *Constitution*, which after considerable difficulty and hardship he succeeded in bringing up the coast from San Francisco. By the fall of the same year, the *Constitution* was making weekly calls at most of the settlements on Puget Sound and twice each month crossed the Strait of Juan de Fuca to pick up mail and passengers from Vancouver Island at Victoria. It took the steamer 14 hours on a normal run to make the one way passage from Olympia to Victoria. Even this operation was sporadic and rather unreliable, and it also turned out to be unprofitable. The vessel was sold to satisfy creditors less than a year later. However, she remained in service with her new owners long enough for news of the discovery of gold on the Fraser River to create a sensation all along the Pacific coast and result in an instant boom in the steamboat business, which secured the short term future of virtually any vessel north of San Francisco that could float.

The Fraser River gold rush changed Victoria and Fort Langley almost overnight. From the small trading outposts of the Hudson's Bay Company, they were transformed into centres of the gold rush — takeoff points for the Interior and the gravel bars of the Fraser. Victoria became a bustling city as a shack and tent town mushroomed around the stockade on the harbour. The most immediate problem was to provide adequate steamer service from Victoria to the Fraser and within the space of just a few months vessels were being sailed north from the Columbia while others were being built in Victoria to capture the lucrative trade awaiting whoever could begin operations first.

By the summer of 1858, the sternwheelers *Umatilla* and *Enterprise*, both built for operation on the Columbia, were transporting eager miners and their supplies up the Fraser and making tremendous profits. The season was short, however, and by late fall most of the miners had returned to Victoria or the United States to wait out the winter, as the weather conditions made further placer mining impossible. Of 25,000 miners who came to the goldfields in 1858 only about 3,000 stayed through the winter, but the following spring the rush was resumed.

A veteran of rate wars, storms, gold rushes and steamboat races, the *Eliza Anderson* served the Pacific coast for half a century.
— PROVINCIAL ARCHIVES

One of the steamboat operators who came north for the rush of 1859 was Captain William Irving, a Columbia River veteran who, as the owner of the Victoria Steam Navigation Company, quickly put the sternwheelers *Colonel Moody, Maria* and *Governor Douglas* into service. Irving's strongest competitor was Captain William Moore with his steamer *Henrietta.* Competition was fierce and rates fluctuated widely, from ridiculously low when the operators were out to get the last passenger away from each other to exorbitantly high when one company succeeded in obtaining a short-lived monopoly by driving the competition from the route.

The gold boom continued into the mid-1860's; the miners had, by that time reached the Cariboo and its fabled creeks. As gold drew the miners further inland, steamboats continued to play a critical role in transporting men and materials from the coast to the head of navigation on the Fraser River at Yale. From that point, everything had to be carried overland along a rough narrow trail known as the Cariboo Wagon Road, which wound its way through the Fraser Canyon to Ashcroft and beyond.

As well as opening up the interior of British Columbia, the gold rush, with its booming economy and dramatic increase in population, also led to significant changes in government for the Colony of Vancouver Island and the British territories on the mainland. In 1858 the mainland became the Crown Colony of British Columbia, and Vancouver Island, over which the Hudson's Bay Company had been given discretionary powers, reverted to the Crown. By 1866, however, the prosperity of the gold rush collapsed and financial difficulties became very real, contributing to the union of the two colonies.

The collapse of the gold rush left many steamers without cargo and a number were laid up or even dismantled. Irving, however, remained optimistic and had a fine new ship, the *Onward,* built in 1865, but as the 1860's drew to a close he found it was necessary to reach an agreement with his closest competitor, Captain Moore, to operate on alternate years until the economic situation improved.

Steamer operations between Vancouver Island, New Westminster (by that time Victoria's rival city in the new Colony), and the communities on the Fraser River continued throughout the lean years. By this time a more reliable service had also been established between Vancouver Island and ports on Puget Sound by the sidewheel steamer *Eliza Anderson,* a vessel to become somewhat of a legend in her own right. The *Eliza Anderson* was also involved in the Fraser River gold rush, but by late 1859 she had been placed on a schedule providing a once weekly sailing from Olympia to Victoria and then to New Westminster and return. The little steamer established the first really dependable service on this route and defied all competition through winter storms and rate wars for nearly a decade.

In 1871, British Columbia became the sixth province in the Dominion of Canada and in the process received the Canadian government's promise of a railroad link with the east. Such a

A veteran of rate wars . . .

massive construction project as this meant nothing but prosperity for the river steamers, since the problems of supply for the construction camps would be critical. However, many political battles had to be fought before work on the long awaited railroad began. On August 28, 1872 the veteran steamer operator Captain William Irving died at New Westminster and was succeeded by his son, John. Although only 18, the young Irving was not inexperienced in shipping and steamboat operations. He proved fully capable of taking over and expanding his father's business and began a career that would see him placed on an equal footing with his illustrious father as one of the province's outstanding transportation pioneers.

John Irving continued to operate vessels on the Fraser River, and in 1874 he had the sternwheeler *Glenora* built for service on the Stikine River, where a short lived gold rush was beginning. Like his father, Irving negotiated an agreement with his competition, and was soon sharing the profits of the Stikine run in exchange for withdrawing his vessel and returning to the Fraser.

The unpredictable nature of rates for passage on the Fraser continued as more rate wars developed and passed, but by 1878, it appeared as though work would finally begin on the new transcontinental railroad, to be known as the Canadian Pacific Railway. After much deliberation, it was decided that the railroad would be built through the Fraser Canyon to Port Moody on Burrard Inlet, east of the present site of Vancouver. However, the actual commencement of construction was still a few years away and in the meantime, Irving was involved in competitive struggles on the Victoria to New Westminster route and also on the Fraser River.

In order to gain control of the lucrative Victoria to New Westminster run, Irving purchased the old sidewheeler *Wilson G. Hunt* and placed her in opposition to the Hudson's Bay Company's steamer *Enterprise* and other vessels that plied the route. The Hudson's Bay Company soon recognized the necessity of placing a large, fast ship on the run to compete effectively with the *Wilson G. Hunt* and purchased the sidewheeler *Olympia* from her owner George S. Wright for $75,000. The 180 foot *Olympia* was a handsome vessel of 932 tons. She was powered by a large, single cylinder walking beam engine with a bore of 46 inches and a stroke of 132 inches. Overall, she reflected the broad beam and profile typical of the sidewheel paddle steamers of the era.

By 1878, the *Olympia* had already operated all along the Pacific coast from California to Puget Sound to Alaska and had been involved in a number of rate wars on the Victoria to Olympia run. She was brought to Puget Sound in late 1869 by Captains Duncan Finch and George Wright, who had operated the steamer *Eliza Anderson* very successfully on the same run. Opposition to the *Olympia* came in 1870 when two brothers from Portland, Edwin A. and Louis M. Starr, provided financial backing to Captain J. T. Nash, who had previously underbid Finch and Wright on the Puget Sound

The sidewheeler *Wilson G. Hunt* was brought to the British Columbia coast from California during the Fraser River gold rush. She eventually became part of the Canadian Pacific Navigation Company's fleet but was sold in the mid-1880's. — PROVINCIAL ARCHIVES

The *Princess Louise*, formerly *Olympia*, operated along the Pacific coast from San Francisco to Skagway. She was the first of the Princess ships. This view shows her docked at Comox about 1890 with the Beaufort Mountains of Vancouver Island in the background. — PROVINCIAL ARCHIVES

The sidewheeler Wilson G. Hunt . . .
The Princess Louise . . .

mail contracts. The Starrs arranged to eliminate competition by paying Finch and Wright $1,400 a month to keep their steamer off the run. However, they hoped to eliminate this costly business expense by ordering a new steamer which, they felt, would give them decisive control of the Puget Sound routes.

This vessel was the *North Pacific*, built by Gates and Collyer in San Francisco. The speedy sidewheeler arrived in Puget Sound in late June 1871 and was in every way comparable to the *Olympia*. Thus, the setting was perfect for one of the most heated races and rate wars of the period. Rates dropped to 25 cents per person on the Puget Sound route. However, the contest would not be finally resolved until the two splendid sidewheelers *North Pacific* and *Olympia* were matched in a race.

The race took place on June 27, 1871 and had been eagerly anticipated all around Puget Sound and southern Vancouver Island. It was reported that Captain Finch even went so far as to sort the *Olympia*'s coal to insure the most efficient operation of his ship's engines. Victorians generally favoured the *Olympia* while their neighbours in Port Townsend, Seattle, and Olympia backed the *North Pacific*. The course of the race was from the mouth of Victoria's harbour to Point Wilson, 36 miles across the Strait of Juan de Fuca. As the steamers were very closely matched, at first neither vessel seemed to gain an advantage, but gradually, the *North Pacific* pulled ahead and by the time she reached Port Townsend, she had outdistanced her rival by about four miles.

By winning the race, the Starrs captured the Victoria to Olympia run, but the race was really more of a symbolic victory than a lasting one, and the opposition was far from crushed. The *Olympia* was still a highly competitive ship and if Finch and Wright continued to operate her both companies would suffer financially. The Starrs felt, therefore, that it would be better to reinstate the subsidy than risk another rate war which they might just possibly lose. In consequence, in July the *Olympia* was once again earning money for her owners by not running. She was withdrawn from the route in accordance with the agreement and was ultimately sold for operations in California. She eventually returned north to Victoria after an absence of seven years, which had netted nearly $50,000 in subsidies, and was acquired by the Hudson's Bay Company. The Starrs eventually sold their interests to the Oregon Railway and Navigation Company, which dominated the intercity services on Puget Sound into the 1890's.

The Hudson's Bay Company renamed the *Olympia* the *Princess Louise* after giving appropriate notice and also changed the ship's port of registry to London. Competition between the *Princess Louise* and the *Wilson G. Hunt* forced fares down, and many people took advantage of the situation to travel between the mainland and Vancouver Island at bargain prices. In August 1879, the *Princess Louise* took time out from the struggle to take a party of excursionists on a cruise

The sternwheeler *Western Slope*, shown here at Yale, was run by Captain William Moore in competition with John Irving's steamers. Eventually, however, Irving bought the vessel and added it to his fleet. Note that she is rigged with sails on the forward mast. — PROVINCIAL ARCHIVES

The *R. P. Rithet* was a classic sternwheeler of the late 1800's. These flat-bottomed, shallow draft vessels were ill suited to operation in open waters but nevertheless many regularly steamed across the Strait of Georgia, Puget Sound and the Strait of Juan de Fuca. The *R. P. Rithet* was one of the most luxurious sternwheelers ever to operate on the lower Fraser, she boasted electric lights, richly upholstered seats in the saloons, and comfortable staterooms. — PROVINCIAL ARCHIVES

The sternwheeler Western Slope . . .
The R. P. Rithet *was* . . .

around Vancouver Island; probably the first such cruise offered. It proved a great success and provided the party with many opportunities for sightseeing in the remote, seldom visited settlements and Indian villages around the Island. Such cruises would be repeated in later years by other ships that, like the *Louise*, would be named *Princess*. The *Princess Louise* also made several sailings to Alaska, being relieved on the Victoria to New Westminster route by the sidewheeler *Enterprise*.

The competition between Irving and the Hudson's Bay Company was finally resolved in 1880 when they agreed to co-operate on the route and develop a healthy monopoly that would be in their mutual interest. As a result, the HBC operated the *Princess Louise* to New Westminster from Victoria and maintained the mail contract for the route. Irving provided a connecting service with one of his river steamers from New Westminster to Yale in what became known as the " 'arf and 'arf" arrangement.

The Victoria *Daily Colonist* could not understand why such a transfer of freight and passengers was necessary. It noted that, "she [the *Princess Louise*] is well adapted to river service during the three months of high water," and concluded that why the vessel terminated her voyage at New Westminster was "an inexplicable mystery." A little more thought might have suggested that the reason was prudent navigation, since side-wheelers were not well suited for the rapidly changing water conditions and shallows of rivers like the Fraser. Moreover, the *Princess Louise* was a large enough vessel to require wharves and proper docking facilities that were unavailable upstream from New Westminster.

While Irving was still involved in the competitive struggle with the Hudson's Bay Company, he lost his sternwheeler *Glenora*. She struck a rock above the Harrison River on the Fraser and was a total wreck. However, a far greater loss occurred two years later in 1881 when his brand new stern-wheeler, the $50,000 *Elizabeth Irving* caught fire at Hope on her second voyage up the Fraser and could not be saved. The beautiful vessel, reputed to be the finest on the river, was uninsured. Irving had had her built to better equip his Pioneer Line, as he called his steamer operation, for the boom in traffic that was starting in the early 1880's as construction commenced on the Canadian Pacific Railway. In the same year the *Elizabeth Irving* was lost, he sold the *Wilson G. Hunt* to Joseph Spratt of Victoria, who placed the old steamer in operation along the east coast of Vancouver Island.

By the time work began in earnest on the CPR, Irving had three steamers to handle the traffic. These were the *Reliance*, the *Royal City* and his newest vessel, the *William Irving*, built at Moodyville in 1880. This fleet was running in competition with Captain William Moore's steamers *Gertrude* and *Western Slope*. By 1883, however, Moore was in financial difficulties and Irving was able to acquire these vessels at auction. By that time Irving had also replaced the wrecked *Elizabeth Irving* with the fine steamer *R. P. Rithet*, built in Victoria in 1882.

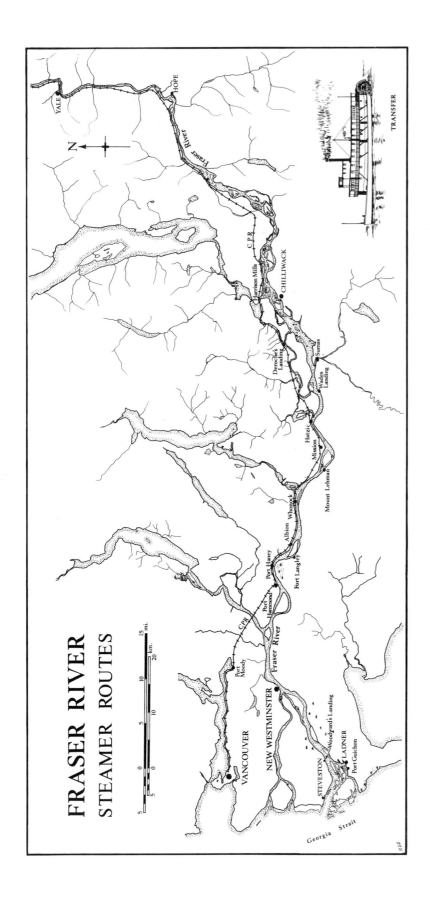

FRASER RIVER
STEAMER ROUTES

N

Georgia Strait

VANCOUVER

NEW WESTMINSTER

Port Moody

CPR

Fraser River

Port Hammond

Port Haney

Albion

Whonnock

Port Langley

STEVESTON

Woodyard's Landing

LADNER

Port Guichon

Mount Lehman

Mission

Hatzic

Dewdney

Deroche's Landing

Wades Landing

Sumas

CHILLIWACK

Harrison Mills

CPR

Fraser River

Fraser River

HOPE

YALE

5   0   5   10   15 mi.

5   0   5   10   20 km.

TRANSFER

8

Yale was the head of steamer navigation on the Fraser River and became an important stop on the route to the Cariboo during the gold rush of the 1860's. John Irving's plush sternwheeler *William Irving* is shown above at the landing ready to unload her cargo.
— PROVINCIAL ARCHIVES

Captain John Irving...
Irving's commercial...

Captain John Irving followed in the footsteps of his father in becoming a riverboat operator. He formed the Canadian Pacific Navigation Company in 1883 and went on to manage it until the turn of the century. — PROVINCIAL ARCHIVES

Irving's commercial ventures paid off well and he built this stately residence in Victoria.
— PROVINCIAL ARCHIVES

*The Canadian Pacific
Navigation Company*

— GERALD E. WELLBURN COLLECTION

John Irving knew that the construction boom that lasted throughout the early 1880's would pass with the completion of the Canadian Pacific Railway and that his sternwheelers would have to make way for the more competitive transportation system they helped to build. Recognizing that steamer services would still be vital between Vancouver Island and the terminus of the railway, and also to small communities along the Fraser, he moved to secure his future position and prospects.

Early in 1883, he dissolved his Pioneer Line and joined his fleet of sternwheelers with the steamers operated by the Hudson's Bay Company, his old adversary turned partner, to form the Canadian Pacific Navigation Company. The Company was capitalized at $500,000 secured in 5,000 shares. The founders of the enterprise included: John Irving, who became director; R. P. Rithet, one of Victoria's leading merchants; William Spring, a trader; P. McQuade, the famous ship chandler from Victoria; M. W. T. Drake, a lawyer; and William Charles and Alexander Munroe of the Hudson's Bay Company. The new steamship line, which began operations in March 1883, had an impressive fleet of vessels at its disposal. There were the sternwheelers *R. P. Rithet*, *William Irving*, *Gertrude*, *Reliance*, and *Western Slope*, the sidewheelers *Enterprise*, *Princess Louise* and *Maude*, and the old Hudson's Bay screw steamer *Otter*. Of these vessels, the *Maude* was acquired from Joseph Spratt, along with the old *Wilson G. Hunt*, which was no longer considered suitable for operation.

With these vessels as a beginning, Irving set out to improve the new Company's fleet by adding new ships better suited to operation in the straits and unprotected waters between Victoria and New Westminster as well as along the coasts of Vancouver Island. His first acquisition was the magnificent sidewheeler *Yosemite*, purchased in 1883 from the Central Pacific Railroad Company, which had operated her on the Sacramento River between San Francisco and the state capital of Sacramento. The *Yosemite* was a beautiful ship, with broad spacious decks and ample cabin, dining and lounge space. She was also powerful and fast, although somewhat unstable in exposed water during rough weather. The *Yosemite* brought with her to the Northwest a reputation for misfortune, resulting from a tragic boiler explosion. While in service on the Sacramento her starboard boiler ruptured and the consequent explosion destroyed the forward half of her superstructure and killed 55 people. Like so many other river steamers, the *Yosemite* was rebuilt, reboilered and returned to service. Fortunately, while in CPN service she suffered no serious accidents and more than returned the Company's investment in her.

That same year, the *Princess Louise* was withdrawn from service and fitted with new boilers fabricated at the Albion Iron Works in Victoria. She was given a thorough overhaul and returned to service before the new year. However, all was not quite "clear sailing" for the new steamship company, as the following rather pointed notice in the *Daily Colonist* of December 5, 1883 indicates:

Take notice, that the Canadian Pacific Navigation Co. having advertised the old steamer *Enterprise* to run on the East Coast route from and after Friday next, I hereby inform freighters and travellers that I have no connection, directly or indirectly, with the said company or the said old steamer *Enterprise*, and I hereby inform the residents of Victoria and the East Coast that the aim of the Canadian Pacific Navigation Co. is to create a monopoly of the carrying traffic on the East Coast of the Island — the same as now exists, to the public sorrow and indignation, on the Fraser and between Victoria and the Mainland, by which the rates of freight within the last twelve months have been nearly doubled by the Canadian Pacific Navigation Co. at the cost of the public. And I hereby caution the public not to contract for passage or freight with the said C.P.N. Co. as I am now completing arrangements for NEW BOATS to run on the Fraser as well as on the East Coast, by which passengers and freight will be carried at the reasonable rates which prevailed before the Canadian Pacific Navigation Co.'s Grab. The said steamers will be managed by obliging and civil officers.

Opposition to the CPN crystallized in 1884 with the formation on May 1st of the People's Steam Navigation Company. Backed by businessmen from Victoria, Nanaimo, and Chemainus, the Company began operations with a capital stock of $100,000. Its first major acquisition was the sidewheel steamer *Amelia*, which had been built in San Francisco for use on the Sacramento River. The vessel was brough north and after duty was paid to the customs collectors in Victoria, was placed in Canadian registry. The necessary formality of crossing the international boundary cost the owners 10 per cent of the value of the hull and a further 25 per cent on the value of the ship's machinery.

Soon after, the *Amelia* was placed on the Victoria to Nanaimo run in opposition to the CPN's *R. P. Rithet*, and predictably the fares on both vessels plummeted to 25 cents per person return. This rate war continued off and on until July 1, 1885, when the two companies agreed that the CPN would withdraw from the route in consideration of 25 per cent of the gross receipts of the *Amelia*. However, the Victoria to Nanaimo route was doomed to a short life since that same summer work had begun on the Esquimalt and Nanaimo Railway. When completed in September 1886, it made the steamboat runs increasingly uneconomical. Consequently, in July 1889, the *Amelia* was sold at auction and the following year was acquired by the CPN, in a turn of events that must have been frustrating to her original operators.

On July 28, 1885, the CPN suffered its first loss when the *Enterprise* was rammed by the *R. P. Rithet* off Ten Mile Point near Victoria. The impact of the collision was so great that the bow of the *Rithet* penetrated nearly to the wheelhouse of the *Enterprise*. Fires broke out and the combined damages were so severe that the vessel was not worth rebuilding. The hulk was towed to Cadboro Bay, stripped, and abandoned.

EAST COAST ROUTE
Caution to the Travelling Public

JOSEPH SPRATT,
Owner of H.M. Mail Steamers on the East Coast.

As canning technology advanced, the salmon fisheries of the Pacific coast developed into a vital industry. Isolated canneries like this one sprang up all along the coast. Steamers like the *Princess Louise* were their only links to the outside world.
— PROVINCIAL ARCHIVES

As canning technology . . .

PRINCESS
LOUISE

The Yosemite *was* ...
The Maude *served* ...

The utilitarian Sardonyx ...

New Ships: the Premier and the Islander

By the late 1880's, the demands of shipping on the Pacific coast were changing and the wooden-hulled sidewheelers and sternwheelers were losing their place to more modern iron and steel-hulled screwdriven steamers. Recognizing this trend and also the possibility of expanding CPN's operations into Puget Sound, Irving set out to enlarge his fleet.

With the completion of the Canadian Pacific Railway to its final western terminus a few miles west of Port Moody at Hasting's Mill, the lumbering community that was to become the city of Vancouver, trade had increased between the mainland, Victoria, and Puget Sound ports. The prospects looked so good that Irving felt justified in purchasing a steamer to operate between Vancouver and Portland as a feeder service for the CPR and in ordering a second vessel to sail from Vancouver to Victoria and Puget Sound. The first vessel was the S.S. *Sardonyx*, a steel-hulled 18-year-old freighter that had been operated by various owners on the Coast since the early 1880's. The *Sardonyx* was a utilitarian vessel, with few of the refinements that Irving hoped to include in the new vessels he planned for his fleet. In contrast to the *Sardonyx*, the new steamer which he ordered from the Union Iron Works in San Francisco featured the most modern fittings and machinery available.

The new iron-hulled 200 foot vessel was christened the *Premier*. She incorporated all of the latest improvements in coastal steamer accommodations, including comfortable staterooms with large berths and even a few with double beds, a spacious, well appointed dining room, saloons, and observation rooms, and, significantly, the still novel convenience of electric lighting. Heavy-duty triple expansion engines and a single 11 foot propeller gave the ship a speed of about 15 knots as well as an economy of operation that the older sidewheelers could not match.

The *Premier* arrived in Victoria on October 5, 1887 under the command of Captain W. H. Ferguson and was prepared for service. United States registry was retained to avoid having to pay customs duty and to allow the ship greater freedom to operate in American waters. Ten days after arriving in Victoria, and before beginning regular service to Port Townsend and Seattle, the *Premier* sailed on her inaugural excursion. Under the auspices of the St. Andrew's and Caledonian Society, 300 citizens of Victoria participated in a day-long trip to Port Townsend, across the Strait of Juan de Fuca.

As the excursionists from Victoria began to tire of sightseeing in Port Townsend, it was suggested that a tug-of-war be organized. There were plenty of visitors on hand to man Victoria's end of the rope and in short order, following a quick round of the local saloons and docks, enough local citizens were collected to provide the opposition. All apparently being fair in a tug-of-war, the Port Townsend men tied their end of the rope to an express wagon and gave the horse a nudge on the rump. However, their scheme was soon uncovered and another round began. This time, the Victorians, not to be outdone,

The *Yosemite* was the largest sidewheeler in the CPN fleet. She was bought by John Irving from the Central Pacific Railroad in 1883 and served with the fleet until 1906. In the scene above, she is berthed at the Company's Wharf Street dock in Victoria. — PROVINCIAL ARCHIVES

The *Maude* served many of the coastal settlements on Vancouver Island during her long career. She is shown here at Nanaimo when she operated as a sidewheeler. The CPN rebuilt her as a screw-driven steamer in 1885. — PROVINCIAL ARCHIVES

The utilitarian *Sardonyx* was acquired for the Portland, Oregon - Victoria - Vancouver route but also served along the north coast where she was lost on a reef in 1890. — CPR COLLECTION

secured their end to a water main, much to the chagrin of their opponents. Finally, a fair contest was fought to a conclusion and the Port Townsend team won convincingly.

The community picnic, and the railway or steamer excursion such as the one of the *Premier* to Port Townsend, was very much a part of life on the West Coast well into the twentieth century. Most people were entirely dependent on public transport and, aside from such outings, had little opportunity for travel even to the nearby countryside. Distances of a few miles had to be covered on foot or by wagon over poor, bumpy roads which were often impassable in bad weather. It is not surprising that the transportation companies had little difficulty in attracting sell-out excursion crowds.

While the *Premier* was still under construction in San Francisco, the CPN proceeded with the purchase of yet another new, even larger and more elegant steamship. This vessel was intended for the Victoria-Vancouver run which after the completion of the CPR had overshadowed the Victoria-New Westminster route in importance. Vancouver, because it was the terminus of the Canadian Pacific Railway, was witnessing a fantastic boom period that would see it rapidly develop into the largest city in western Canada.

The new steamer, named the *Islander*, was built in Glasgow by the firm of Napier, Shanks & Bell at a cost of $200,000. She had a displacement of nearly 1,500 tons, was 240 feet long and had a beam of 42 feet. Powered by triple expansion engines and twin screws, the steel-hulled vessel was capable of about 15 knots. Her interior fittings were magnificent and made her the finest vessel on the Coast when she arrived in Victoria from the builders on December 9, 1888.

On December 30, 1888, the *Islander* made her first trip between Victoria and Vancouver under Captain Rudlin, her new commanding officer. Also on board for the special trip were Captains Irving and Robertson, the latter having brought the vessel to the Pacific coast from Glasgow. Irving had offered a reduced fare for the inaugural trip and as a result, the vessel was packed with several hundred passengers. The *Islander* demonstrated a capacity for speed, soon overtaking and passing the American sidewheeler *T. J. Porter*, a vessel which was itself known for speed and later the *Princess Louise*. Irving's new steamer arrived in Vancouver four hours and forty-five minutes after leaving Victoria. The passengers were allowed to spend the afternoon in Vancouver before the scheduled return sailing to Victoria at 3:35 p.m.

While Vancouver was booming, it was still only British Columbia's second city, trailing behind Victoria in size, influence, and attractiveness. The rivalry between the cities was intense. It appears that this state of affairs gave Vancouver's Mayor McLean an inferiority complex, for he went to considerable lengths to disuade people for going on to Victoria once they had arrived in his city. In mid-October 1887 he went a bit too far, at least in the opinion of John Irving. During an address to an excursion party of 350 from Winnipeg, the

The drydock at Esquimalt was an important defence installation for the Royal Navy during the late 1800's, but also served commercial shipping. In the foreground is the steamer *Cariboo and Fly* while behind her is the CPN's much more modern *Premier*. — PROVINCIAL ARCHIVES

The CPN's beautiful *Islander* was the finest ship on the Coast when she arrived in 1888. Fast, economical and elegantly appointed, she set a new standard for passenger travel.
— PROVINCIAL ARCHIVES

The drydock at Esquimalt . . .
The CPN's beautiful Islander . . .

vociferous mayor declared that the CPN's steamer *Princess Louise* was unsafe and advised them to spend the remainder of their tour in Vancouver.

This accusation was, of course, unfounded since the vessel was well maintained, had a licensed capacity of 500, and had demonstrated her seaworthiness. In fact, the *Princess Louise* would serve with the CPN and CPR for another 19 years before being retired in 1906. John Irving considered the mayor's rash utterances to be criminal libel and he announced to the papers that he planned to take legal action against McLean. In the meantime, he issued an order that McLean was not to be allowed on board any of the CPN's vessels.

Less than a week later, Mayor McLean and several Vancouver aldermen went down to the docks to inspect Irving's new steamer *Premier* before she departed on her first sailing from Vancouver. The mayor apparently paid no attention to a written request from Irving that he not board the vessel until he had explained his earlier remarks. On boarding the *Premier*, McLean and his party were met by First Mate Munroe, who had definite ideas about not letting the mayor on the vessel. McLean was unceremoniously removed from the steamer, much to his chagrin. The newspapers were quick to seize on the incident, Victoria's papers siding with Irving, Mate Munroe and the CPN, while their journalistic rivals in Vancouver naturally took the side of McLean.

Victoria's *Daily Colonist* described the *Premier*'s mate as "a most genial gentleman and a good mariner," while the Vancouver *News-Herald* portrayed him as "a big blustering bully, that is evidently a good specimen of the San Francisco hoodlum and who, we are sorry to say is the mate of the boat . . . and . . . who in a grossly insulting and threatening manner ordered the mayor off the boat."

McLean did not remain in office too long after this incident and was succeeded by David Oppenheimer, who apparently also had designs for the expansion of Vancouver and also cared little for the Canadian Pacific Navigation Company. Once again, the *Premier* was the centre of an altercation on the Vancouver docks.

The second dispute began on January 5, 1889 when a doctor named Beckingsale, a passenger on board the *Premier*, made a tentative diagnosis of a smallpox case on the ship. The vessel was prohibited from landing in Vancouver and was sent to the quarantine station off Albert Head near Victoria. There, she waited until January 11, when she received clearance to proceed to Vancouver. However, on arriving in Burrard Inlet, the vessel was met with a most inhospitable welcome. Captain O'Brien, master of the *Premier*, was greeted by Vancouver's Dr. Robertson of the City Board of Health and was informed that the vessel would not be permitted to dock. The doctor requested that the steamer anchor in the harbour for the night so that the situation could be discussed further the next day.

"There's no smallpox on board; there never was," retorted Captain O'Brien. "I have my instructions from Captain John

The *Islander* is shown above in Esquimalt Harbour. Apparently it is a holiday excursion that has taken her off her regular run. A band is seated behind the bridge playing for the passengers.
— PROVINCIAL ARCHIVES

The Islander *is . . .*

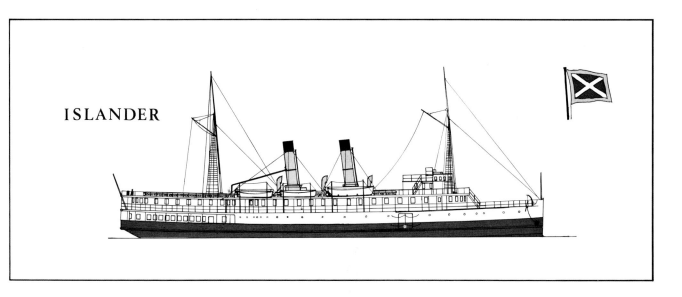

ISLANDER

Vancouver was the terminus of the CPR's main line. From there CPN steamers provided a connecting service to Victoria. In the 1899 view above the *Islander* has just arrived from Victoria and is tied up ahead of one of the CPR's first Empress liners — the *Empress of China*, *Empress of Japan*, or *Empress of India*, all of which were built for trans-Pacific service in 1891. Royal Navy warships are anchored in Burrard Inlet. The photo was taken looking down Granville Street. — BAILEY BROS. PHOTO, CPR COLLECTION

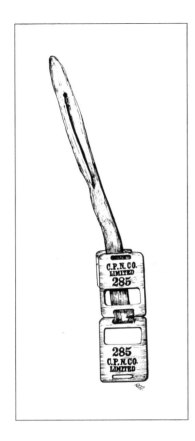

A CPN baggage check from the British Columbia
Provincial Museum's collection.
— ROBERT D. TURNER

Irving to land my passengers. I shall not anchor out in the
stream."

Anticipating the arrival of the *Premier*, the city had decided
to act strictly in accordance with its by-laws and prohibit the
docking of the steamer or the landing of any of its passengers.
Accordingly, the police were on the alert and a number of
"specials" had been sworn in should trouble arise.

As the *Premier* touched the dock, several frustrated passengers tried to jump ashore but were quickly forced back on the
vessel by the police. At this point, the delay was greeted with
some humour by the passengers, although their patience was
nearing exhaustion. Various opinions from CPR authorities
and customs officials supported the position that the ship should
be allowed to dock, but Dr. Robertson remained adamant in
his view that the vessel could not dock that evening. Even
Dr. Beckingsale, now greatly distraught at his forced confine-
ment on the steamer, was specifically refused permission to
come ashore, even though he had received a telegram from the
Deputy Minister of Agriculture in Ottawa stating: "If vacci-
nated and clothes thoroughly disinfected detention for observation not necessary." Determined, he tried to land but was soon
returned to the ship. With finality, Robertson declared, "No
one can land tonight!"

The ship was given permission to sail to Moodyville to take
on water, but under the strict injunction that no one was to go
ashore. At this point Mayor Oppenheimer arrived on the
docks and made it clear that he too felt no one should land
that evening. Near midnight, the *Premier* sailed to Moodyville
where she was met by a contingent of police to enforce the
mayor's ruling. However, Dr. Beckingsale and one other
passenger made their escape into the night unnoticed by the
local constabulary.

Captain O'Brien then took his vessel back to Vancouver and
stood offshore until 8:30 the next morning. He then took his
ship away from the dock towards the middle of the inlet. Later
in the morning the *Islander*, under command of Captain
Rudlin, arrived in the harbour from Victoria with Captain
Irving aboard. The vessel did not dock as usual, but came close
inshore and Irving himself proceeded to the customs office in a
small boat. Irving then returned to his ship with a customs
official and steamed over to the *Premier*, to be met by the
cheers of the frustrated passengers. Passengers from the *Premier*
were then transferred to the *Islander* and both vessels headed
back towards the docks. Irving hoped that the passengers
would then be allowed to go ashore, but he had not counted
on the determination of Vancouver's mayor.

Before either vessel could dock, Irving was informed that he
had now endangered the *Islander* and no one from that steamer
would be allowed to set foot in Vancouver. Growing increasingly impatient, Irving swung his ship around and steamed
full speed for the dock at Hastings Mill. Immediately, there
was a mad rush of police, "specials," city officials and spectators to beat the steamer to the dock. Once again Irving was

frustrated, arriving just after the Vancouver police and was prevented from landing any of his passengers.

Irving then steamed back to the CPN wharf where more police were waiting. He tried to secure his vessel between the liners *Mexico* and *Parthia*. Boats were lowered from the *Islander* and lines were secured to the pilings below the waterline. To counter this offensive, the mayor sent men with axes down onto the pilings with orders to cut the lines. While attention was being focused on the attempts to secure the *Islander*, Irving and Captain Rudlin hurriedly ran out a gangplank from the forward shell doors and the two officers tried to land. Then the battle began in earnest. Police met Irving on the dock and a scuffle followed in which one man "had his hat crushed in by a blow from a truncheon" and Irving was roughly handled. Finally the contest centred on the gangplank, the police attempting to push it back into the steamer while the *Islander*'s crew made every effort to keep their link with the dock secure. Ultimately, however, the police won out.

Realizing that he could be held responsible for not delivering the mail carried on the *Islander*, Irving then offered to land the mail sacks but was refused, so that it then became the fault of the city for any delay that might result.

The climax came when observers onshore noticed fire hoses being broken out on the *Islander*. Immediately, the mayor rang the fire bell and a pumper was dispatched to the corner of Hastings and Granville. The firemen played out sufficient hose to reach the docks and give them enough manoeuverability to sweep the decks of the steamer. Meanwhile, the docks were cleared of spectators. It was a standoff. Crew members of the *Islander* had originally connected the fire hoses to the ship's hot water system, providing a very potent weapon that could have cleared the docks in short order. However, Irving felt that this might be pushing the situation too far. The hoses were then connected to the cold water outlets in readiness for action. As water from the *Islander*'s hoses began to reach out for the docks, and as the city firemen began to retaliate from shore, Irving gave orders to "hold fire" and turned off the water himself. Whether he recognized defeat, had second thoughts, or was initially unaware of his crew's actions, as he later claimed, is open to speculation.

As the eastbound passenger train was about to depart from the CPR station, time was running out for the mails to be transferred. A written request for delivery of the mails was made by E. H. Fletcher, who was responsible for the exchange, and was given to Dr. Robertson, who made several unsuccessful attempts to get it to Irving onboard the steamer. Irving eventually came forward and was then informed by the doctor of the contents of the dispatch. However, by that time, more than thoroughly disgusted, he suggested that the letter be mailed to him at his Victoria office!

Meanwhile, Captain O'Brien had tried once again to dock the *Premier*, only to have her lines cut by Sergeant McLaren and his squad of police. The only casualty in this minor skirmish was Special Officer Frank Granville, who suffered a direct hit of "ancient hen-coup" which ruined his "fine coat."

By this time, telegrams from Ottawa had been received by both the customs official and Mayor Oppenheimer, stating that the quarantine regulations had been complied with in all respects and that since the *Premier* was cleared at Victoria she should not be interfered with. City solicitors were of the opinion that the city was within its powers to expand the quarantine provisions of provincial or federal laws. Fortified by this declaration, the mayor remained adamant. The vessels would not be permitted to dock in his city! While the skirmishes continued on the docks, lawyers fought verbal battles over the legality of the actions of both parties.

Irving then made it known that he was taking the *Islander* back to Victoria so that the passengers could be put ashore. In preparation, baggage was transferred from the *Premier* to the *Islander*. However at about 3:00 p.m. a man named Rand and his wife were lowered over the side of the *Islander* and made their escape in a small boat. Half an hour later, the mails were finally unloaded after being thoroughly fumigated and cleared by health officers and turned over to the CPR for shipment east. While neither Irving nor the mayor was willing to give in, both recognized the legal difficulties that might arise if the mail were illegally delayed.

At 4:30 p.m. the *Islander* sailed, but instead of steaming towards the First Narrows on a course for Victoria, she headed east up Burrard Inlet, towards Port Moody. There, 16 passengers were landed and made their way by train to New Westminster that evening. She then returned to Moodyville, where six more passengers disembarked and boarded the tug *Etta White* for Vancouver. Irving had won his fight with Oppenheimer to land his passengers. He then took his steamer back to Victoria.

It was rumoured that Irving would sail the *Islander* around to New Westminster to disembark the rest of the passengers and as a result, the militia was called out to prevent the landing. However, this event did not take place. Following the *Islander*'s return to Victoria, her remaining passengers, freight and express were transferred to the *Princess Louise*, which was to sail to New Westminster the next day. On arriving in New Westminster, the passengers were not interfered with and made connections with the CPR passenger train leaving for the east.

The war was not quite over, however. Irving had threatened not to bring the *Islander* back to Vancouver until the dispute was settled one way or another. On Sunday, he cancelled the steamer's regular sailing although this action infringed on his contract commitments with both the CPR and the federal government for movement of passengers and mail between Victoria and Vancouver for connection with the eastbound passenger trains.

On Monday Irving returned to Vancouver on the *Islander*,

armed with a court injunction prohibiting any interference with his vessels. He also instituted a $40,000 lawsuit against Mayor Oppenheimer and the City of Vancouver for protection against any damage actions that might be pressed against the Canadian Pacific Navigation Company. By this time, Oppenheimer had recognized defeat and did not interfere with the steamer further. The bitterness subsided and Irving allowed the damage action to drop. After all, it would have been very bad public relations to sue an already disgruntled city which provided a large proportion of the steamship company's business.

Three and one-half years later, there was yet another smallpox scare that involved the CPN and the City of Vancouver. This time, in July 1892, the *Yosemite* was barred from docking on two trips from Victoria and again passengers were landed farther up Burrard Inlet. Vancouver officials were eventually cited for contempt before they relented and after a brief suspension of service, the *Yosemite* resumed her run.

The *Premier* continued in service on the Tacoma-Seattle-Vancouver route after John Irving's battles with Mayor Oppenheimer, making two round trips each week. Southbound, the steamer left Vancouver at 2:00 p.m., arriving in Port Townsend at 9:30. One and a half hours later, she sailed to Seattle, arriving the next morning at about 2:00. After a four-hour layover, she proceeded south to Tacoma, docking at 12:00 noon. A three-hour stop was made at Tacoma before the *Premier* retraced the route, steaming north towards Vancouver and arriving there at 5:30 p.m. the day after her departure. However by mid-1891, the *Premier*'s stop at Vancouver was eliminated and she was operated between Whatcom (Bellingham), Seattle and other Puget Sound ports.

At this time, either the *Islander* or the *Yosemite* operated between Vancouver and Victoria and other CPN steamers, usually the *Princess Louise* or the *R. P. Rithet*, sailed between Victoria and New Westminster. Additionally, Company sternwheelers provided service to the small communities along the Fraser River between New Westminster and the mouth of the Fraser and as far upstream as Hope. Finally, the little steamer *Maude* sailed once each month between Victoria and the lumbering community of Alberni at the head of Barkley Sound on the west coast of Vancouver Island.

The assignment of ships to the various coastal routes was very flexible and variations were made to permit regular overhauls and to provide for excursions and special cruises. Irving himself often took command of the *Islander* for the cruises. In late May 1889, he took her on her first trip to Alaska. This ten day cruise was under charter to an eastern millionaire named Webb who, with his wife, three children, six guests and their attendants, made up the party. On May 18th the ship left Victoria for Vancouver, where the passengers embarked with great quantities of baggage. She continued north the same day,

The CPN in the 1890's

A celebration of the anniversary of the Battle of the Boyne prompted the local Orange Lodge to take an excursion on the CPN sternwheeler *Transfer* in the mid-1890's.
— PROVINCIAL ARCHIVES

The 887 ton *Danube* was purchased by the CPN to replace the *Sardonyx* lost in 1890. In 1869, the year she was built, she was in the procession of ships that opened the Suez Canal. This photo was taken at Port Essington in the 1890's.
— PROVINCIAL ARCHIVES

making good time. Brief stops were made at Alert Bay, Bella Coola and Fort Simpson, where freight was discharged. From there the ship sailed on to Sitka, Alaska, through the inlets and fjords characterizing the north coast of British Columbia and the Alaska Panhandle.

At that time, Sitka was a small community of about 1,600 about half of them white and half native. The town had been an administrative centre for the Russian Governor before the United States purchased Alaska and thus contained a number of buildings of interest to the travellers from the south, including the large, ornate Greek Orthodox church that dominated the main street. John Williams, the *Islander*'s mate, who reported the cruise for the *Daily Colonist*, was most impressed, noting that, "The walls are hung with fine old paintings imported by the Russians during their sovereignty here, one painting alone of the Madonna being reputed to be worth $10,000. The vestments of the altar and also the pontifical robes are on account of their antiquity as well as splendor, well worthy of inspection." He also visited Baranof Castle, a large wooden structure that had once been the Russian Governor's mansion, but was by then in a state of decay.

A celebration of . . .
The 887 ton Danube . . .

After a short visit the *Islander* sailed from Sitka with most of the town's population turning out to see her off. On the isolated North Coast, the arrival or departure of any ship was a most important event, as it provided the only connection the residents had with the outside world. From Sitka, the ship steamed past Glacier Bay and on to Juneau, where Williams noted, "Nothing predominates but mud." Several gold and silver mines were operating in the vicinity perhaps giving a slight indication of the boom that would occur in Alaska and the Yukon within the decade. After visiting Wrangell, the *Islander* headed towards Vancouver, arriving on the 27th of May.

The Hudson's Bay Company's old *Otter*, in her last years relegated to freighting and ultimately to use as a coal barge, was finally burned for her copper in Victoria Harbour in 1890. In that same year the steamer *Sardonyx*, in operation for the CPN since 1887, struck an uncharted reef off the east coast of the Queen Charlotte Islands and sank without loss of life. The loss of this vessel forced Irving to acquire yet another ship for the CPN's fleet. This was the screw driven steamer *Danube* of 887 tons.

This historic steamer was built by J. Elder & Company on the River Clyde in Scotland in 1869 and saw service in many parts of the world before being purchased by Irving. In 1869 she had been one of the ships in the procession that opened the Suez Canal and later was chartered to return the body of David Livingstone to England from East Africa. The *Danube* was acquired to operate between Portland, Oregon and Vancouver, maintaining the feeder service for the CPR formerly provided by the *Sardonyx*. She was to lead a particularly long life with a career spanning 67 years before finally being broken up for scrap in 1936 as the *Nervion*, registered in Spain.

In 1890 the CPN also acquired the steamer *Rainbow* from the firm of Turner, Beeton and Company of Victoria, which had operated the vessel between Vancouver and Nanaimo. This ship was originally Captain William Moore's *Teaser*. He had been forced to sell the vessel during a period of financial difficulties. The CPN ran the *Rainbow* to northern ports in opposition to the Union Steamship Company of Vancouver. Four years later, the CPN sold the ship, which was then renamed the *Eva Marie* and used in sealing in the North Pacific.

By the early 1890's steamer service between Vancouver Island and Puget Sound had progressed a long way from the sporadic and unreliable operations that had characterized the routes during the 1850's and 1860's. Several vessels of different companies were running regularly, carrying mail and passengers in increasing quantities between the Canadian and American communities, closely knit despite the international boundary. In addition to the CPN's *Premier*, which still sailed from Vancouver to Puget Sound ports, the fine new steamers *City of Kingston* and *City of Seattle* were in operation between Tacoma, Seattle and Victoria. These two ships, in many ways comparable to the CPN's *Islander*, had been acquired in Philadelphia by the Puget Sound and Alaska Steamship Company in 1890 and were sailed to the West Coast around Cape Horn.

On the *City of Seattle*'s arrival in Seattle, nearly 27,000 people attended the open house held on the vessel. Initially it was intended to place the *City of Seattle* on the Seattle, Tacoma, Whatcom route and the *City of Kingston* on the run to Victoria, but, as often happened, the vessels were operated on both routes interchangeably. On the Victoria route, a daily except Sunday service was provided. These two ships were not without competition. The Union Pacific Railroad's steamers *Olympian*, *North Pacific*, *T. J. Potter* and others vied for the business on similar runs on Puget Sound. These rivalries culminated in a race to determine which vessel ruled the route. In this contest the *City of Seattle* decisively defeated the sidewheeler *Olympian* in an exciting run between Seattle and Tacoma.

Ships like the *Premier*, *City of Seattle* and *City of Kingston* reflected the advances in marine engineering that had occurred since the 1860's. Screw driven steamers with compound or even triple expansion engines were proving faster, and much more efficient than the sidewheelers with their single cylinder walking beam engines and exposed paddlewheels. As more technologically advanced ships came to the North Pacific, the old paddlewheelers lost their supremacy on the important intercity runs and many were laid up or used for a few final years on less lucrative and competitive routes to the smaller ports along the coast.

Early in October 1892, the *Premier* was involved in an incident that nearly ended her already noteworthy career. Steaming south from Port Townsend towards Bush Point en route to Seattle, the vessel encountered heavy fog. Full speed

The elegant steamship City of Seattle . . .

was maintained in order to stay on schedule but standard precautions were taken. Foghorns were sounded regularly at 20-second intervals, and as the *Premier* passed the steamer *City of Kingston*, the CPN liner's course was altered one and a half points starboard to keep her well to the right of the channel. However, foghorns of another vessel could be heard from somewhere to port. Unable to locate the other vessel, Captain Bernard Gilboy, master of the *Premier*, and the ship's pilot went out on deck to try to determine the relative position of the two ships. Suddenly there were two long whistle blasts, followed by a shorter one as a large steamer, the collier *Willamette*, loomed out of the fog and crashed into the port side of the unlucky *Premier*.

At the first sound of the whistle, the *Premier*'s engines had been reversed, but it was too late to avoid a collision. The steel bow of the collier cut deeply into the passenger steamer, tearing through the hull and wooden superstructure to the ship's centre line. The *Premier*'s bridge was twisted and moved off position as the two steamers locked together.

As one passenger on the *Premier* later related to the *Daily Colonist*:

I was sitting in the smoking room when someone exclaimed: "Good God! They will be down on us in a minute!" I and the others crushed forward to the saloon entrance, when there was a tremendous crash and everything was sent flying forward. I got to the stern where the ladies were, and from there, went forward to where the *Willamette* was interlocked. Just then everybody seemed to be making a wild scramble to get on board the collier. Some of the scenes were heartrending, particularly the wild grief of D. J. Wynkoop over the loss of his young son ...

Three were killed and 21 injured in the collision and a fourth died the next day. Surviving passengers and crew members of the *Premier* quickly made their way to the *Willamette*. The crews of the two vessels acted quickly and efficiently to do whatever possible to help the passengers.

So tightly interlocked were the two steamers that the *Willamette* was able to keep the *Premier* afloat. The two vessels were slowly manoeuvered to Bush Point where the *Premier* was grounded in 24 feet of water. Passengers from the *Premier* were taken onboard the tug *Goliah* and were ferried to Seattle. For over 24 hours the two ships remained locked together until the *Willamette* was finally freed at about 5:00 p.m. on October 9th by tugs *Goliah*, *Tacoma*, and *Tyee* and made her way to Seattle for repairs. There, part of her cargo of coal was unloaded to lighten the forward part of the ship, revealing the full extent of the damages. A jagged gash, ten feet long and five feet wide testified to the force of the impact. While one and a half feet of the hole was below the waterline, the bulkheads had held, preventing the vessel from sinking. Had the opening extended further aft, however, the collier would have sunk quickly, taking the *Premier* with her.

Later investigations into the accident resulted in the licenses of both Captain Gilboy and Captain Hansen, master of the *Willamette*, being revoked. Captain Gilboy was censured

The elegant steamship *City of Seattle* and the nearly identical *City of Kingston* brought new standards of service to the Victoria - Seattle run when they were placed in operation in 1890 by the Puget Sound and Alaska Steamship Company. — PROVINCIAL ARCHIVES

primarily for proceeding at high speed when the position of an unidentified vessel in the vicinity of his ship was uncertain. Captain Hansen was criticized for his decision to attempt to pass ahead of the *Premier*.

The fog signals of the *Premier* were distinctly heard by people on Bush Point, and, as the sound passed over the *Willamette*, all of the signals from the *Premier* must have been heard by the officer and lookout on board of the *Willamette*. It appears that Captain Hansen did hear signals, but paid no particular attention to them, as the weather was clear where the ships must have been within a mile of each other, and several more blasts were exchanged before they collided. At the time Captain Hansen heard the *Premier*'s fog signal, he certainly must have known that the course he was then steering would either cross the *Premier*'s track or go very close to her. He had plenty of room north of the vessel, and, had he ported would not have collided but would have passed very close to each other.

Because of the heavy cargo in the *Willamette* at the time, Hansen had been reluctant to run any closer to shore. However, had he swung to port when he heard the signals of the *Premier*, the two vessels would not have collided.

The day after the accident, Captain Irving, Captain Biondo of Seattle, Captain Bryant, the local inspector, and Alexander Allan of the drydock inspected the beached, partially submerged *Premier*. The surveyors felt that the ship could be pumped out and taken to drydock, but Irving questioned that it would be worth the trouble as the hull was badly twisted from the collision. However, further investigation indicated that the ship might be salvageable after all.

Irving stated that if the steamer could be raised he wanted to have it repaired at Esquimalt rather than in an American shipyard. Captain John O'Brien was given the contract to raise her and during the last week of October completed his preparations. He estimated that it would cost under $20,000 to refloat the ship. However, there were difficulties and the work progressed slowly. O'Brien subcontracted the work to the Grant Brothers of Tacoma, who planned to use a type of inflatable canvas pontoon to float the vessel. By October 31st, John Irving was becoming disheartened, and commented:

"I'm disappointed and just a little bit disgusted with the Grant process — it will never raise the *Premier*. They have ten more days to try it in and then if they are not successful, I'll go over again myself and try to get her up."

However, after many hours of determined effort, the Grant Brothers were successful, floating the damaged ship with their canvas pontoons at 2:00 a.m. on November 8th. The vessel was then beached and the gaping hole in the hull boarded up. The steamer was pumped out and floated at high tide and then towed to Victoria. There she was tied up at the R. P. Rithet Wharf in the Inner Harbour. She was drydocked soon after and repairs were carried out. However, apparently to avoid impending lawsuits against the vessel, the CPN changed her registry from American to Canadian and never let her return

As the report stated:

The unlucky Premier . . .

The unlucky *Premier* was involved in a tragic collision with the collier *Willamette* in 1892. The wrecked CPN vessel is shown at Victoria after she was refloated and salvaged. She was repaired and renamed *Charmer*. — PROVINCIAL ARCHIVES

The *Charmer*, ex *Premier*, emerged from the shipyards fully refitted and apparently none the worse for the collision that nearly ended her career. Here, she is leaving Victoria with a full complement of passengers — many of them soldiers. — CPR COLLECTION

28

The Charmer, *ex* Premier . . .

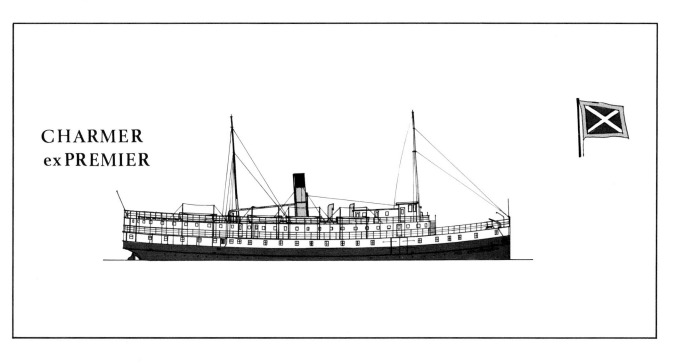

CHARMER
ex PREMIER

to United States waters. As a Canadian steamer the *Premier* was renamed *Charmer*, and was assigned to the Victoria-Vancouver service.

It seems likely that other factors besides possible legal action weighed in favour of reregistering the ship. Competition was heavy on the runs to Puget Sound and with the vessel damaged and depreciated from her new value, customs duty would be much lower than if the *Premier* had been brought under Canadian registry when new.

In 1886, Irving purchased a small steamer, the *St. Pierre*, from Halifax interests for use on the west coast of Vancouver Island. However, on the voyage to Victoria, the vessel, which fortunately was insured, was lost in an Atlantic storm. She was replaced the following year by the larger, sturdier S.S. *Tees*, a 569 ton, four-year-old steel-hulled vessel that had been operated by the Hudson's Bay Company. Irving made an excellent choice in purchasing the *Tees*, as she was a well built, efficient steamer and served the CPN and subsequent owners well.

The 1890's marked a period of steady business for the CPN, disrupted only by the depression of 1893 and the usual fluctuation in the salmon pack of the coastal canneries which provided good cargos for the Company. In 1893 a new sternwheeler, the *Transfer*, was built for operation on the lower Fraser route from New Westminster to Steveston and other settlements near the River's mouth.

The year 1897 changed the entire future of the CPN and of almost every other shipping company on the Pacific coast when word was received from Alaska that gold had been discovered on the Klondike River near Dawson in the Yukon Territory. The famous rush was on and as in previous gold rushes, virtually any vessel that could float was enlisted to carry the miners to the gold fields. Many old relics, including the *Eliza Anderson*, were patched up and sailed to Alaska carrying as many people and as much cargo as could be fitted aboard. Recognizing the tremendous potential existing in this latest gold rush, the CPN began expanding its fleet.

The three-masted wooden schooner *Queen City* was acquired in 1897 and an order was placed with the Albion Iron Works of Victoria, in which Irving was a shareholder, for compound engines so that the vessel could be rebuilt as a steamer. With these new engines, she was capable of 8.5 knots and was licensed to carry 150 passengers. She was ready for service by the summer of 1898.

Irving could not resist the urge to take a sternwheeler north to the Yukon River, and to this end had a new vessel prefabricated at Victoria and shipped north to St. Michael, Alaska, at the mouth of the Yukon River, for assembly. By June 1898, it seemed as if half the CPN fleet was sailing north to Alaska as the *Princess Louise*, *Danube* and *Tees* departed from Victoria. The *Danube* carried the engines and machinery for Irving's new steamer, which was by that time nearing completion at

The Klondike and Alaska Gold Rush

The *Queen City* was typical of the small, wooden-hulled coastal steamers that were used by the CPN, CPR and other shipping companies. She started life in 1894 as a sailing vessel but was rebuilt as a steamer by the CPN in 1897.
— PROVINCIAL ARCHIVES

The Klondike gold rush of 1898 saw nearly every ship on the North Pacific head for Alaska. Here the CPN's *Tees* and *Islander*, loaded with prospectors, prepare to leave Victoria.
— PROVINCIAL ARCHIVES

The Queen City *was . . .*
The Klondike gold rush . . .

St. Michael. It was Irving's intention to outfit the new stern-wheeler, which he named the *Yukoner*, and take her up the river himself for the first voyage.

At the same time as preparations were being made for the departure of the three ships from Victoria, a new sternwheeler, the *Beaver*, named to commemorate the Hudson's Bay Company's vessel, was placed in service on the CPN's upper Fraser route, sailing upstream from New Westminster.

Yet another new addition to the CPN fleet was the steamer *Willapa*, a wooden-hulled vessel of 331 tons built at Astoria on the Columbia River in 1891 as the *General Miles*. Soon after completion, the ship was sold to the Alaska Steamship Company to run from Puget Sound north, and was renamed the *Willapa*. She was wrecked early in 1896 and abandoned, but was salvaged and acquired by the Canadian Pacific Navigation Company, which repaired her. The *Willapa* proved to be invaluable to the CPN during the Klondike rush. She was placed on the service to the west coast of Vancouver Island, freeing other vessels for the Alaska trade.

The CPN also announced that it was negotiating with builders in Great Britain for the construction of a 21 knot "first class" vessel for the Victoria-Vancouver route. The projected ship was to be about 270 feet in length and have a breadth of 34 feet. Her estimated cost was $375,000. However, this ship was never built. This was not the first such proposal not to materialize as a projected sistership to the *Islander*, to be appropriately named the *Mainlander*, was planned by Irving but did not develop beyond the discussion stage.

With his preparations completed, John Irving entered the Yukon River trade in grand style. His *Yukoner* was launched with the traditional bottle of champagne and on its first trip up the river, he entertained a crowd estimated at 300. He showed off his fine new steamer to all who cared to look and drink a toast to her success. The trip up the Yukon was a profitable venture but on returning to St. Michael he sold the stern-wheeler and returned to Victoria. Not long after, he resigned his position as general manager of the CPN and concentrated his energies on developing more steamer services in the north.

He planned to build two more sternwheelers to operate from Lake Bennett to the White Horse Rapids, while a third was planned for use on Atlin Lake and a fourth to run from the head of Bennett Lake to Taku Arm, where connection would be possible, via a two-mile portage, with steamers on Atlin Lake. To carry out these plans, he established the John Irving Navigation Company. However in 1901, one year after the completion of the White Pass and Yukon Route, Irving sold his interests in the river steamers to the railway.*

---

*The White Pass and Yukon Route was actually composed of three railway companies — the Pacific and Arctic Railway Co. (in Alaska), the British Columbia Yukon Railway Co. (in B.C.), and the British Yukon Railway Co. (in the Yukon) — and one steamboat company, the British Yukon Navigation Co. These companies were operated as the Rail and River Divisions of the Y.P. & Y. Route.

Victoria was the headquarters for the Canadian Pacific Navigation Company. The Company's steamers, *Willapa*, *Princess Louise*, *R. P. Rithet*, and *Danube* are berthed along the Wharf Street docks. — PROVINCIAL ARCHIVES

Victoria was the headquarters ...

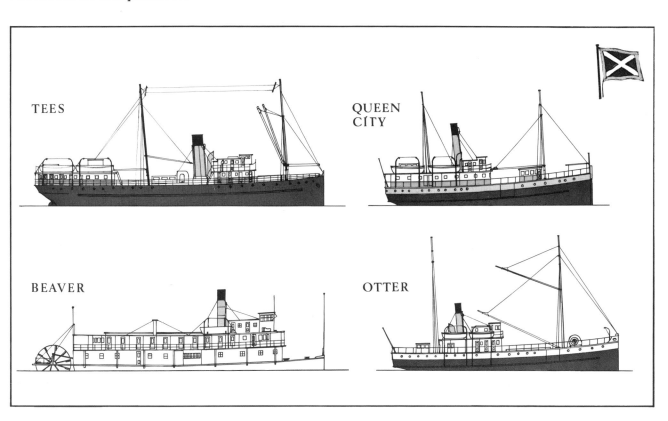

TEES

QUEEN
CITY

BEAVER

OTTER

33

The sternwheeler Beaver ...
The Amur *would* ...

The wooden-hulled Willapa ...

The excitement of the gold rush years was contagious. Miners from all over the world flocked to the West Coast as the first stage in their journey north. Virtually every steamer sailing north for Alaska carried capacity crowds and where possible the ships brought return cargoes south.

The *Princess Louise* returned from the north early in September 1898 with 8,100 cases of salmon picked up at Alert Bay, but it was a saddened crew that landed in Victoria on the completion of the voyage. Three seamen had fallen overboard while leaning on the rail posing for a picture and had been swept under the steamer's sidewheel and lost without a trace.

However, such personal tragedies did little to lessen the pace of these hectic years. The *Princess Louise* was fueled and provisioned and set off once again for the north with another capacity load of miners and their supplies. Included on her passenger list was a party of 16 men from Minnesota who boarded the vessel with over $5,000 worth of equipment. Others of the same group were to follow on a later sailing of the *Islander*, which by that time was also engaged in the Alaska trade. In September the newspapers estimated that as many as 20,000 more miners were on their way to the Coast, hoping to reach the Klondike before winter closed in. By early October, however, the peak of the traffic for that year had passed and ships sailing north for Alaska carried only light cargoes and small numbers of passengers.

By the spring of 1899, the steamship companies had reached agreements on new rate structures to the north with the White Pass and Yukon Route, a narrow gauge line being completed from Skagway on the Pacific to Whitehorse in the Yukon. The new freight and passenger rates marked a dramatic reduction in transportation costs to Dawson from any of the ports in southern British Columbia or Puget Sound. In contrast to 1898, when freight took from a month to six weeks and cost 60 cents a pound or $1,200 per ton to be shipped to Bennett and from 20 to 30 per cent more to Dawson, on completion of the railway, the new services could deliver goods to Bennett in less than two weeks and at a fraction of the cost.

The agreement worked out between the Alaska Steamship Company, the Canadian Pacific Navigation Company, the Canadian Development Company (in connection with which Irving's lake and river steamers were to operate) and the White Pass and Yukon Route provided that once the railway reached Bennett, about halfway between Skagway and Whitehorse, the following tariff schedule went into effect: from any port in Puget Sound or southern British Columbia, a first class through ticket to Dawson would cost $135, with second class and children's fares also available. The ticket included 150 pounds of free baggage. Freight rates to Atlin were set at $100 per ton, with a 10 per cent reduction on shipments of second class freight over ten tons. Rates to the Klondike, though higher because of the greater distance, were still significantly lower than in the previous year. First class merchandise, including perishables, was $160 per ton, while second class cost $155 and

The sternwheeler *Beaver* was the last vessel of this type acquired by the CPN and operated on the Fraser River until 1913, when competition from the B.C. Electric Railway made her continued use unjustified. — CPR COLLECTION

The *Amur* would certainly rate as the ugliest ship in the CPN fleet. Nevertheless, the 12 knot steamer was an important addition during the Klondike gold rush and served with the CPN and later the CPR until 1912. — PROVINCIAL ARCHIVES

The wooden-hulled *Willapa* was another vessel acquired by the CPN during the gold rush years. She is shown here on the west coast of Vancouver Island at Clayoquot around the turn of the century. As the *Bellingham*, she survived until the 1950 Seattle Seafair, when she was burned as part of the celebrations. — PROVINCIAL ARCHIVES

Sketch of *R. P. Rithet* — ROBERT D. TURNER

Many vessels sailed . . .

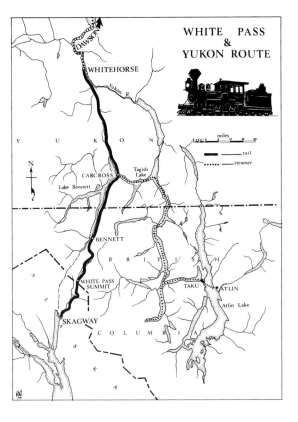

WHITE PASS
&
YUKON ROUTE

miles

——— rail
••••••• steamer

third class $136 per ton. Livestock was carried, when in car-load lots of 14 head or more, at $82 per head.

It is not surprising that with these significant changes in the freight rates, the prices of goods and supplies in the north dropped quickly and where once shortages and inflated prices had been the rule, surpluses began to accumulate. By this time too, many miners found the best claims staked and, with little chance of profit, began to return to the south.

By 1900, the Klondike boom had passed and the slower, more lasting development of both the north and the Pacific coast continued. In that year, the CPN acquired two more small coastal vessels to augment its fleet. These were the *Amur*, a 907 ton steel cargo vessel which had been operated to Alaska by the Klondike Mining Company between 1898 and 1900, and a new wooden-hulled steamer named the *Otter*, after the early Hudson's Bay vessel, one of the CPN's first ships. The second *Otter* was built in Victoria and displaced 366 tons. While somewhat larger, she closely resembled the *Queen City* in appearance and was used in the coastal trade, supplying isolated canneries, whaling stations and agricultural settlements. She was in service early in 1901.

It was at this point that the Canadian Pacific Navigation Company began negotiations with the Canadian Pacific Railway Company for the takeover of the CPN's steamship services on the Pacific coast. The CPN was at a critical stage in its development, requiring very significant infusions of capital to assure its position in the years ahead. The CPR had plenty of capital, and furthermore it was interested in expanding the service and in extending its influence along the coast and onto Vancouver Island.

Many vessels sailed to Alaska during the gold rush. Here the *City of Seattle* skirts the Foster Glacier in Taku Inlet in a Case and Draper photo. While the glaciers were a popular attraction they also produced icebergs that caused the loss of many ships. — PROVINCIAL ARCHIVES

The *Princess May*, first vessel acquired by James Troup after the CPR's takeover of the Canadian Pacific Navigation Company, emerged from an extensive refit in 1906 with enlarged and improved passenger accommodations. In gleaming white, she is recorded here at Esquimalt as the engineering crew is working, no doubt, to overcome the conspicuous black smoke, a good indication of poor coal or improper combustion.
— CANADIAN FORCES PHOTO

The CPN Pass for 1901 featured the ill-fated *Islander.* — PROVINCIAL ARCHIVES

CHAPTER II

THE FORMATION OF THE CANADIAN PACIFIC RAILWAY'S B.C. COAST SERVICE

The CPR Buys the CPN

JANUARY 1901 brought dramatic changes to the steamer operations on the Pacific coast. On the 12th, it was announced that the Canadian Pacific Railway Company had purchased controlling interest in the Canadian Pacific Navigation Company and that plans were being formulated for upgrading the CPN's services along the British Columbia and Alaska coasts. Initially, however, work would be directed towards improving the Victoria-Vancouver run and the services to Alaska from Victoria and Vancouver, which were proving particularly lucrative following the Klondike gold rush.

On March 5th of the same year, new directors and officers were elected for the Company, reflecting the change in ownership of the steamship operations, and Captain James W. Troup was appointed manager. This arrangement, whereby the CPN continued to exist, albeit in name only, as an independent company continued until May 1903, when it was officially absorbed into the Canadian Pacific Railway Company. The CPN fleet, purchased by the CPR in the $531,000 transaction included the following vessels: *Charmer, Islander, Danube, Amur, Yosemite, Princess Louise, Willapa, Tees, Queen City, Otter, R. P. Rithet, Beaver, Transfer* and *Maude*.

At the time of the purchase, these ships were being operated on seven different coastal routes. The *Charmer* (formerly *Premier*) made daily sailings between Victoria and Vancouver, leaving Victoria at 1:00 a.m. and, after a leisurely passage through the Gulf Islands, arriving at the "Terminal City" at breakfast time. The return trip commenced at 1:15 p.m., following the arrival of the CPR's Train No. 1 from the east. If the train was late, the steamer was normally held so that the mails could be transferred and passengers could make connections through to Victoria.

The sternwheeler *R. P. Rithet* connected Victoria with New Westminster and points along the lower Fraser River, covering the route three times a week. During the winter, the service was taken over by the sidewheeler *Princess Louise* and the frequency of sailings was reduced to two return trips each

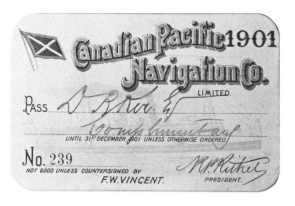

The CPN Pass . . .

week. The steamer *Tees* sailed from Victoria to Alberni and other Barkley Sound points, beginning the 1st, 10th and 16th of each month. The two latter sailings were extended to include a service to Quatsino Sound and Cape Scott further north along the west coast of the Island.

The *Amur*, augmented by the *Princess Louise* during the summer months, sailed north to settlements such as Rivers Inlet, Port Simpson and ports on the Queen Charlotte Islands. Steamers on this run departed Victoria at 11:00 p.m. on the 1st and 15th of each month, making a stop at Vancouver en route early the next morning. In addition, the *Queen City* sailed to the Nass River canneries and other points on the north coast of British Columbia.

The luxurious *Islander* and the more utilitarian *Danube* alternated on weekly sailings from Victoria via Vancouver to Skagway and Wrangell, Alaska. Departure time from Victoria was scheduled for 8:00 p.m. Additionally, two local services were maintained on the Fraser River. The sternwheeler *Transfer* served the lower Fraser River route, sailing from New Westminster each day, calling at Steveston, Ladner and other landings. On market days, when agricultural produce was sold at New Westminster, two trips were made to carry the extra cargos and heavier passenger traffic. The sternwheeler *Beaver* sailed on the upper Fraser River route from New Westminster to Chilliwack. She steamed upriver on Mondays, Wednesdays and Fridays, making return trips each following day and laying over at New Westminster on Sundays.

The steamers *Maude*, *Otter*, *Willapa* and *Yosemite* provided an adequate reserve fleet to replace the regular ships in case of refits or groundings, which were not infrequent. These ships also augmented the other steamers during the busy summer seasons and were available should sudden traffic develop or for charter business and excursions. In addition to relief duties, the *Maude* was used as a collier for the fleet.

While the service was satisfactory, it really did little to encourage tourist travel on the Coast and provided no links to Puget Sound or many ports in the Strait of Georgia. While other shipping lines such as the Union Steamship Company and the Pacific Coast Steamship Company served some of these routes, it was clear that there were ample opportunities for improving on the efforts of the Canadian Pacific Navigation Company which were coming under increasing criticism from the public.

However, before much could be done to extend the services, replacements were necessary for some of the aging ships in the fleet. The *Yosemite* was nearly 40 years old and the other sidewheeler, *Princess Louise* was over 30. Moreover, all of the larger steamers were at least 10 years old. The smaller vessels were slow and not well suited to the needs of intercity travel and were proving inadequate on some of the coastal freight and passenger runs as well.

To James Troup, the new manager of the CPR's recently acquired shipping line, the actions needed to improve the

The Tees *became . . .*

The Otter *was built . . .*

The *Tees* became the regular vessel on the Vancouver Island west coast route during the early 1900's. She is shown here pulling away from a dock on Barkley Sound. — PROVINCIAL ARCHIVES

The *Otter* was built by the CPN at Victoria in 1900 and resembled the *Queen City* in appearance. She served on a number of the coastal routes, including the Gulf Islands run. Schedules on these sailings were flexible. Some stops were made at "company convenience" and others on "flag", all of course with weather and tides permitting. Off the stern is *Princess Alice*. — JOE D. WILLIAMSON

The CPN's Maude *was ...*

The CPN's *Maude* was sold in 1903 for use as a salvage vessel. Her 42-year career ended at the scrap yard in 1914. — PROVINCIAL ARCHIVES

operation were clear and he persuaded his superiors to follow his suggestions and acquire new faster ships. Captain Troup was an excellent choice for the position of manager. He was experienced, having operated river steamers on the Columbia River, both in Oregon and in British Columbia. He was an imaginative, capable administrator and a man of vision. During the first few years he held office he developed a keen insight into the needs of the coastal cities and communities and left his mark on both the design of the new ships and the standards established for the service.

Since traffic on the northern route to Alaska was heavy, it was decided first to acquire a vessel capable of complementing the *Islander* in this service. Instead of building a new vessel, Troup determined to purchase a suitable steamer already available and thus avoid the delay of a year or more in construction time. The *Hating*, a relatively new, steel-hulled vessel built for the Chinese coastal trade, was found to fill the CPR's requirements and was acquired early in 1901. The 1,708 ton steamer was built by Hawthorne, Leslie and Company of Newcastle-on-Tyne in 1888 as the *Cass*. In her 13 years in the Far East, she had been the scene of a mutiny and had survived an attack by pirates. Being sold several times, her name had been changed from *Cass* to *Arthur* to *Cass* to *Ningchow* and finally to *Hating*, the name she carried on her arrival on the Pacific coast in May 1901.

The CPR had one more name change in mind for the *Hating*. Having a fleet of ocean liners carrying the name "Empress," the Company decided to name new additions to its coastal fleet after Princesses. With this decision, the famed Princess fleet came into being. It was announced even before the *Hating* arrived that she would be renamed the *Princess May* in honour of the wife of the Duke of Cornwall and York. However, the actual formalities took some time to complete, so that for the first few months of her career on the Coast, she retained her former name.

Under the command of Captain A. O. Cooper, the *Hating* made an uneventful crossing of the Pacific. Heavy seas and thick fogs were encountered but the ship was still able to maintain a speed of about 12 knots for most of the voyage and arrived two days ahead of schedule. While the ship's appointments were somewhat below the standard the CPR planned to set for its new fleet, they were quite adequate until she could be refitted. There were accommodations for 60 first class passengers and a much greater number of second class travellers, although her dining room space was quite limited.

It was planned to place the new Princess on the Alaska run as soon as she could be made ready, replacing the smaller steamer *Danube*, which was serving the route at the time. The *Islander* was also being readied to resume her regular runs north following her annual overhaul. In the absence of the *Islander*, the *Amur* had been placed on the service. However, the heavier summer traffic required the services of the larger steamers. The *Islander*'s first departure for the north was announced for May 20th, with the *Hating* to take the next sailing a week later. This schedule provided sufficient time for the *Islander* to relieve the *Charmer* on the Victoria to Vancouver service for a few days so that the latter could be given her annual cleaning and painting.

Meanwhile, Captain Troup was busy making plans for further additions to the fleet. He saw great potential in developing the tourist trade on the Pacific coast. With a warm, mild climate, beautiful scenery and steady commercial trade, the area had all the requirements for establishing a lucrative business. He recognized that the present schedules were inadequate for tourists and that revisions would be required. Passengers on the late night sailing from Victoria to Vancouver missed all of the attractive scenery of the Gulf Islands, the views of Mount Baker and the Olympic Mountains, and caught only a glimpse of the entrance to Vancouver Harbour. In consequence, Troup spent the spring months of 1901 working on possible schedule revisions and on the designs of new steamers for the Coast Service. The new *Princess May* was a real boon to the fleet, but the ambitious and far-sighted Captain Troup had greater things in mind.

He envisioned an 18 to 20 knot steamer that would be the swiftest and most luxurious vessel on the entire Pacific coast. He carried his ideas to his superiors in the CPR and won their approval. As a result, bids were opened early in 1901 for construction of the next CPR Princess, to be named the *Princess Victoria*.

Development of the Princess fleet progressed smoothly throughout the first six months of Captain Troup's capable management, but events were to intervene and brutally disrupt his plans.

The Sinking of the Islander

If there was any part of the rugged, indented North Pacific coast that seemed to hold particular antipathy for ships of the CPR's coastal service, it was surely the rock- and ice-strewn Lynn Canal on the Alaska shipping route. Lucky indeed was the vessel that did not at some time experience the hazards presented by that long, stormy fjord. For three ships of the CPR service, the Lynn Canal was a graveyard.

The S.S. *Islander*, sleek, steel-hulled and luxurious, was long a favourite on the Coast. When the Klondike gold rush began in the late 1890's, the speedy *Islander* was assigned to the northern route to carry the miners and their following to Skagway and Juneau where their long inland treks began.

She was the biggest ship in the CPR's coastal fleet, and while not the most modern, she certainly was one of the most attractive. Two hundred and forty feet long and 42 feet at the beam, the hull was subdivided into six watertight compartments separated by heavy steel bulkheads. Many people thought her to be practically unsinkable.

At 7:30 p.m. on August 14, 1901, the *Islander* was leaving Skagway, Alaska for points south. Captain Hamilton Foote,

PRINCESS
MAY

The first addition . . .
The Princess May *was . . .*

The first addition the CPR made to its fleet was the steamer *Hating*, renamed *Princess May*, which served on the Alaska route.
— PROVINCIAL ARCHIVES

The *Princess May* was overhauled by the CPR and given many improvements over the years. In this view, she is making about 15 knots in Johnstone Strait. The lack of smoke indicates that there is a good fire on the boilers with little fuel being wasted. — PROVINCIAL ARCHIVES

the master, ordered the head and spring lines cast off and then rang up Full Ahead. To his chagrin, the ship did not budge, except to rock from side to side and to pull down at the stern. In his haste to sail, he had forgotten to let go his stern line, and, as one passenger recalled, to relieve his frustrations and restore his dignity, "He regaled all on deck with a loud rendition of the complete encyclopedia of nautical profanity." Such was a captain's prerogative in times of embarrassment or duress. The situation was soon rectified and after clearing the confines of the harbour, the *Islander* worked up to a speed of about 14 knots. The course was southwest, down the long narrow Lynn Canal towards Juneau.

Since it remained light in these northern waters in the summer months until midnight, the passengers were in no hurry to retire. On board the *Islander* were 110 passengers and a crew of 62. After a leisurely dinner in the ship's restaurant, many congregated in the main saloon for card games and dancing. It was time for a celebration, for many on board had not left the Yukon since 1897 or '98 when word of the gold rush had first spread down the coast. Undoubtedly, many in the happy gathering had made their first sailing north on the *Islander*.

Even during the summer, care had to be exercised when navigating in the north. Ice from glaciers was always a threat and sudden, unexpected squalls could quickly change an inlet from placid to storm-whipped and perilous. However, as darkness settled over the *Islander*, the only hint of danger was a low, thin layer of fog hanging just above the water. Otherwise, visibility was good and the sea was calm. Meanwhile, Captain Foote had retired to the ship's saloon to socialize with the passengers. Captain LeBlanc, the ship's pilot, was left in charge on the bridge. Captain Foote had left no specific instructions relating to the speed or course of the vessel in the event that ice or other hazards should appear.

About 2:00 a.m. off Douglas Island, LeBlanc sighted floating ice off the bow and swung to clear it. He maintained the ship's speed at about 14 knots. Only 15 minutes later, there was a rending crash on the port bow. The ship had hit an iceberg. LeBlanc immediately ordered the engines stopped, fearing the ship's screws would also hit and the ship would be disabled. Reports soon reached the bridge that the vessel was taking water rapidly. Setting course for Douglas Island, three-quarters of a mile away, LeBlanc prepared to beach the steamer.

Captain George Ferey, ship's quatermaster was at the wheel. LeBlanc ordered full ahead, and then realizing the extent of the damage and the rapid rate of flooding, ordered full astern, hoping to take pressure off the bulkheads and beach the *Islander* stern first, but the ship was unresponsive, due to water in the port side counteracting the rudder. Meanwhile, Captain Foote had reached the bridge.

At first the officers hoped that the ship might not sink, merely settling by the bow, but Foote ordered the boats swung out over the sides of the ship. He felt the bulkheads would hold as they had two years previously when his ship *Tees* had run into ice and suffered only light damage. However, within minutes, it was apparent that the graceful *Islander* was doomed. The screws and rudder had lifted clear of the water; the engines thrashing uselessly. Ferey said to the ship's master, "Captain, I guess we will have to go." and Foote replied, "I guess we will have to." They left the bridge and joined the passengers and crew hurrying to the boats.

During this period, the crew was standing by the boats and attempting to rouse passengers in their cabins. Horace Fowler, second steward, rushed below in a vain attempt to reach cabins in the lower decks. He was never seen again. Within five minutes of the crash, the engines were useless and the chief engineer, Alex L. Brownlee, ordered his men to aid the passengers in abandoning the ship and then to save their own lives. In hopes of slowing the rush of water through the ship, the coal bunkers were sealed off, trapping 11 stowaways who had been quartered there; no one knew they were still inside.

As often happens in times of great danger, there was confusion in getting the passengers and crew evenly distributed among the boats. While theoretically there was ample capacity for all aboard, many found themselves without a boat. Indeed, one boat left the ship little more than half full. As the *Islander* suffered her final agonies before slipping under the icy water, passengers and crew members still on board made frantic efforts to clear the ship so that they would not be pulled down by the suction of the plunging vessel.

Struggling from their stateroom up the steeply inclined decks, Dr. W. S. Phillips of Seattle, his wife and daughter finally reached the upper deck. However, the suction caused by the rapid inrush of water was so great that all three were sucked into one of the ventilators and Mrs. Phillips and her daughter were carried to their deaths. Fortunately, the doctor's chin caught on the rim of the ventilator and he was able to extricate himself. Then the *Islander* took her final plunge, carrying the doctor with her. When he surfaced, he was pulled onto a life raft and later taken to shore. There, to his horror, he found the body of his little girl washed onto the beach.

As the engine rooms flooded, the boilers exploded, shattering the saloon and upper decks and sending a shower of debris down on the survivors in the water. Only 15 minutes had passed since the steamer had struck the iceberg. Captains Foote and Ferey and many others were carried overboard by the force of the explosion and managed to cling to pieces of wreckage until they could make their way to larger rafts or boats. However, for many the night of agony was far from over.

Passenger Joseph W. MacFarlane recalled the scene:

I could hear voices all around me shouting for help. Some were women's voices; and once I thought I heard a child cry out. The loudest of all of these was a Swede's shouting hysterically every breath, "For God's sake; somebody come and save me . . . For

God's sake; somebody come and save me..." He kept this up ten minutes, I believe, his crazed cry slashing the darkness with agony. It was becoming more nerve-racking than the urgent waters we were all fighting against, when I heard someone say, "You fool; if you can't swim, float!" Everyone laughed, in spite of imminent death; the climax of tension snapped under the wry humour of such advice.

Gradually the survivors congregated on the larger pieces of wreckage and the life rafts. The boats had struck out for shore. There the passengers were landed and some of the boats returned to the scene of the wreck to look for more survivors. However, in the darkness with broken fog hanging over the water, they found few until morning. Meanwhile, Second Officer Powell had made his way to a raft where Captains Foote and LeBlanc had taken refuge. On grasping a lifeline, he was confronted by a large man on the raft pointing a revolver at him ordering him off the raft. "Shoot anyway," replied the officer, "for I guess you'll soon follow me. Anyhow, I believe your cartridges are wet." Later, finding a floating door, Powell abandoned the raft. About the same time, LeBlanc also found a better float, but Captain Foote, who stayed on the raft, received the brunt of remarks from the man with the revolver.

The captain is reported to have replied, "Oh I've lost my ship; I suppose I will have to take my medicine, but I can die as game as many of you!" The other man hastened to add that the raft was overcrowded. Then Foote said, "I guess there is too many of us on the raft. Good-bye boys," and he slipped off the raft and swam away. Not long afterwards the captain was seen to slip from his lifejacket and disappear. Later, the man with the revolver denied that he had forced anyone from the raft, claiming that the captain, delirious from the cold, had slipped away from the raft.

As the night wore on many others succumbed as the biting cold of the waters took its toll. By morning when the last of the survivors was rescued, the extent of the casualties was apparent. Captain Foote, 16 members of his crew and 23 passengers had perished along with the proud *Islander*.

Later, an inquiry into the disaster commended the crew of the vessel on its heroic efforts to save the passengers. No evidence could be found that any of the ship's officers had been drinking. However, the inquiry did conclude that had the extent of the damage to the steamer been appreciated immediately after the collision, more lives could have been saved. In addition, they criticized the apparent lack of orders left for the bridge watch in the event of ice being encountered. Furthermore, Captain LeBlanc was censured for maintaining the *Islander*'s high speed when ice had been sighted in the vicinity of the vessel.

The tragic loss of the *Islander* saddened people all along the Coast. It was one of the worst wrecks in the history of steam navigation in these waters. However, the story of the *Islander* is not concluded with her loss. Returning from the north, she often carried large quantities of gold. At the time of the wreck, Vancouver's *Daily Province* reported that she carried $275,000 worth, of which $175,000 was held by the purser while the balance was carried by the passengers. Such stories of lost treasure resulted in a number of attempts to locate and raise the vessel. Finally in July 1934, she was brought to the surface and eventually scrapped, but only approximately $40,000 in gold was recovered and that was not enough to pay the salvage costs.

The New Princesses

The loss of the *Islander* greatly increased the need for replacement vessels for the CPR's B.C. coast steamship operations. Several new ships were required if the service was to be maintained and improved. Fortunately work was about to proceed on Captain Troup's new vessel, the *Princess Victoria*. She was to be built for the Victoria-Vancouver route at the Newcastle yards of C. S. Swann and Hunter Company in England. This firm received a contract to built the 1,943 ton, 300 foot, 20 knot steamer, and by mid-1902 work on the ship was well advanced. The triple expansion, 5,800 horsepower engines were provided by Hawthorne, Leslie & Company Limited and were comparable to those installed in contemporary warships.

On November 18, 1902, Mrs. Archie Baker, wife of the European traffic manager of the CPR, christened the new vessel the *Princess Victoria*. The Company sent T. G. Mitchell, chief engineer of the *Charmer*, to England to supervise the installation of the ship's machinery and prepare her for the long voyage to the Pacific coast. As strikes were pending in English shipyards, it was decided to complete the *Princess*'s wooden superstructure in British Columbia so that the vessel could begin operation in time for at least part of the 1903 summer season. As a result, the *Princess Victoria* sailed from Newcastle on January 29, 1903 looking more like a torpedo boat than a smart new coastal liner. At this stage in her career, she was little more than a sleek hull, with a rudimentary canvas bridge built in front of the ship's funnel casings. On seeing her, few would have guessed that she would soon be one of the most beautiful and elegant vessels on the Pacific coast.

After two months at sea and an uneventful passage through the Straits of Magellan, the *Princess Victoria* arrived in Victoria on March 28, 1903. She was immediately taken to shipyards in Vancouver to be completed. The work, for which the local yards were well qualified, included fitting out all the cabins, lounges, staterooms and boats, and providing all interior furnishings. It was a considerable undertaking and one that had to be carried out with dispatch. The work proceeded throughout the late spring and early summer.

Meanwhile, at the B.C. Marine Railway shipyards at Esquimalt, a second new Princess was under construction. This ship was of wooden construction and was intended to replace the *Islander* on the service to Alaska and northern British Columbia ports. The new single-screw steamer was 193 feet long, 37

The incomparable *Princess Victoria* set the pattern for the CPR's
revitalization of the coastal steamship services of the Canadian
Pacific Navigation Company. She was fast, graceful and had
luxurious accommodations. There was not a coastal liner on the
Pacific that could successfully compete with her for speed and
elegance. — PROVINCIAL ARCHIVES

Looking more like a torpedo boat than an elegant coastal liner, the *Princess Victoria* is shown shortly after her arrival at Victoria on March 28, 1903. All of her wooden superstructure and passenger accommodations had yet to be fitted before she could enter service.
— PROVINCIAL ARCHIVES

Looking more like ...

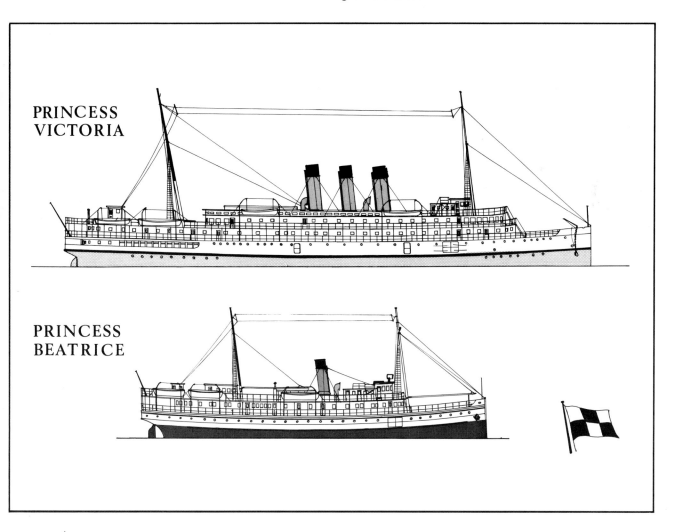

PRINCESS
VICTORIA

PRINCESS
BEATRICE

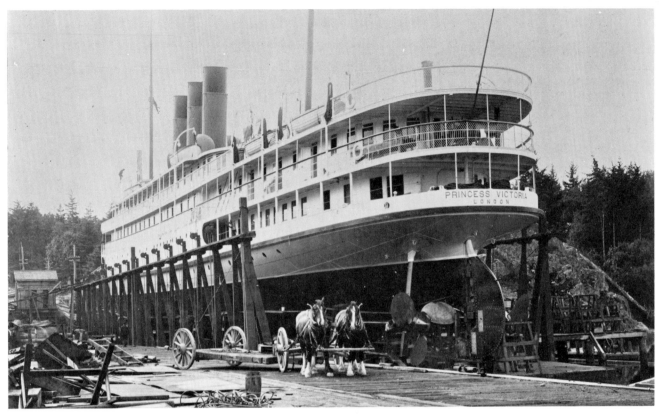

The British Columbia Marine ...
The Princess Beatrice ...   *Completing the hull ...*

The British Columbia Marine Railway at Esquimalt did most of the CPR's repair work. Here the *Princess Victoria* is shown out of the water not long after completion. Note that she is registered in London. All of the Princesses were eventually registered in Victoria, their home port. — PROVINCIAL ARCHIVES

The *Princesses Beatrice* and *Victoria* . . .

The launching . . .

The *Princess Beatrice* was the first CPR Princess built in British Columbia. These photos illustrate the progress of her construction. In the first scene, the framing of her wooden hull is well advanced at the B.C. Marine Railway's Esquimalt yard. As work progresses on the *Beatrice*'s superstructure in 1903, the *Princess Victoria* is also being worked on. The launch of the *Princess Beatrice* took place on September 10, 1903 and she underwent her trials, shown in the final photo, early in November of that year. — ALL PROVINCIAL ARCHIVES

feet in breadth, and had a displacement of 1,290 tons. With a design speed of 13 knots, she was not comparable to the much faster *Princess Victoria* and hence never received as much publicity. Nevertheless, the *Princess Beatrice*, as she was to be named, was a fine, seaworthy steamer.

On August 17, 1903, the *Princess Victoria* was ready for her sea trials. Two hundred and fifty invited guests boarded the gleaming white liner at the dock of the B.C. Marine Railway Company at Esquimalt, anticipating an exciting three hour cruise in Juan de Fuca Strait. The weather was perfect for the occasion, with calm seas and almost no wind. Clear skies accentuated the rugged outline of the Olympic Mountains to the south. Promptly at 3:00 p.m., Captain Troup gave the order to cast off and the new steamer eased away from the pier.

Once clear of Fort Rodd Hill and the anchored sailing ships off Royal Roads, the steamer swung to port off Brochie Ledge and Full Ahead was ordered. The *Princess Victoria* sprang to life. Coal smoke rolled from her three slightly raked funnels as below decks, stokers fired her six boilers. The well balanced engines produced almost no vibration as she worked up to 15, then 19 knots. Under Chief Engineer T. G. Mitchell, the engine room staff was, in the words of the *Daily Colonist* reporter, "As proud of the engines as a mother of a child."

To the delight of those on board, the steamer's sleek hull cut through the calm water producing remarkably small bow waves and an even wake. A proud Captain Rudlin held the wheel of the ship that would soon be his new command, as Captain Troup, master of the ship until the trials were completed, looked on. The official speed on the *Victoria*'s timed runs was 19 or perhaps 19½ knots. It was a fine speed and few questioned that she would improve on that by a considerable margin. Off Trial Island, the steamer swung around and then raced back to William Head, again making 19 knots. Then she turned south towards Port Angeles, Washington.

On the afterdeck, the band of the Fifth Regiment, Canadian Garrison Artillery, played and refreshments were served in the saloon. The ship's officers and the guests then gathered in the dining room where toasts were made to Captain Troup, the CPR service, the *Princess Victoria*, Captain Rudlin, Sir Thomas Shaughnessy, president of the CPR, Chief Engineer Mitchell and others. Victoria's pioneer doctor, J. S. Helmcken, spoke to the party and Troup responded, not neglecting to mention that in the past Victoria had spurned any suggestions that the CPR establish steamer service between Victoria and Vancouver. However, after the numerous toasts all present were willing to forget past differences and turn their attention to the beautiful ship that had carried them to within sight of Port Angeles. The *Princess Victoria* then headed back to Victoria's Inner Harbour and tied up at the CPR docks at about 6:00 p.m. As the delighted guests left the liner, preparations were made for her first regular run to Vancouver, scheduled for that night.

Whistle of the *Princess Victoria*.
Drawing — ROBERT D. TURNER

After a leisurely, uneventful passage to Vancouver, the *Princess Victoria* was readied for her return to Victoria. Captain Rudlin and his crew eagerly awaited their departure, for it was evident that the ship had the potential to easily capture the "blue riband" for the fastest run between the two cities. With a strong flood tide running against her, the *Princess* commenced her trip at 1:30 p.m. By 2:45 she had cleared Sand Heads at the harbour mouth and 38 minutes later, she skirted Gossip Reef. On this 12 mile portion of the run, she had averaged between 18 and 19 knots. Nearing Victoria, she passed Ten Mile Point at 4:51 and at 5:18 rounded the Outer Wharf, where compulsory speed restrictions were obeyed. The elapsed time for the 72 nautical mile crossing was three hours and 48 minutes, fully 13 minutes better than the record, set by the Union Steamship Company of New Zealand's trans-Pacific liner *Moana* in 1901. The previous record had been set by the old sidewheeler *Yosemite* in 1883, when Captain Broadhurst had made the run in four hours and 20 minutes.

Delighted by his ship's performance, Captain Rudlin knew that she would do better yet. During the trials, the engines had run at 155 revolutions per minute, while on the record run a maximum of only 145 revolutions per minute had been reached. The *Princess Victoria* was quickly establishing a reputation as the fastest merchant steamer on the Pacific coast. In fact, only navy torpedo boat destroyers were faster.

The *Princess Victoria* took time out from the Victoria-Vancouver run for her first excursion, carrying the Native Sons of British Columbia from Victoria to Tacoma and back on Saturday, August 22, 1903. Not surprisingly, she set a new speed record for the Puget Sound run, clocking a fast time of four hours, 40 minutes and 30 seconds. Troup was well aware of the promotional value of such record runs; he was anxious to develop the steamship line and advance Victoria as a tourist centre.

The *Victoria* was by no means fully finished when she began service in the summer of 1903. Much work still remained to be done to the cabins and furnishings. However, Troup felt it was important to show off the new vessel for publicity purposes and also to capture at least a portion of the heavy summer traffic. In this way, the ship was able to produce considerable revenue simply by having her finished work delayed until winter, when she could be withdrawn with little loss of patronage.

By September 9, 1903 the vessel under construction at Esquimalt was ready for launching and at the ceremonies was christened the *Princess Beatrice* by Mrs. Fitzherbert Bullen, wife of the shipyard owner. The *Beatrice* was at that time one of the largest vessels to be built in British Columbia and demonstrated the abilities of the local craftsmen to produce splendid vessels. After her launching, final fitting out was carried on and the steamer was ready for trials by early November.

Like the *Princess Victoria* and nearly all subsequent Princesses, the *Beatrice* was luxuriously appointed. As the *Daily Colonist* noted, "Her saloons and staterooms are marvels of richness — her decorations could hardly be better were she the private yacht of a millionaire." The paper also noted that "Everyone was delighted with the *Beatrice*'s speed and luxury. She was a gentlemen's club afloat with a special lounge for ladies so they could get away from male stares and smoke." Despite such praise, she could not be compared to the *Princess Victoria*; overall she was a much smaller, less elegant vessel.

It was Troup's intention to operate the *Princess Beatrice* between New Westminster and Victoria until the following spring, when she would be placed on the run to the Nass River and Alaska, but events were to dictate otherwise.

A Victoria to Seattle service had been maintained throughout the 1890's by the beautiful steamer *City of Kingston*, owned during her last years by the Oregon Railway and Navigation Company. The Company also operated the large steamer *Victorian* on the route. She had been built under the supervision of Captain James Troup especially for the run, during the period before he moved to Canada to work for the CPR. However, the *Victorian* proved to be too expensive to operate, having inefficient engines, and was withdrawn. The *City of Kingston* met a worse fate in 1899, when she sank following a collision with the steamship *Glenogle* in Tacoma Harbour. The *City of Seattle*, which had also sailed the Seattle to Victoria route as a relief vessel had in the meantime been sold to the Pacific Coast Steamship Company which operated her from Seattle to Alaska.

Following the sinking of the *City of Kingston* the Seattle-Victoria route was taken over by the Puget Sound Navigation Company of Seattle (PSN), which was affiliated with the Alaska Steamship Company, and which at various times during the early 1900's was referred to as the International Steamship Company and the Inland Navigation Company. This company placed the wooden-hulled steamers *Rosalie* and *Majestic* on the run during the summer, providing a twice-daily service. During the winter months, the much smaller *Garland* was substituted for reasons of economy, but the service she provided was inadequate, at least in the minds of Victoria residents. In 1903 the PSN placed its brand new steamer *Clallam* on the route, along with the *Majestic*, which had been given an overhaul and renamed *Whatcom*. The *Clallam* was a fine ship, but if one takes cognizance of maritime superstition, she was marked for bad luck. At her launch, the traditional bottle of champagne missed her bow and failed to break. Then when the ensign was unfurled, it was found to be upside down — a jinx if ever there was one.

Less than a year later, on January 8, 1904 the *Clallam* was crossing the Strait of Juan de Fuca bound for Victoria when she ran into rough weather. As the storm worsened the engine room began to flood. The pumps could not check the water and before long power was lost. The ship began to wallow in the swell, despite the fact that a jib sail had been rigged for-

The Clallam, *shown . . .*

The *Clallam*, shown above, was placed on the Seattle - Victoria route by the Puget Sound Navigation Company. Tragically, the unlucky steamer foundered and sank with the loss of 54 lives in January 1904. Shortly after, the CPR placed the *Princess Beatrice* on the route.
— JOE D. WILIAMSON

ward. The captain ordered the women and children into the lifeboats when the *Clallam* appeared about to go down. Ironically, she stayed afloat, but all in the lifeboats were lost. The steamer survived through the night and was taken in tow the next morning, only to founder a short while later. Fifty-four persons, most of them women and children, were lost in the tragedy. It was reported that the day before the loss of the *Clallam*, the bell-sheep used to lead other animals aboard refused to step onto the ship and had to be left behind.

Most of the mutton used on the Island and in Vancouver was supplied through Seattle on ships like the *Clallam*. The sheep were shipped alive by steamer since refrigeration was primitive and expensive at that time. For years the CPR had an old ram named, not unexpectedly, Billy, which led the sheep from the stock cars onto the night steamers. As many as 500 or 600 sheep would be handled in this way on one sailing. It is said that Billy would wander around the docks until he heard the ship's whistle when he would race back to be on board for the departure. Apparently, he also got into the habit of breaking into the fresh produce shipped on the steamers and developed a taste for fresh lettuce and tomatoes. Eventually, he was retired to a farm on the outskirts of Victoria. Live cattle were also carried on the ships and as might be imagined they also created problems. On occasion they would break loose and once found their way through the shell doors on the side of the ship and fell overboard into Victoria Harbour only to be rounded up by one of the ship's boats.

Following the *Clallam* tragedy, residents of Victoria were determined to have a more reliable service established between the Island and Puget Sound. They therefore asked the CPR to place the newly finished *Princess Beatrice* in operation between Victoria and Seattle. The CPR was sympathetic to the proposal and agreed to it. The *Beatrice* was immediately put in service on the route; on January 20, 1904, she initiated the run that eventually became part of the famous "Triangle Route" between Seattle, Vancouver and Victoria.

While the CPR was undoubtedly pleased to extend its operations into the Puget Sound area, the move contributed to the already severe shortage of vessels. With the *Beatrice* committed to the Seattle route, another steamer would be required to augment the Alaska service. Troup therefore ordered another wooden steamer, larger than the *Princess Beatrice*, from the B.C. Marine Railway Company at Esquimalt. This newest addition would be named the *Princess Royal*.

Meanwhile, the CPR was working to establish a critical link in its hotel chain by opening a luxury hotel in Victoria. Since the completion of the railway through the Rocky Mountains, the CPR had vigorously promoted tourism as a means of attracting passengers. Hotels and chalets were built at suitable locations, such as Lake Louise, Glacier and Banff to provide luxury accommodations for travellers. It is no coincidence that Canada's first National Parks were established in the Rockies along the route of the railway.

In 1908, the CPR . . .
Carriages await . . .

Victoria, at the southern tip of Vancouver Island, was another area that had great potential for tourist promotion, due to its warm climate and attractive scenery. It was a natural extension of the CPR's hotel system to include one in Victoria to provide accommodations for passengers using the B.C. Coast Service steamers from Washington and mainland British Columbia.

Following an active promotion campaign by Victoria's mayor, Frank Barnard, the city agreed to grant the CPR tax exemptions if a hotel costing at least $300,000 was built. The CPR agreed and commissioned architect Francis Mawson Rattenbury to design the structure, to be called the Empress Hotel.

Construction of the magnificent building began in July 1904 and continued for three and a half years before it was formally opened on January 20, 1908. The CPR more than fulfilled its obligation to Victoria, as the Empress finally cost more than $1,600,000 to complete. The Empress Hotel became a symbol of Victoria, traditionally visited by the rich and famous, from royalty and presidents to film stars. It has also been a popular hotel for the less affluent. Today it is still, in consort with the Provincial Legislative Buildings, one of the most famous and imposing structures in western Canada.

By mid-April 1904 the *Princess Victoria*, after spending several months at the B.C. Marine Railway having her interior passenger accommodations finished, was finally ready to resume service. Throughout, she was a picture of elegance and comfort. The layout and high quality of the fittings set the pattern and standard that was to exemplify the CPR's coastal steamers for the next half century.

With the *Princess Victoria* having demonstrated a remarkable record of dependable high-speed performances during her brief operations the previous summer, Captain Troup planned to take full advantage of the potential for improving the service offered by the steamer. Since the sailing between Victoria and Vancouver or Seattle could be completed in under four hours, it seemed reasonable to expect the vessel to be able to make at least four one-way voyages in a 24-hour period. As a result, a new service was established. The *Victoria* was scheduled to leave Victoria at 7:30 a.m., arriving in Vancouver four hours later. There, a 90 minute layover was made before she returned to Victoria for a scheduled 5:00 p.m. arrival time. This sailing provided good connections with the CPR's passenger trains arriving in Vancouver from the east in the mornings and leaving in the afternoons. The liner then had ample time to make a night trip to Seattle, leaving Victoria at 7:00 p.m. and returning by 4:00 the next morning. The three and a half hour layover in Victoria provided adequate time for coaling and provisioning the vessel.

To enable her to cover the 325 miles in a 24-hour period, the *Princess Victoria* carried a double crew on board. It was a rugged schedule, but Troup staked his reputation on her ability to perform to his expectations. The service was inaugurated in

In 1908, the CPR opened its famous Empress Hotel in Victoria. Several large additions were soon made to the building, making it one of the outstanding hotels on the Pacific coast.
— PROVINCIAL ARCHIVES

Carriages await passengers outside the CPR's steamship offices in Victoria in the early 1900's.
— PROVINCIAL ARCHIVES

mid-June 1904 and from then on Troup was never to regret his decision to place the *Victoria* on the run. It proved highly successful despite minor interruptions when the ship was out of service for repairs.

Rivalry on Puget Sound

All Victorians knew that their *Princess Victoria* was the fastest steamer on the Pacific coast, but in Seattle there were those who questioned this claim — notably the owners and crew of the Puget Sound Navigation Company's new oil-fired steamer *Indianapolis*. In Seattle, this vessel had been advertised as "the White Flyer, fastest steamer in these waters." Crews of the two liners had exchanged numerous challenges.

"Wait until the *Indianapolis* starts about the same time as the *Princess Victoria*!" was the taunt. Actually, one only needed to compare the service speeds of the two steamers to recognize that the *Princess* held the edge, having attained a speed of 22 knots, while the *Indianapolis* had managed only 16 knots. Ah, but who would believe statistics when the reputations of two ships were at stake! A race would be the only acceptable course of action to end the rivalry once and for all. Of course, two companies' liners did not just race; a contest had to come about through circumstance. Needless to say, it was not long before an appropriate situation presented itself.

On Tuesday, July 10, 1906, conditions seemed ideal. The *Indianapolis* was in Victoria Harbour with an excursion party of 623 people from Seattle. Her scheduled departure time was 6:00 p.m., 45 minutes ahead of the *Princess Victoria*'s usual sailing. Captain Carter of the *Indianapolis* was impatient to get as much lead over his rival as possible, and to the consternation of some of his passengers, sailed early, leaving several on the dock. These stranded passengers found space on the *Princess Victoria* and quickly changed sides in the impending contest. The *Princess Victoria* sailed promptly on schedule, but by 6:50 when Captain Griffin ordered Full Ahead, the *Indianapolis* had gained a substantial lead.

Shortly before the *Princess Victoria* steamed past Brochie Ledge at 6:55, smoke was sighted ahead. Excitement grew as the distance gradually closed. Passengers took time for a hurried dinner as they prepared for a long chase. The *Princess* passed Discovery Island at 7:09 and Point Wilson at 8:22, as evening closed in on the racing steamers. The *Indianapolis* was still several miles ahead and intent on maintaining the lead, but by 9:15, when the *Princess* cleared Point No Point at the northern end of the Kitsap Peninsula, the lights and billowing smoke of the *Indianapolis* were clearly in sight.

Twenty minutes later, the distance separating the steamers had closed to less than one mile. Excitement on the *Princess Victoria* was fast reaching a peak as passengers and crew lined the ship's railings to witness the closing minutes of the long chase. From below the engine room crew was constantly shouting, "Have we passed her yet?" At 9:44, as the two steamers swept past Jefferson Head, the cheers of those on deck answered

The Indianapolis *was . . .*

their queries. With three blasts of her distinctive whistle, the *Princess Victoria* left her defeated rival in her wake. A trumpeter on the *Princess* blew a defiant rendition of the Retreat, while the *Indianapolis* answered with a respectful blast of her whistle. Taunts from passengers of the *Princess*, most notably those left behind by the *Indianapolis*, sealed the victory. "We'll tell them you're on the way!" "If you don't get in until the last car leaves Tacoma, come over in the morning! . . . " The stokers and deckhands provided a more colourful and explicit harangue which remains unprintable.

Leaving the *Indianapolis* to find her way to port, the *Princess Victoria* steamed on ahead, docking in Seattle at 10:26 p.m. Her sailing time was three hours and 24 minutes, fully seven minutes longer than her own record crossing made the previous year. Several minutes later, the chastened *Indianapolis* steamed into port at full speed, the claims of her owners and crew thoroughly shattered.

Taking on a more dignified air, the *Princess Victoria* resumed her regular tri-city service without interruption. However, just over a week later, on July 21, 1906, she was involved in a tragic collision with the steam tug *Chehalis* near Vancouver Harbour's Brockton Point.

The Chehalis *Tragedy*

The *Chehalis*, a 50-foot vessel owned by the Union Steamship Company of Vancouver, was chartered to carry eight people on a cruise to the North Coast. Under the command of Captain James House, she sailed from North Vancouver at 1:55 p.m. and proceeded at a speed of eight knots towards the First Narrows at the harbour mouth. Just after 2:00, the *Princess Victoria* sailed from her berth at Shed No. 1 on the CPR pier with 219 passengers on board, bound for Victoria. It was a fine sunny day, with a light westerly breeze blowing and some fog hanging over the Narrows. The *Chehalis* was steering for the north side of the Narrows against a strong tide, flowing at about six knots. As a result, her actual headway was only about three knots, and her manoeuverability was severely impeded.

Apparently, the *Princess Victoria*'s officers noticed the *Chehalis* far off to starboard and turned their attention to clearing Brockton Point, as the steamer worked up to Full Ahead at 2:06. Their attention was then fixed on avoiding a small launch passing through the south side of the Narrows. Meanwhile, the courses of the *Chehalis* and the *Princess Victoria* had converged; the *Chehalis* had been forced towards the centre of the channel by the force of the tide, while the *Princess* had swung to starboard in clearing the launch, bringing her much closer to mid-channel than she otherwise would have been. In addition, her headway was reduced by the strong force of the tide.

Captain House of the *Chehalis* assumed that since he was ahead of the *Princess Victoria*, she would pass astern. However, those on the bridge of the *Princess* had failed to notice the *Chehalis* until a collision was imminent. On seeing the

The *Indianapolis* was placed on the Puget Sound - Victoria service by the Puget Sound Navigation Company. She was a fine, modern steamship but not a match for the larger, faster *Princess Victoria*.
— JOE D. WILLIAMSON

danger, Captain Griffin sounded the *Victoria*'s whistle twice and ordered Half Ahead at about 2:11, followed at 2:13 by Stop Engines, and then Full Astern. The helm was held amidships and the steamer came to a shuddering halt, but it was too late for the *Chehalis*. Suffering a glancing blow near the stern, she rolled to starboard and capsized. Nine of the 13 people on board went down with her. A boat lowered from the *Princess Victoria* and small craft in the area quickly rescued the survivors.

Subsequently, a Court of Inquiry was held to review the causes of the collision. The court felt that had the *Princess Victoria* manoeuvered to either side in addition to slowing her speed when the *Chehalis* was sighted, the collision might well have been avoided. It concluded that the collision resulted from lack of care in the CPR vessel's navigation, but went on to commend the rescue operations carried on by the steamer's crew. Captain Griffin was given a six month suspension of his Board of Trade Certificate. The court also felt that detailed regulations needed to be established for the navigation of ships in the confined entrance to Vancouver Harbour. At the time of the accident, small craft had equal rights with large ships, creating numerous problems for the bigger, less manoeuverable vessels.

The year 1906 held still one more trial for the *Princess Victoria*. On October 16th, the steamer ran aground on Lewis Rock off Oak Bay near Victoria in a heavy rain squall. There were no injuries, and the passengers were taken off by the *R. P. Rithet* and carried to Victoria. The next day at high tide, the *Victoria* was pulled free by the salvage steamer *Salvor* and the tug *Lorne*. Repairs to her damaged bow took about a month, and were carried out at the B.C. Marine Railway at Esquimalt.

Meanwhile, the new vessel under construction at the B.C. Marine Railway's Esquimalt Yards had reached an advanced stage of construction and was ready for launching. On Saturday, September 2, 1906 all was in readiness. The vessel was covered in flags and bunting and facilities were ready to accommodate Company officials and guests for the launching.

Shortly after 3:00 p.m. workmen began to knock away the blocks holding back the hull on the ways. Finally, the "dog shore" was removed and the vessel slowly began to move. The traditional bottle of champagne was released to christen the vessel — the *Princess Royal*. She slid down the throughways, but the bottle only grazed the bow and fell unbroken against the side of the ship. However, aside from this minor mishap, which might have been interpreted as bad luck, the launch was perfect. Tugs secured the vessel and towed her to the dock, where a reception was held. The trim wooden-hulled ship measured 227 feet long, had a beam of 40 feet and a moulded depth of 17 feet. The large triple expansion engines that were to power the new Princess at 15 knots were ready for

The Princess Royal
is Launched and the
E & N Steamers Join the Fleet

The *Joan*, a twin-screw wooden-hulled steamer of 831 tons, is pictured on the ways at Victoria, undergoing an overhaul.
— PROVINCIAL ARCHIVES

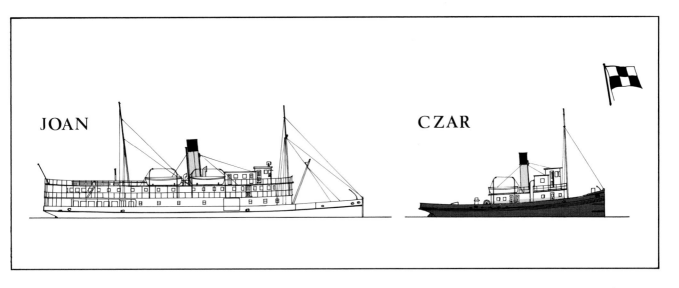

JOAN

CZAR

The Joan, *a* . . .

Nanaimo, the coal . . .
The steel-hulled Nanoose . . .

The tug Czar *was ...*

Nanaimo, the coal mining centre of Vancouver Island, was linked to Vancouver by the steamer *Joan*, owned by the Esquimalt and Nanaimo Railway Company. When the CPR purchased this line in 1905 the *Joan* and *City of Nanaimo*, both shown above, and the tug *Czar* were taken over and eventually added to the CPR's own coastal steamship service. — PROVINCIAL ARCHIVES

The steel-hulled *Nanoose* was built by the CPR for the railway barge service and is pictured at Ladysmith. The wharves in the background are for loading coal from the mines at Extension. — PROVINCIAL ARCHIVES

The tug *Czar* was used by the E & N Railway and the CPR to tow railway car ferries between Vancouver and Ladysmith. — CPR COLLECTION

installation, loaded on a scow. Since there was still a great deal of work to be done on the vessel, completion was not anticipated until the following summer, when the *Princess Royal* would sail on the Alaska route.

In 1905, while the *Princess Royal* was being built at Esquimalt, the CPR acquired the Esquimalt and Nanaimo Railway and all its holdings on Vancouver Island. With this purchase, the E & N's steamships *Joan*, which operated between Nanaimo and Vancouver, and *City of Nanaimo*, used along the east coast of the Island, as well as the tug *Czar*, became a part of the CPR's fleet.

The *Czar* had been employed by the E & N in towing railway car barges between Ladysmith and Vancouver, a service which enabled the Company to ship carload freight to and from the mainland without having to load and unload the cargo onto steamers. The consequent savings in time and labour were significant and contributed to keeping many Island enterprises competitive with firms on the mainland. With the growth in traffic on the E & N Railway following its takeover by the CPR, it soon became apparent that the barge service to the Island would need to be increased, and an order was placed with the B.C. Marine Railway Company in Esquimalt for the construction of a steel-hulled tug.

The new $75,000 tow boat was christened the *Nanoose*, after a bay near Nanaimo, and was ready for trials on July 11, 1908. She was painted in the standard CPR colours, with black hull, white bridge and upperworks and a yellow, black-topped funnel. She measured just over 120 feet in overall length and had a beam of 24 feet. Loaded, she drew 11.5 feet of water. She was powered by a single 600 horsepower engine, giving her a full speed of 12 knots.

Under the eye of H. F. Bullen, representing the builders, and Captains Troup and McGowan from the CPR, the *Nanoose* carried out trials in the Strait of Juan de Fuca, then tied up at the CPR's Belleville Street wharf in Victoria for final fitting out and public inspection. Later, she took dignitaries on a picnic excursion. The new tug then replaced the *Czar* on the barge service from Ladysmith to Vancouver so that the former E & N vessel could be given a refit as part of the CPR's routine maintenance program.

The *Princess Victoria* on the left and the *Chippewa* on the right
were arch rivals in the rate war between the CPR and the Puget
Sound Navigation Company. Both ships were fast, modern vessels
with attractive, spacious accommodations, but the *Chippewa* was
never able to match the speed of the CPR's three-funneled liner.
In this scene, at the height of the rate war, the two ships are
about to steam out of Seattle's Elliott Bay in a race for Victoria.
— JOE D. WILLIAMSON

Joshua Green posed for this portrait as a young
man in 1901. — SEATTLE HISTORICAL SOCIETY

CHAPTER III

THE GREAT RATE WAR

*The PSN Buys New Ships
and the Rivalry Increases*

Joshua Green . . .

THE EXCITING RACE in 1906 between the CPR's *Princess Victoria* and the Puget Sound Navigation Company's *Indianapolis* was but one aspect of the growing rivalry between the two steamship companies. While the public enjoyed and eagerly followed the racing and considered it great sport, the Companies were deadly serious in their determination to win in the competition for the lucrative Puget Sound to Victoria trade.

With the completion of the new Princesses, the CPR had a clear advantage over its rival, but the PSN soon took steps to improve its position. The Company's president, Joshua Green, purchased the modern steel-hulled Great Lakes steamers *Chippewa* and *Iroquois*. These ships arrived on the West Coast in the spring of 1907. Originally built for excursions, they had proven so popular that their owners had decided to sell them and acquire larger vessels for the prosperous trade that had developed. Before entering service with the PSN, the sleek, twin-funnelled steamers were converted to burn oil and were given a general cleanup and painting. While not as luxuriously appointed as the *Princess Victoria*, they were nonetheless attractively fitted out. The observation lounges were pannelled with mahogany and tastefully furnished with rattan and brown velvet upholstered seats. Their modern dining rooms could accommodate 109 people at a sitting and featured inlaid hardwood decor. The decks were spacious and the staterooms were comfortable.

Of the two vessels, the *Iroquois* was slightly larger, displacing 73 tons more than the 996 ton *Chippewa*. The *Iroquois* also had a slight edge in speed over the *Chippewa*, but both vessels were reported to be capable of about 18 knots. Triple expansion engines fed by four Roberts boilers drove their single screws. The Company had every reason to be proud of its new acquisitions.

On July 14, 1907, the *Chippewa* made her first run to Victoria, leaving Seattle's Pier One at 8:30 a.m. and arriving at the British Columbia port at 1:30 p.m., putting in briefly at Port Townsend en route. Returning, the *Chippewa* sailed from Victoria at 4:30 p.m. and tied up at Seattle five hours later.

When she arrived from the Great Lakes in 1907, the well
proportioned *Chippewa* was one of the most modern steamships
on Puget Sound. A favourite with excursionists, as this photo
attests, she was an able competitor in the rate war on the Seattle -
Victoria route. — JOE D. WILLIAMSON

Captain W. O. Hughes . . .
Number 324 . . .

Captain W. O. Hughes on the right was the first master of the *Princess Royal*. On his left is Captain J. W. Troup, manager of the CPR's coastal steamship operation. This photograph was taken in 1912 on either the *Princess Alice* or the *Princess Adelaide* shortly after their arrival on the coast. — PROVINCIAL ARCHIVES

Number 324 Maitland Avenue was the Troup residence in Victoria. The spacious house was built in 1905 and was finally demolished in the early 1960's to make way for construction of the Princess Patricia apartments.
— PROVINCIAL ARCHIVES

At the same time as the *Chippewa* went into service, the CPR coastal fleet was increased by the addition of the locally-built *Princess Royal*. She was a fine vessel of wooden construction featuring all the refinements for which the CPR was becoming well known. She had 72 comfortable staterooms, large airy observation lounges, a spacious dining hall and ample deck space. Resplendent in fresh white and grey paint with buff trim, the new steamer made a striking sight as she entered Victoria's Inner Harbour. Captain W. O. Hughes, a veteran mariner with 42 years experience, took command of the *Princess Royal* and prepared the vessel for her first cruise to Alaska, scheduled for July 18th. The *Royal* was to alternate with the *Princess May* to provide a weekly service to Alaska, while the *Princess Beatrice* was to be diverted from her winter Victoria-Seattle route to the north coastal run to Prince Rupert for the summer months.

The *Princess Royal*'s first cruise to Alaska was most successful; the steamer was widely acclaimed all along the Coast. One hundred and twenty people had the distinction of making the first trip north, while 136 sailed south on the return voyage. Captain Troup, who went along on the cruise, was pleased with the steamer's performance. She was able to hold to the schedule of the *Princess May*, which at the time was regarded as the fastest vessel on the Alaska run. The *Princess Royal* had little difficulty in maintaining a respectable speed of 14 to 14½ knots while remaining reasonably free from vibration.

The new Princess's second voyage north was more eventful. As she steamed into Dixon Entrance on the east coast of the Queen Charlotte Islands, she rammed an undetected obstruction, breaking off one of the propeller blades. While her speed was necessarily reduced, the incident did not prevent the *Royal* from completing the cruise. The usual coaling stop at Nanaimo was omitted on the southbound trip and the steamer proceeded to Esquimalt for repairs.

The keen rivalry between the CPR and the PSN continued throughout the summer and early fall of 1907, but since the heavy tourist trade was at its peak, neither company had any reason to try to force its competitor from the run. However, as the tourist business diminished in the late fall and winter months, the economic pressures on both companies grew.

The CPR replaced the *Princess Victoria* with the *Princess Royal* after the latter vessel had been fitted with a new propeller, giving her a speed of 15 knots. The *Princess Royal* took over the regular daily service between Seattle and Victoria in competition with the PSN's *Chippewa*. While the scheduling of the two steamers was actually complementary, since the *Royal* sailed from Victoria about the same time the *Chippewa* was departing Seattle, the business was insufficient to maintain the operation of both ships on a paying basis. Clearly some agreement between the two companies was needed to reduce the losses on the winter sailings. Yet neither company wished to compromise its chances of being the only operator on the

The Princess Royal *was . . .*
The Princess Ena *was . . .*

Puget Sound route. Rumours of an impending rate war were heard increasingly along the waterfronts of both Seattle and Victoria. If a struggle did develop, it was evident that it would be bitter and protracted.

Meanwhile, the CPR received the newest addition to its growing coastal fleet. She was the squat little *Princess Ena*. The new steamer arrived on January 22, 1908 after an 83 day voyage around Cape Horn from Liverpool. Captain A. O. Cooper, who had brought both the *Princess May* and *Princess Victoria* to the West Coast, was her master. Designed by the resourceful Captain Troup, the *Ena* was a coastal freighter with accommodation for only five passengers. The 1,368 ton vessel was a product of the Garston (Drydock) Shipbuilding Company of Garston, England. She embodied a number of features specially incorporated for the peculiar requirements of the CPR service. The hold was capable of carrying any size of lumber that could be produced by the mills of the day. In addition, the vessel could accommodate up to 300 head of cattle under cover. The *Ena* was a sturdy, 10 knot vessel with a double bottom, and was ballasted with 270 tons of fresh water. For the most part, the ship remained out of the limelight, plying the coastal trade year after year with efficiency but little publicity.

The Rate War Begins

The Puget Sound Navigation Company was faced with more than one competitive struggle in 1908 as the *Indianapolis* was trying to take over the Seattle-Tacoma service from the express steamer *Flyer*, owned by the Columbia River and Puget Sound Navigation Company (not related to the PSN). This dispute continued for several years with neither company able to drive its opponent's vessel from the run.

In order to cut extra expenses during the 1907-08 winter season on the Seattle-Victoria route, the PSN decided to withdraw the *Chippewa* for a few months and replace her with the smaller, more economical *Rosalie*. This ship had operated on the route several years before, but had been replaced by the *Indianapolis* when it first arrived from the Great Lakes. At the same time as the Company announced that the *Rosalie* would return to the run, rates were cut to 50 cents per person each way, thus undercutting the CPR's fare for the same route by $1.50.

The *Chippewa* was then docked for a refitting and overhaul and was afterwards placed on the Company's Seattle-Vancouver service. The CPR remained steadfast in its position, maintaining that people would rather pay the higher rates to travel on the faster, more luxurious Princesses. For the most part, it was right, since many people who travelled at that time were wealthy enough not to be affected by the price difference. The low fares on the *Rosalie* attracted those who would otherwise not have been able to travel the Puget Sound route. In fact, the Puget Sound Navigation Company maintained that

The *Princess Royal* was the second vessel built for the CPR by the B.C. Marine Railway at Esquimalt. She joined the Princess fleet in July 1907, the same month the *Chippewa* made her first sailing to Victoria. She was generally larger and had more spacious accommodations than the *Princess Beatrice*. The *Royal* had 72 staterooms with 144 berths compared to the *Beatrice*'s 40 rooms with a total of 114 berths.
— CPR COLLECTION

The *Princess Ena* was the first coastal freighter built for the Princess fleet. She entered service in 1908 and had a varied career that saw her cross the North Pacific in 1916 to carry munitions to the Russians at Vladivostok, and again in 1918 to take explosives to Japan. — JOE D. WILLIAMSON

it was not attempting to start a rate war, but only adjusting its fares to reflect the quality of service offered.

CPR officials stated that they were doing all the business they could handle and saw no reason to adjust their fares in line with the new rates of the competition. They further added: "The Seattle travelling public are standing by us well and the Victoria people are with us to a man. They do not regard the move of the other company favourably and it has helped rather than hurt us."

In reply, the Puget Sound Navigation Company released the following statement: "The *Rosalie* is going out every day with full berths and a large cargo. The cut rate seems to make business where there was none before and we have been happily surprised at the way things have been coming our way. There will be no change in the rate for the present at least."

The Seattle-Victoria route was a critical link between the communities, as there were many personal and business ties joining the two cities. In addition, the steamers carried the mails and a considerable quantity of freight. While travel dropped off significantly during the winter, the traffic that remained was particularly important.

The *Rosalie* remained on the run for the rest of the winter and into the early spring months of 1908, while negotiations between the two companies proceeded. Neither the CPR nor the PSN was prepared to withdraw from the run or accept a compromise proposal. The Puget Sound Navigation Company claimed priority rights to the run because it had first established service and also suggested that an agreement should be reached to permanently reduce the fares on the Puget Sound route in order to encourage offseason travelling by residents of both Victoria and Seattle. Joshua Green of the PSN proposed a fare cut of $1.25 each way or $2.00 for the return ticket, in addition to a special weekend excursion rate of $1.00 return. The CPR was not interested in this suggestion, but the PSN gave notice that it would institute the low fares regardless of whether or not an agreement could be reached.

The rate war had begun in earnest and there was no turning back. The Puget Sound Navigation Company announced that its *Chippewa* would return to the Seattle-Victoria run on April 23rd, and that the low fare of 50 cents each way would be maintained. Since the *Chippewa* was comparable to the *Princess Royal* and *Princess Beatrice* used by the CPR on this route, the low fares took on real significance.

To bring further pressure to bear on the CPR, the PSN stated that it planned to establish a service between Victoria and Vancouver in direct competition with the CPR. The Seattle company contemplated a 50 cent fare on the run, coupled with convenient sailing times. It planned to transfer one of its steamers, probably the *Iroquois*, to Canadian registry to begin the service, even though it would be forced to pay a customs duty of 30 per cent of the ship's value to accomplish the change.

In response, the CPR announced on April 18th that it was making preparations to place one of its fast steamers on a daylight run from Victoria to Seattle. Furthermore, the Company would institute new low fares that would, it felt, effectively counter the opposition on the run. The PSN then increased the stakes by stating that it was considering, in addition to its proposed Victoria-Vancouver service, a new north coast route from Vancouver to Prince Rupert using the *Rosalie* and that it was prepared to pay the estimated $30,000 customs duty to change the registry of the steamer to make the service possible.

To maintain its hold on the Victoria-Vancouver traffic, the CPR announced that it would add a second ship to the run during late April. The *Princess Royal* and the *Charmer* would both be used on the expanded service. It was further planned that the *Princess Victoria* would relieve the *Princess Royal* early in May following her annual refit and would remain on the run throughout the summer months.

At times, it seemed as if luck was on the side of the CPR. On April 27th, the *Chippewa* arrived as usual in Victoria Harbour at 1:30 p.m. but was unable to dock successfully until nearly 3:00.

The *Daily Colonist* provided the following vivid description:

While the passengers with their valises ready crowded at the bow ready to land, while bus drivers, hotel runners and others waited impatiently ashore, Captain Clancy backed and tilted with the steamer. She would run to within less than a stone's throw of the wharf and then backed astern again, sometimes toward Laurel point, sometimes toward the CPR wharf.

"Say au revoir, but not good-bye," shrieked the gramophone, which the fruit and cigar dealer at the corner of Wharf and Government streets had thoughtfully started for the amusement of the belated passengers.

"Here she comes," said Joe Montare, as straight as an arrow from a bow, the gleaming white bows approached the wharf.

"There she goes," said Billy Burns the customs man, as the two-funnelled steamer slid away as fast as she had approached.

"If at first you don't succeed, try try again," chirped the phonograph.

There was a faint cheer from the thronged passengers waiting at the bow as the boat seemed to handle a little and swerve toward the dock.

"Is the *Chippewa* in yet, please?" enquired a young lady from the patient agent, who was trying to hide in the cellar.

"No, she's going — excuse me, oh yes, she'll be tied up in a minute," said Mr. McArthur in his most dulcet tones.

"Honey Boy, I hate to see you leaving," whined the phonograph at the hilltop.

A half hour passed. The local supply of patience was almost exhausted. The bus drivers had fallen asleep after telling their comrades to awake them when the steamer was landed. The steamer still flirted with the wharf without any serious attachment.

An hour passed. The phonograph still making its canny melodies heard over the water. The selections were good. Now a dreamy waltz as the *Chippewa* slid backwards again toward the harbour mouth, then a lively march as she came to again getting near the wharf, then a furtive musical protest such as "Good bye Beloved" or another.

The Puget Sound...
The 657 ton Whatcom...

An hour and a half passed. The sleeping bus drivers were awakened by a cheer...

Shortly after, the *Princess Victoria* was ready to return to the Seattle-Victoria run. On May 9th, the day of her first sailing, the papers announced one of the CPR's more ingenious ploys in the battle with the Puget Sound Navigation Company. The *Princess Victoria* would carry chambermaids on the Seattle-Victoria run. Six "dainty young ladies" would attend to preparing the staterooms for the passengers. Stewards would continue to attend the dining room and saloon.

The Races Between the Chippewa and the Princess Victoria

Since the *Chippewa* and the *Princess Victoria* were scheduled to leave Victoria in the late afternoon on May 9th, there was considerable interest in both Seattle and Victoria as to which vessel would reach Seattle first. The *Chippewa* left Victoria nearly an hour before the *Victoria*'s 5:30 p.m. sailing time, but she had to make a call at Port Townsend. Thus it seemed that the vessels were evenly matched.

Seattle newspaper advertisements praising the *Chippewa* stated, "We promise you it is worth your while to see this spic and span packet, 'The Witch of the Waters' which is the talk of marine men all over America . . . the finest, fastest, daintiest craft in existence, and she advertises Seattle." In a critical rate war like this one, the PSN saw little point in understating the assets of its steamer.

Despite the best efforts of the *Chippewa* and the claims made by the PSN, the *Princess Victoria* passed her before either vessel had reached the entrance to Puget Sound, and by the time the *Chippewa* had made her scheduled stop at Port Townsend, the *Princess* had a commanding lead. In fact, bettering past performances, the *Victoria* arrived in Seattle an hour ahead of the rival steamer.

Fifty-cent fares were now effective on both steamship lines, and the people of Seattle and Victoria were taking full advantage of the new opportunities for travel. The *Chippewa* and the *Princess Victoria* were both heavily patronized as the competition intensified throughout the spring of 1908.

In one respect, the PSN had a significant advantage over the CPR. Since the *Chippewa* operated under U.S. shipping regulations, which were more generous in calculating the carrying capacity of steamers, she was permitted to carry 1,250 passengers. On the other hand, the *Princess Victoria*, a considerably larger vessel, was limited by the stricter Canadian regulations to carrying only 1,000 people.

To be sure of getting all possible business away from the CPR on the Sunday, May 11th sailing of the *Chippewa*, the PSN offered fares cut to 25 cents per person (50 cents return). However, the CPR did not follow this lead. By the time the *Chippewa* sailed from Seattle's Elliott Bay at 8:30 a.m., 1,132 passengers had crowded aboard. Every inch of deck space was

The Puget Sound Navigation Company's steamer *Rosalie* was a veteran of the Klondike gold rush and played a key role in the rate war with the CPR. She was outclassed by her rivals but being small and economical to operate she was used to advantage during the winter when traffic was light. — JOE D. WILLIAMSON

The 657 ton *Whatcom* was also used by the PSN during the winter on the Seattle - Victoria route. She ended her days in 1939 as the auto ferry *City of Bremerton*. — JOE D. WILLIAMSON

occupied as the heavily laden steamer pulled away from the dock to the music of a local band.

Meanwhile, at the CPR pier, an even larger assembly waited to board the *Princess Victoria*. In fact, a squad of police was required to restrain the crowd. Over 500 were turned away and the CPR's agents were forced to repurchase many tickets. At 9:00 a.m., the *Princess Victoria* sailed with a capacity crowd of 983 aboard. Quiet Victoria was due for an invasion of tourists.

Rapidly working up to full speed, the *Princess* overtook the *Chippewa* near Point No Point, well before the entrance to the Strait of Juan de Fuca. She raced by the smaller steamer at over 22 knots, or, as one passenger commented, "30 of the same kind of knots" as the *Chippewa* was claimed to be capable of. Gaily decked out in flags, the *Princess Victoria* passed the *Chippewa* at such close quarters that the overcrowded Seattle steamer was left rolling in her wake. In fact, Captain Clancy of the *Chippewa* was forced to stop his ship and swing the bow into the swell. Eleven hundred and thirty-two seasick passengers were more than he cared to contemplate.

In the fleeting moment of the encounter, the passengers on the *Princess Victoria* did their best to heap abuse on top of indignity, showering the *Chippewa* with a barrage of pointedly worded derision. *Chippewa* passengers answered in kind as the *Princess* steamed out of sight. Some eager *Princess* passengers even went so far as to cast a line over the stern railing of their steamer, offering the *Chippewa* a tow!

The *Princess Victoria* arrived in Victoria at 1:00 p.m. and her crowd of excited passengers swarmed ashore, taking advantage of all the available carriages and streetcars to see the city. One and a half hours later, the *Chippewa* steamed into Victoria's Inner Harbour, listing heavily as her passengers crowded near the railing, each wanting to be the first ashore. However, since the *Chippewa* was forced by her slower speed to leave in only two hours, their sightseeing was cut short. In contrast, the tourists from the *Princess Victoria* not only had the advantage of an earlier arrival, but they did not sail until one hour and twenty minutes after the *Chippewa*.

There were skeptics who thought the *Princess Victoria* could never again overtake the *Chippewa* with that much of a handicap, but off West Point in Puget Sound, the *Princess* once again left the *Chippewa* rolling in her wake as the passengers demonstrated that the morning's encounter had not exhausted their vocabulary of abusive phrases. To make the defeat even more decisive, the *Princess Victoria* overtook and passed the PSN's steamers *Whatcom* and *Indianapolis* before reaching Seattle. Many of the *Princess*'s Seattle passengers waited for the *Chippewa* to dock before leaving the waterfront for home.

While it was evident that both vessels could carry sellout crowds on the weekends, it was the daily weekday traffic that would ultimately determine which company would win the rate war. It was soon apparent that at least in the early stages of the war, the CPR was winning. The *Princess Victoria* frequently carried five times as many travellers as the *Chippewa*, even though the latter had added business to and from Port Townsend.

Winning the support and patronage of the public was an all important consideration to the companies. Officials of both the CPR and the PSN were quick to plead for loyalty — often on both sides of the border — on grounds of nationalism, allegiance to one's city, and simple justice. Newspapers in Seattle and Victoria were equally quick to editorialize on the issues of the war and almost invariably came out strongly on the side of the company based in their city.

Shortly after the May 11th excursions, the PSN was warned by Canadian immigration authorities that despite the fact that the *Chippewa* was licensed to carry 1,250 passengers, such overcrowding would not be tolerated in Canadian waters. Under the authority of the Canadian Immigration Act, officials in Victoria limited the *Chippewa* to a maximum of 1,000 passengers on the Victoria-Seattle run.

There was still optimism that the *Chippewa* could beat the *Princess Victoria* to Seattle. On May 21st, it was learned on board the *Chippewa* that the next sailing of the *Princess* from Victoria was likely to be delayed. The added lead that this delay might give the *Chippewa* could just be all she needed. The usual stopover at Port Townsend was cancelled and the *Chippewa* steamed out of Victoria in a cloud of heavy oil smoke fully five minutes ahead of schedule.

Unfortunately for Captain Clancy and the *Chippewa*, word of the impending coup reached the *Princess Victoria*. One hour and 20 minutes after the *Chippewa* raced out of port, the *Princess* slipped away from the CPR pier at Belleville Street, cleared the harbour, and quickly worked up to 19 knots.

By the time Sparrowstone Point was sighted, the outcome of the race was a foregone conclusion. Captain Troup's "pocket liner" churned by the *Chippewa* in a decisive burst of speed. Beating the *Chippewa* by 15 minutes, the *Princess Victoria* was tied up at the CPR pier in Elliott Bay by the time the PSN ship reached port. The *Princess* had cut two minutes off her previous record and had completed the 76-mile run in three hours and 14 minutes. Thereafter, the officers of the *Chippewa* were reluctant to submit themselves and their ship to further humiliation and subsequently avoided races with the *Princess Victoria*.

The Battle of the Signs and Attempts at Settlement

On May 23rd, two days after the last decisive race, the schedule of the *Princess Victoria* was accelerated for the four days of the Victoria Day holiday, an annual event celebrating the King's birthday. For this period, the *Princess* ran two return trips a day between Victoria and Seattle. The CPR planned in this way to capitalize on the heavy holiday traffic and also to afford excursionists the opportunity to see the Great White Fleet, the squadron of U.S. Navy warships visiting Puget Sound ports at the time. The PSN, for its part, replaced the

Chippewa with the *Rosalie* on the regular service for the holiday period and ran the *Chippewa* on special excursions between Seattle and Victoria, passing the U.S. fleet en route. Both companies were rewarded with heavy patronge on their excursions.

The May 24th holiday traffic instigated a new and unprecedented phase of the rate war. In Seattle, the CPR erected a large sign on the north side of Pier A, informing the public of the reduced fares on the *Princess Victoria* and the schedule of the steamer. The sign was painted in flaming red letters a foot high, with capitals twice that height. It was situated so that anyone coming down Yesler Way could not help but see the advertisement. Adjoining Pier A, however, was Pier One, which the Alaska Steamship Company and the PSN occupied. The relative positions of the two piers made it possible for the PSN to block off the view of the CPR sign by erecting a barricade, and that is exactly what it proceeded to do. A billboard company was hired to construct a barrier capable of obstructing the view of a six-foot six-inch man from Yesler Way. Of course, the CPR officials were not about to stand idly by and let their vigorous advertising campaign be thwarted so easily. They moved their sign to the roof of the sheds on Pier A, where its view was unobstructed. To emphasize his determination to keep the sign visible, A. P. Calder, general agent for the CPR, told the *Seattle Post-Intelligencer* that if the Alaska Steamship Company and PSN tried to raise its barricade higher, the CPR would hang its sign from an airship or balloon!

Meanwhile, members of the Seattle and Victoria business communities tried, without success, to arbitrate a compromise to end the rate war. Despite the immediate advantages of a rate war for the travelling public and commercial interests, it was better for all concerned to have a stable, reasonable rate structure than the uncertainties of the rate war. Moreover, if one company was driven from the run, a monopoly might develop and that was not looked upon with favour.

On May 28, 1908, the same day that the *Princess Victoria* reverted to one round trip sailing a day, the fares on the *Chippewa* were cut to 50 cents return. This was the PSN's final rate cut in this phase of the struggle, and it was not met by the CPR. The passengers soon demonstrated that they would rather pay the additional 25 cents to ride the more luxurious CPR vessel, so that despite the higher price of the CPR tickets, the Company continued to carry significantly greater numbers of passengers than the PSN. On Sunday, May 31st, the *Princess* carried 761 to Victoria while the *Chippewa* brought only 583, and on Monday the *Chippewa* attracted only 153 passengers to the *Princess Victoria*'s 751.

To make matters worse for the PSN, on the 31st, the *Chippewa* broke down twice before arriving in Victoria, causing a two hour delay. Furthermore, the weather was rough, with strong breezes blowing in Puget Sound and the Strait of Juan de Fuca. Unfortunately, the *Chippewa* was a poor sea boat

The *Princess Beatrice* was the CPR's smallest vessel used in the rate war. She could not match the larger PSN vessels in speed but was faster than the *Rosalie* and *Whatcom* and had better passenger accommodations. She is shown above at Nanaimo. — B.C. PROVINCIAL MUSEUM

Resplendent in white, with red and black funnels, the *Iroquois* was the best the PSN could offer. Her career spanned six decades and saw her return to the Great Lakes between 1920 and 1925 before being rebuilt as an auto ferry for the Seattle - Victoria route. — JOE D. WILLIAMSON

The Princess Beatrice was . . .
Resplendent in white, with . . .

and it was a green-faced, unhappy crowd of excursionists that made its way ashore that afternoon. Returning to Seattle, the steamer broke down once again, delaying her arrival until nearly midnight. This was the worst kind of publicity for the Company. The public might be tempted to save 50 cents on the return ticket, but not at the price of long delays and seasickness.

On June 4th, the CPR announced its next move in the dispute. The *Princess Royal* was to be placed on the Vancouver-Seattle route in direct competition with the PSN's *Iroquois*. Service was to begin on June 15th, when the *Princess Victoria* would be operated on the tri-city run connecting Victoria with both Seattle and Vancouver.

Joshua Green retaliated by announcing that if the *Princess Royal* were placed on the Vancouver-Seattle run, fares on the *Iroquois* would be cut to 25 cents each way from the established rate of $2.50. Such a drastic price reduction might well have brought the Great Northern Railway into the rate war, since the proposed low rates would significantly undercut the prices charged on the passenger trains running between Vancouver and Seattle. Green continued to state his intention to transfer one of his vessels to Canadian registry for a direct service between Victoria and Vancouver and proposed as an interim measure to have the *Iroquois* stop at San Juan Island's Roche Harbour on the Vancouver to Seattle run. A connection would thus be provided between Roche Harbour and Victoria, since the *Rosalie* stopped there on her way from Bellingham to Victoria. Fares were to be 50 cents per person and meals would be served for 25 cents. For leisurely summer travel, this route would provide an enjoyable alternative to the direct route through the Canadian Gulf Islands provided by the CPR.

Despite Green's threats, the CPR went ahead with its plans and placed the *Princess Royal* on the Vancouver-Seattle-Victoria run in the first true "triangle service." On June 14th, this new operation that was to become so famous on the West Coast began. It was also the first time since the Canadian Pacific Navigation Company had withdrawn the *Premier* from the Seattle-Vancouver run that CPN or CPR ships had operated regularly between these two ports. Recognizing that his bluffing had done him no good, Green decided to maintain the *Iroquois* on her previous schedule and content himself with a rate cut from $2.50 to $1.00 for the one-way fare between Vancouver and Seattle. After a few days, the CPR followed suit and the fares stabilized at that figure. To further its cause, the PSN even made arrangements with a Seattle area brewery to supply a free bottle of beer with each ticket.

In late June, Green met again with Troup and tried to reach a settlement. He proposed that the CPR limit its service to one boat on the Seattle run. Green anticipated heavy traffic because of the Alaska-Yukon-Pacific Exposition to be held in Seattle in 1909 and suggested that this would form the basis of a reasonable compromise. However, the CPR took a different view. With a new steamer, larger than the *Princess Victoria*, under construction in Scotland, the Company was not about to restrict its activities and forego the possibility of establishing a double service on the Triangle Route just to bring a quick end to the rate war that it was winning anyway.

Victoria to Vancouver
in Almost Three Hours

On June 28, 1908, the *Princess Victoria* once again demonstrated the excellence of her design by steaming from Victoria to Vancouver in three hours and nine minutes, fully five minutes better than her previous record. Overall, the liner averaged 22.9 knots, a truly remarkable speed. On that day, when the *Princess* arrived in Victoria from Seattle with 488 Sunday travellers on board, conditions seemed favourable for a particularly fast run to Vancouver on the northern leg of the Triangle Route. Captain Griffin and Chief Engineer Brownlee hoped that with a good tide, the run could be made in under three hours. The engine room crew was briefed and at 12:45 p.m. the steamer sailed from Victoria. However, the tide did not aid the steamer until James Island was cleared and then it was disappointingly weak. Nonetheless, the engines were worked up to 164 revolutions, giving the steamer a maximum speed over 23 knots. With a more favourable tide, Griffin's hopes of a three hour crossing would certainly have been met.

The only vessel to have beaten the *Victoria*'s speed on the run up to that time was the torpedo boat destroyer H.M.S. *Sparrowhawk*, which while working under forced draft, crossed the Straits in two and a half hours. At the time, the naval vessel was in hot pursuit of a paymaster from the Esquimalt Naval base who had absconded with the payroll and was trying to escape to Alaska aboard the steamer *Alpha* leaving from Vancouver.

Maritime observers could not help speculating on the speed of the new *Princess Charlotte* being built for the CPR in Scotland. The new vessel had a design speed two knots higher than the *Princess Victoria*'s. She might well prove to be, they thought, the fastest coastal steamer in the world. The *Charlotte* was to disappoint them, however, as she had difficulty attaining her design speed when she arrived on the Coast.

Meanwhile, a shipping broker was making inquiries for Joshua Green with Canadian customs officials about the possibility of returning the steamer *Bellingham*, formerly the CPN's *Willapa*, to Canadian registry for operation between Victoria and Vancouver. Customs ruled, however, that the purchasers or present owners of the vessel would be assessed 25 per cent duty on her appraised value to satisfy recent changes in Canadian shipping laws. Prior to 1902 it had been possible to return a former Canadian vessel to Canadian registry without duty. Thus, once again Joshua Green was thwarted in his efforts to place a vessel in opposition to the CPR on the lucrative Victoria-Vancouver route. Although he continued to state this intention, it became increasingly apparent that his opposition was paying little attention.

July 1908 was a bad month for the Puget Sound Navigation Company. On Saturday, the 4th, the *Chippewa* and *Whatcom* carried over 1,300 Victorians across the Strait to Port Angeles on an excursion. However, the Company failed to make adequate provision for the return of the travellers. Only the *Chippewa* came back to Port Angeles to pick up the excursionists in the evening and nearly 150 people had to be left behind. They were assured by the *Chippewa*'s crew that they would be picked up later that evening, but as the evening progressed, it became all too apparent to the now tired and disgruntled tourists that they would not get back to Victoria that night. Some Port Angeles residents opened their homes to the visitors and the saloons stayed open all night, allowing people to sleep on the tables and on the floor. Others walked the streets all night. Finally at 10:00 the next morning the *Whatcom* returned to pick up the thoroughly disgusted travellers. On arriving in Victoria the passengers cheered as they passed the CPR docks and a number threatened to bring legal action against the PSN. There was little doubt in the minds of these people which steamship company they would patronize in the future.

The next day, July 5th, the *Rosalie* collided with the ferry *West Seattle* about a mile from the ferry's Seattle terminal and the PSN steamer had to be withdrawn from the Victoria-Seattle route for repairs. Even though she was an economical boat to operate, the *Rosalie* was losing money on the run, so that when the repairs were completed the service was not resumed and only the *Chippewa* remained to compete with the CPR on the key Vancouver Island operation.

Then, on July 10th, the CPR cut its fares on the Victoria-Seattle run to 25 cents each way, posting the lowest rates on the run since the rate wars of the 1800's. While the PSN fares were 50 cents return, a one way fare was also 50 cents. To make matters worse for the PSN, the Seattle papers were reporting rumours that CPR agents were looking into the possibilities of acquiring various American vessels to compete on the Puget Sound shipping routes. While taking the offensive by cutting the rates on the Victoria route, the CPR was going ahead with plans to cut fares dramatically on the Vancouver-Seattle route as well. Assistant general pasenger agent for the Company, C. E. E. Usher, met with officials of the Northern Pacific and Great Northern Railways to discuss the rate war with them and try to allay their concern. Both railroads were operating passenger services between Vancouver and Seattle at the time and were worried that the proposed cuts would affect their business. While the CPR could maintain a fight with the PSN, it was not anxious to engage in a war with two major American railroad companies.

The next day, Saturday, July 11th, Joshua Green met the CPR's rate cut and lowered the fares on his steamer to 25 cents each way. However, at this time the CPR announced significant cuts in charges for berths on the *Princess Royal*. Sunday saw record crowds of Seattle residents availing themselves of

The 1908 Summer Season

The Chippewa *is* . . .

the new low fares. The *Princess Victoria* was sold out fully an hour before sailing time and over 400 were turned away from the ticket offices on Pier A. Many of these people finally found space on the *Chippewa*, which also carried a capacity crowd. In total, the two competing steamers carried nearly 2,000 people to Vancouver Island. On Monday, July 13th, the *Princess Victoria* carried 581 passengers to the *Chippewa*'s 177. It was apparent that when fares were equal, people preferred to ride on the more luxurious *Princess*.

On July 20th, the CPR made its next move in the rate war. The fare on the direct Seattle-Vancouver service was slashed from $1.00 to 25 cents. The fares had reached rock bottom; they could go no further.

Green maintained the $1.00 fare on the *Iroquois* between Seattle and Vancouver despite the CPR's rate cut to 25 cents. He felt that his steamer was still competitive, since the CPR vessel, operating on the Triangle Route, offered only a direct Seattle to Vancouver service at 25 cents. On the return, a passenger had to travel to Victoria, paying a $2.50 fare and sail from there to Seattle for an additional 25 cents. Frequently passengers would take the *Princess Royal* to Vancouver from Seattle for 25 cents and then ride the *Iroquois* back to Seattle for the old $1.00 fare. This rate cut by the CPR did not hurt the PSN badly and produced no real advantage for the CPR.

Recognizing the weakness in its strategy, the CPR soon took measures to force its opposition to cut rates on the Seattle-Vancouver service. On July 30th, the schedule of the *Princess Royal* was changed so that the vessel operated on the Triangle Route only on Sundays. Instead, a Vancouver-Seattle service in direct opposition to the *Iroquois* was initiated. However, this change forced the CPR to abandon its afternoon sailing from Victoria to Seattle which competed directly with the *Chippewa*. Green quickly increased the fare to $1.00 on this run, hoping that people taking the *Princess Victoria* to Victoria in the morning would take his vessel back to Seattle to avoid waiting until the CPR vessel's 1:00 a.m. departure.

The final result of the many schedule and rate changes was that in order to compete effectively on the Vancouver-Seattle route, the CPR was forced to lose some of its business on the Victoria-Seattle service.

All the rate changing and schedule shuffling left the travelling public at times somewhat bewildered, particularly when the newspapers were sometimes delinquent in keeping their published schedules up to date. On the whole, however, most people took the rate war good naturedly, particularly since they benefited from the low prices. As long as the fares were kept down, few people really cared whether or not the dueling companies lost money.

In late August, a new and curious phase of the rate war developed. For some time the CPR had been shipping freight from Puget Sound ports to Vancouver for movement east by rail. In order to comply with U.S. shipping regulations, American vessels had to be used. However, the ships providing the

The *Chippewa* is shown above arriving at Seattle in 1909. — PROVINCIAL ARCHIVES service had come under the ownership of the PSN, and the CPR was not happy providing its rival with freight traffic worth considerable revenue. To rectify this situation, the CPR chartered the steamer *Alaskan* of the Ketchikan Steamship Company. This vessel soon proved to be too small for the service and was eventually replaced by the larger *Morning Star*, owned by the same company.

With September came a gradual decline in the summer tourist travel that had helped both steamship lines sustain their efforts in the rate war. Instead of cutting back on its service for the coming off-season, however, the CPR announced an accelerated service. With the *Charmer* providing an extra Victoria-Vancouver service, both the *Princess Royal* and the *Princess Victoria* were placed on the Triangle Route. Sailing in opposite directions around the triangle between the three cities, Victoria, Vancouver and Seattle, they offered an excellent service that overcame the weakness in the summer schedule. Fares between Victoria and Seattle were kept at the low rate of 25 cents one way, but on the Vancouver-Seattle run they were increased to $1.00 one way, $1.25 return. These fares were matched by the PSN and went into effect on Wednesday, September 23, 1908.

The double triangle service of the two Princesses was maintained throughout the winter, except for two interruptions. The first was caused when the *Princess Royal* rammed the cargo vessel *Fukui Maru* in Vancouver Harbour and had to be withdrawn for two weeks to be repaired. The second disruption occurred when the *Charmer* side-swiped a barge and had to be dry-docked at Esquimalt. During the same period, the *Princess Victoria* had rammed the fishing schooner *Ida May* but had not been damaged.

In mid-October, the *Whatcom* replaced the *Chippewa* on the Victoria-Seattle run for the winter. The CPR then raised its fares on the route to $2.00 one way and $3.00 return as it did not consider the *Whatcom* real competition.

In the early morning hours of December 30, 1908 the newest addition to the CPR's Princess fleet arrived at the William Head quarantine station off Victoria. The next morning she sailed to Victoria's Outer Wharves where Captain Troup, sporting a bowler hat, mustache and a broad grin, boarded the vessel. Shortly after, the *Charlotte* was moved to the Company's Belleville Street wharf where crews began removing the planking installed to protect the observation rooms during the passage around Cape Horn. Despite the long voyage from Scotland, the engines were running perfectly.

The interior of the *Princess Charlotte* was cleaned, carpets laid, and stores taken onboard and in less than two weeks, the new coastal liner was ready for service. Troup apologized for her slightly rust-streaked exterior, but explained that a period

The CPR's Double Service on the Triangle Route

The Charmer *operated* . . .

The Princess Charlotte

The *Charmer* operated on the Victoria - Vancouver leg of the Triangle Route during the rate war. — CPR COLLECTION

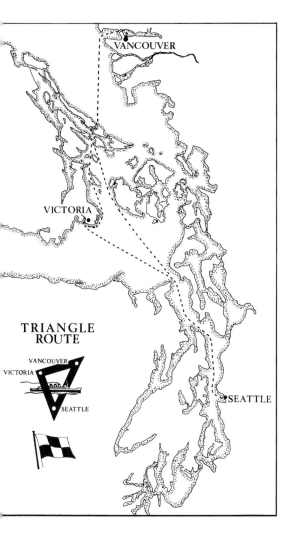

VANCOUVER

VICTORIA

TRIANGLE
ROUTE

VANCOUVER
VICTORIA

SEATTLE

SEATTLE

of unusually cold weather had prevented work crews from repainting the hull.

The *Charlotte* was licensed to carry 1,500 day pasengers and provided accommodations for 275 overnight travellers in 130 two-berth staterooms and four large suites. She was fitted out in the lavish Edwardian tradition established by the *Princess Victoria*. The builders at Govan, Scotland were so impressed by the accommodations that they nicknamed her the "bridal ship." The four luxury suites were patterned after those on the CPR's trans-Pacific Empress liners and featured brass bedsteads, oak dressers with plate glass mirrors and adjoining bathrooms.

On January 10, 1909, Captain Troup opened the vessel to public inspection. Twenty-five cents was charged each guest to aid the Seaman's Institute and the Lifeboat Association. The Ladies' Guild of the Seaman's Institute and other volunteers raised additional money by selling soup, sandwiches, and souvenirs of the occasion. A popular item was a commemorative badge designed by Mrs. Troup. In the forward saloon, a band played for the guests. The enthusiastic visitors were allowed to inspect virtually every feature of the ship from the most luxurious staterooms to the engine room. The 140 seat dining room and the adjacent galley, which featured electrically heated dish washers and automatic egg cookers, were particularly impressive.

During the previous July, the *Princess Victoria* carried a record 28,000 passengers on the Triangle Route and with the Alaska-Yukon-Pacific Exposition scheduled to open in Seattle in June 1909, it was virtually certain that the *Charlotte* would break the *Victoria*'s passenger record in her first year of service. No one doubted that the ship would quickly repay the nearly three quarters of a million dollars invested in her.

On January 12, 1909, the *Princess Charlotte* was ready to enter regular service and began operations on a leisurely schedule making one round trip a day between Victoria and Vancouver. Consequently, the *Princess Victoria* was able to return to the Triangle Route with the *Princess Royal* to provide a double service and direct sailings between Seattle and Vancouver.

New Competition Appears and the Rate War Ends

During the fall of 1908, the Grand Trunk Pacific Railway, a new transcontinental line being built to the Pacific Ocean port of Prince Rupert, announced that contracts for two 21 knot coastal liners had been awarded to shipyards in Great Britain. These vessels were to be used to connect Seattle, Vancouver and Victoria with Prince Rupert. While Troup could not dismiss this new rival, a more pressing concern was the still unsettled rate war with the Puget Sound Navigation Company.

While the issues in the rate war were far from settled, the late winter and spring months of 1908-09 were generally quiet. It was reasonably clear that a continuation of the rate war would work to the detriment of both companies during the coming summer when they would each be assured of capacity crowds even with normal fare schedules. Nonetheless, when the *Chippewa* replaced the *Whatcom* while the smaller vessel was refitted in January, CPR fares were quickly cut to match the *Chippewa*'s 25 cent rate. However, after a short time the *Whatcom* returned to the Seattle-Victoria route and the CPR fares were raised to the previous higher levels.

By the spring of 1909, Joshua Green had made arrangements with the Union Steamship Company of Vancouver to provide through tickets from Vancouver to Prince Rupert for PSN passengers travelling north from Seattle. The Union Steamship Company was a well established operation on the British Columbia coast, with a fleet of small passenger and cargo steamers. It served innumerable logging camps, fish canneries, mines and coastal settlements from Vancouver to the Alaska Panhandle. At this time, the Union's largest ship was the 1,344 ton *Camosun*, a modern steamer normally employed between Vancouver and Prince Rupert. The agreement between the PSN and the Union Steamship Company led to some loss in traffic on the CPR's sailing to the North Coast, but the impact was not great. Overall, Union's service was really directed to the small industrial settlements along the Coast and while it competed with the CPR for this trade and in later years for the Alaska cruise business, it was never a serious rival of the CPR.

In April the final round of the rate war began. The *Princess Charlotte* replaced the *Princess Royal* on the Triangle Route, so that both of the CPR's beautiful three-funneled liners were on the Puget Sound run. With these two vessels setting a new standard of speed, luxury and service on the Triangle Route, the CPR felt it had little to fear from the comparatively spartan *Chippewa*, *Iroquois*, and *Indianapolis*. Thus, when the *Chippewa* returned to the Seattle-Victoria run in late April for the summer season with a 25 cent fare, the CPR made no move to cut its rates. Seeing an opportunity to raise its rates, the PSN increased its fares to $1.00 one way and $1.25 return. The CPR began to have second thoughts and soon matched this rate. By the end of the month, both companies were back to charging 25 cent fares.

Meanwhile, the *Princess Charlotte* left the Triangle Route to carry a party of 250 excursionists to Prince Rupert and the Queen Charlotte Islands on the North Coast. The 1,050 mile excursion took just under a week to complete and introduced the CPR's newest vessel to many people all along the Coast.

The beginning of May saw a cautious armistice develop as both companies raised their fares to pre-rate war levels. At the invitation of the Northern Pacific Railway Company, Troup and Green met with its officials in St. Paul, Minnesota. The atmosphere was conciliatory as Northern Pacific President J. M. Hannaford opened the proceedings. Passing around cigars, he did not realize that Joshua Green did not smoke. Not wishing to offend his host, Green endeavoured to smoke his cigar anyway, but the results were predictable. He was

The Princess Charlotte *had . . .*
The open upper decks of . . .

The *Princess Charlotte* had difficulty making her design speed in trials, pictured above off Victoria in 1909. — PROVINCIAL ARCHIVES

The open upper decks of the *Princess Charlotte* were popular during the warm summer months. — AUTHOR'S COLLECTION

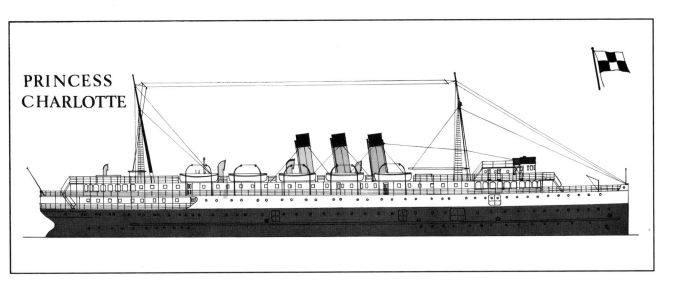

PRINCESS CHARLOTTE

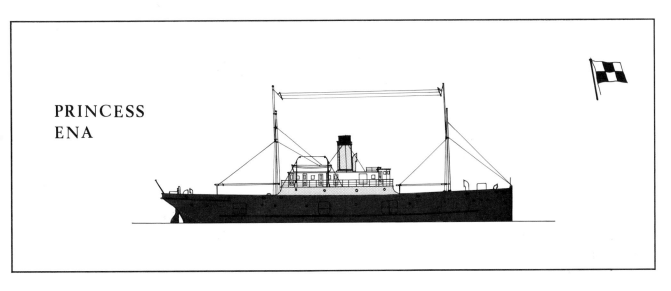

PRINCESS ENA

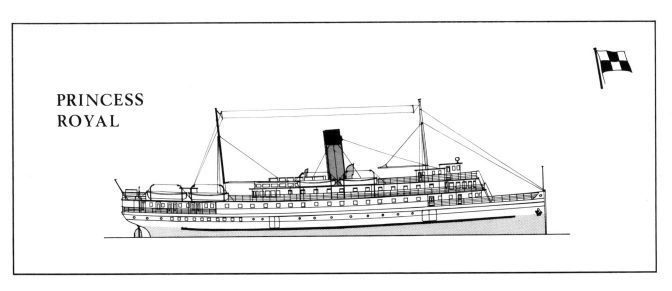

PRINCESS ROYAL

Cruises to Alaska were popular and the *Princess Charlotte* was used in this service from the time of her arrival on the Coast. The ship's stamp was taken from a brochure of her May 1909 trip to the Queen Charlotte Islands. — BOTH PROVINCIAL ARCHIVES

forced to excuse himself in order to recover some stability in his bewildered stomach. The effect on the gathering was to create an even more congenial atmosphere in which a verbal understanding ending the rate war was concluded.

It is worth noting that throughout the dispute, Joshua Green and James Troup had remained friends, each respecting the other's integrity and ability. Both agreed, as the rate war reached a peak in 1908, not to discuss it in order to avoid becoming personally involved.

Soon after the meeting, the Seattle-Vancouver fares were raised still further to $3.00 one way and $5.00 return, or, on the CPR ships running via Victoria, $4.00 one way. Near the end of the month, the *Iroquois* was withdrawn from the PSN's Vancouver-Seattle service and was transferred to the Victoria-Seattle route, replacing her near sister ship *Chippewa*. The *Princess Victoria*'s old rival was then assigned to the PSN's Seattle-Bellingham run. While neither company publicly admitted the fact, it was apparent that the rate war was over.

It took a lot of courage for any company to take on the CPR in an all-out rate war and Joshua Green and his associates had put up a good fight. The long struggle had cost both companies a considerable amount of money and energy, but the greater resources of the CPR, the opening of the Exposition in Seattle, and the need for greater stability in the transportation industry had all worked to end the conflict.

In the long run it was the CPR that benefited most from the rate war. It became soundly established on the service between Seattle and Vancouver and dominated the routes to Vancouver Island from both Washington and the British Columbia mainland. The famed Triangle Route had proven remarkably successful and other services had not suffered. While not in as favoured a position, the Puget Sound Navigation Company became increasingly concerned with operations in and around Puget Sound. Its vessels were chartered to provide relief for the CPR ships on the Seattle-Vancouver service during layover days and its excursion business was brisk. In 1912, PSN re-established the service between Port Angeles and Victoria using the *Whatcom* and the *Sol Duc*. This latter vessel remained on the run until 1928 when she was replaced by the *Iroquois*, by then rebuilt to carry automobiles.

PSN operated on the Seattle-Victoria route without major interruption until the 1950's using the *Sol Duc, Olympic, Iroquois, Malahat, Chinook* and *Kalakala*. In the 1920's, the CPR and PSN produced joint advertising brochures for their services to Vancouver Island marking a dramatic change from the days of the rate war. In addition, from the 1920's, until the eventual formation of Washington State Ferries, PSN operated a ferry service between Anacortes and Sidney, B.C. using such vessels as the *Puget* and *City of Angeles*. This route competed directly with the operations begun in the mid 1920's by the CPR using the ferry *Motor Princess*. PSN continued to try new routes and briefly operated the *Olympic* on a direct Bellingham-Victoria run in the early 1930's.

CANADIAN PACIFIC
RAILWAY
MAY
8
1909
—
S.S. PRINCESS CHARLOTTE

Photographer Leonard Frank made this strikingly beautiful portrait of the *Princess Charlotte* passing through the First Narrows into Vancouver Harbour in 1920. In her long career on the Pacific coast, she underwent few external changes. Today, the hills in the background of this scene are covered with shopping centres, apartments and suburban homes.
— VANCOUVER PUBLIC LIBRARY

CHAPTER IV

GROWTH
OF THE FLEET

*The Operations of
the B.C. Coastal Fleet*

WHILE THE LARGER VESSELS in the Princess fleet were concentrated on the highly publicized, busy Triangle Route, the Company's smaller ships maintained the less glamorous coastal trade. The *Princess Beatrice, May* and *Royal* (when not on the Triangle Route) usually operated to the North Coast and on the Skagway, Alaska route, carrying supplies and passengers to the numerous mining, lumbering and fishing communities. Gold was still an extremely important cargo, and steamers frequently left Alaskan ports with over a million dollars in bullion in their safes. The *Tees* operated regularly on the west coast of Vancouver Island, serving lumber camps, fish canneries and whaling stations between Jordan River and Kyoquot Sound. The *Otter* sailed regularly to small settlements on the Strait of Georgia and along the east coast of the Island.

Cargos on these runs reflected the significance of the fishing and whaling industries on the Coast. Frequently, the steamers would reach port with holds full of canned salmon or several hundred barrels of whale oil from the West Coast. On one occasion, for example, the *Tees* brought, in addition to 25 passengers, 550 barrels of whale oil from Sechart. The Pacific whalers were, at this time, bringing in record catches of the giant sea mammals, slaughtering them in numbers far greater than the whale populations could sustain. Ultimately, the animals were driven to near extinction and with them the whalers disappeared, ironically bringing about their own demise as an industry. Resources were plundered, fortunes made and a magnificent form of life all but destroyed. It was a process that unfortunately would be repeated.

Steamers like the *Tees* also ferried native peoples from their coastal villages to canneries at Good Hope, Brunswick, Rivers Inlets, and other points along the Coast. These people were recruited annually by cannery operators to provide cheap labour during the peak of the fishing season when large quantities of salmon had to be processed. Referred to as "Siwashes,"

Fated to a short, tragic life on the Pacific coast, the *Princess Sophia* sailed under the CPR checkerboard house flag for only seven years. Leonard Frank took this photo, probably the best surviving view of this ship. — VANCOUVER PUBLIC LIBRARY

In this photograph of the Coast Service facilities in Victoria, taken from the Parliament Buildings about 1910, the *Tees*, *Princess Charlotte*, *Amur* and *Princess Victoria* are all in evidence.
— PROVINCIAL ARCHIVES

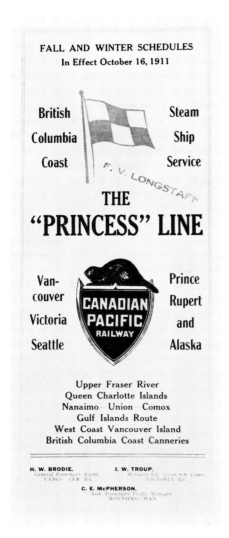

In this photograph of ...

they received low wages and little respect. In fact, the *Daily Colonist* referred to 115 Indians onboard the *Tees* as "cargo."

Loading facilities at many of the small ports served by the steamers were primitive, as one incident at Scow Bay on the northeast coast of Vancouver Island demonstrates. In May 1909, the *Queen City* called at the small logging camp to pick up an injured logger. However, the night before her arrival, a tug had dragged the steamer's landing float into shallow water. As a result, when the tide went out while the *Queen City* was tied up, the vessel was left stranded in the mud. At high tide, several hours later, the steamer was refloated and continued on her voyage, apparently none the worse for the experience.

At some places, like Clo-oose near Nitinat Lake, on the west coast of Vancouver Island, the steamers did not even have the benefit of a wharf. There, the *Tees* was forced to lie offshore and unload her cargo into dug-out canoes manned by Indians from the village. Highly skilled, these men would meet the steamer in virtually any weather and deliver the precious supplies to shore.

To many people in the small coastal settlements, the arrival of the CPR steamer was a major social event of the week, if indeed they were lucky enough to have weekly service. The little coasters provided the only link with the outside world for these people. All mail, supplies, news and gossip came on them. It was little wonder that to long-time residents of the Coast, the *Tees, Otter, Queen City, Amur* and others were remembered with such affection.

On the lower Fraser River, where CPN and CPR stern-wheelers had served continuously since the gold rush, the days of the paddlewheelers were drawing to a close. In August 1908, the *Transfer* was laid up when the mail contract she was operating under was lost and daily except Sunday sailings between New Westminster and Steveston were terminated. By this time, the British Columbia Electric Railway was operating an electric interurban line to Steveston from Vancouver and much of the sternwheeler's traffic had been diverted to this route. A service was maintained by private operators on the lower Fraser, using the gasoline boat *J. C. Bruce* and the steamer *Favorite*. However, the latter vessel sank in heavy ice during the winter of 1908-09 and was not salvaged. In February 1909, the CPR sold the *Transfer* to Robert Jardine, who planned to re-establish service on the route. Her purchase price was approximately $7,000. Ultimately, she ended her days as a power plant for a salmon cannery at Redonda Bay near Powell River. Also in 1909 the CPR sternwheeler *R. P. Rithet* was sold to the Terminal Steam Navigation Company of Vancouver and renamed *Baramba*.

Thus, with the sale of the *Transfer* and the *R. P. Rithet*, only the newer steel-hulled *Beaver* remained of the former CPN sternwheelers taken over by the CPR in 1901. The *Beaver* worked on the Fraser River between New Westminster and Chilliwack until 1913 when she was withdrawn from service. As had been the case with the *Transfer*, competition from the B.C. Electric Railway made continuation of the sternwheeler operation uneconomical. In 1919, she was sold to the British Columbia government for use as a ferry.

By this time several of the smaller former CPN coastal freighters and the sidewheelers *Yosemite* and *Princess Louise* had also been sold. The first ships to be disposed of were the *Willapa* and *Maude*, which were sold in 1902 and 1903 respectively. The *Willapa* was acquired by the Bellingham Bay Transportation Company, was renamed *Bellingham*, and used in the coastal trade between Bellingham and Tacoma. The *Maude* was acquired by the B.C. Salvage Company after the old steamer was rebuilt as a salvage vessel by the B.C. Marine Railway Company at Esquimalt.

The *Danube* was the next former CPN vessel to be sold. In October 1905, she was, like the *Maude*, bought by the B.C. Salvage Company. She was renamed the *Salvor* and kept in service on the West Coast until 1918, when she was sold to a Montreal based company. Two years later she was resold to Spanish owners, who renamed her *Nervion* and operated her until 1934.

In 1906, the sidewheelers *Princess Louise* and *Yosemite* were sold by the CPR. The *Louise*, the first "Princess" ship, was acquired by Marpole Macdonald of Victoria and was resold in 1908 to the Vancouver Dredging and Salvage Company for use as a barge. In 1916, this company sold the hull to the Britannia Mining and Smelting Company. Finally, in 1917, the *Louise* was beached at Woodfibre on Howe Sound by the Whalen Pulp and Paper Company, which had acquired the hull in that year.

The *Yosemite* was sold to the Puget Sound Excursion Company of Seattle for cruises and excursions in connection with the Alaska-Yukon-Pacific Exposition. Her career ended in 1909, when, under the ownership of a real estate promotor named Hillman, she ran aground and was wrecked in Port Orchard Narrows about two miles from Bremerton, Washington.

Since several of the smaller vessels of the CPR's fleet had been sold and still others were due for replacement, the Company was in need of a number of new coastal freight and passenger vessels. Furthermore, traffic on nearly all of the steamer routes was increasing to a point where larger, more efficient vessels were required on the inter-city runs just to handle the growth of business. In consequence, the CPR's British Columbia Coast Service, as the "Princess Fleet" was officially called, embarked on the most ambitious construction program in its history.

Initially, two steamships were required for the Victoria to Vancouver route to provide a regular night boat service between the two cities. In addition a steamer was needed for the west coast of Vancouver Island service, a cargo liner was required for the Alaska route and another vessel was necessary to augment the operations to Powell River, the Gulf Islands and northern ports. On the Nanaimo to Vancouver service, taken over in 1905 with the purchase of the E & N Railway,

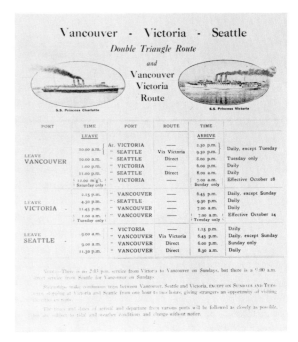

— BOTH PROVINCIAL ARCHIVES

By 1913 the *Princess Royal* had received a black hull, replacing the light grey and white paint scheme applied during her first years.
— LEONARD FRANK PHOTO, VANCOUVER
PUBLIC LIBRARY

At some of the small ports of call, cargo was moved to and from shore by dugout canoe. Here the *Queen City* is shown in Barkley Sound on the west coast of Vancouver Island about 1900.
— PROVINCIAL ARCHIVES

By 1913 the Princess Royal . . .
At some of the small . . .

the steamer *Joan* was proving inadequate for the traffic and a larger, faster passenger vessel was needed as a replacement. With the growth in Vancouver Island rail traffic, additional tugs were also required to tow railway car barges from Vancouver to the E & N's transfer slip at Ladysmith. Ultimately, new larger vessels would also be necessary on the daylight services of the Triangle Route. To fulfil the needs of this ambitious program, the following vessels were acquired by the CPR in the years immediately preceding World War I:

Vessel	Date Launched	Primary Service
Princess Adelaide	July 1910	Victoria-Vancouver night boat
Princess Alice	May 1911	Victoria-Vancouver night boat
Princess Mary	September 1910	Powell River-Comox, north coast
Princess Sophia	November 1911	Alaska
Princess Maquinna	December 1912	Vancouver Island, west coast
Princess Patricia (ex *Queen Alexandra*)	April 1902 (purchased 1911)	Vancouver-Nanaimo
Princess Irene	October 1914	Triangle Route
Princess Margaret	June 1914	Triangle Route
Nitinat (tug) (ex *William Jolliffe*)	1885 (purchased 1914)	Vancouver-Ladysmith barge
Qualicum (tug)	1904 (purchased 1911)	Vancouver-Ladysmith barge

Thus, between the summer of 1910 and the fall of 1914, a total of eight new Princess ships and two tugs were built or purchased by the CPR.

Captain Troup's influence was evident in the designs and standards of accommodation incorporated in nearly all of these new ships. Quality in design and construction was such that many of the steamers remained active with the CPR's Coast Service and successive owners for over 40 years. The *Adelaide* and *Alice* were nearly identical single-funneled steamers designed especially for the night service on the Victoria to Vancouver route but they also proved versatile enough to eventually operate effectively on the daylight runs and on the north coast services to Prince Rupert and Alaska. Their tall, slender funnels made them appear deceptively small at sea, when in fact they were nearly as long as the *Princess Victoria* and had considerably greater displacement. Their overall design and layout reflected the steady refinement of features first incorporated by Troup in the *Princess Beatrice* and *Princess Royal*.

The two new night boats were not designed for speed, but rather for quiet, economical operation, since the nighttime

The Princess Adelaide *was . . .*
The Princess Alice *was . . .*

The *Princess Adelaide* was built for the Victoria - Vancouver night run in 1910, but saw service all along the coast except on the west coast of Vancouver Island.

The *Princess Alice* was nearly identical to the *Princess Adelaide*. The most noticeable difference was the *Alice*'s more enclosed forward deck.
— CPR

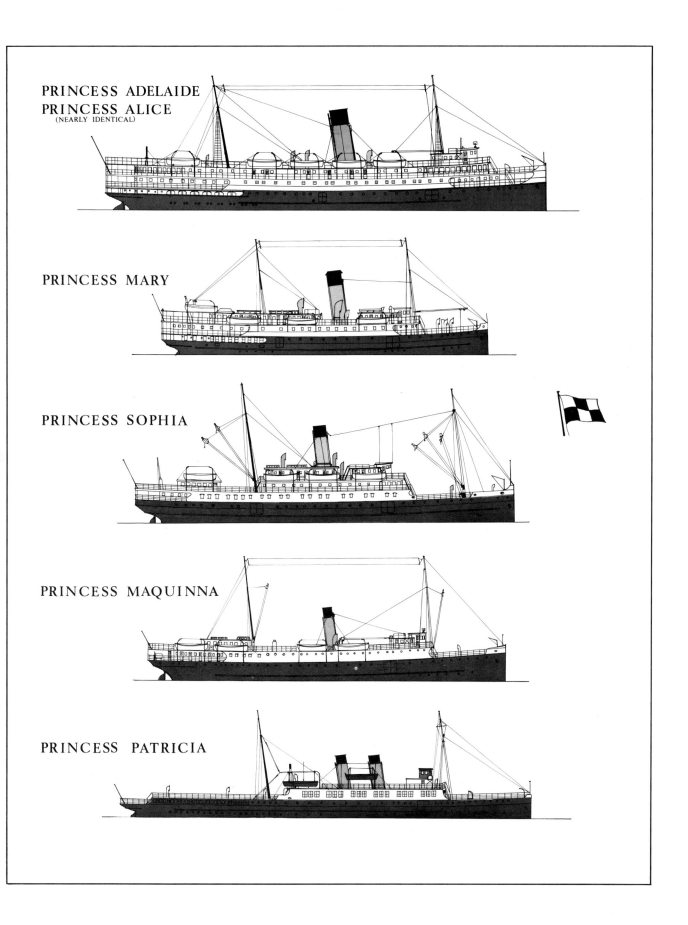

PRINCESS ADELAIDE
PRINCESS ALICE
(NEARLY IDENTICAL)

PRINCESS MARY

PRINCESS SOPHIA

PRINCESS MAQUINNA

PRINCESS PATRICIA

95

Prince Rupert was . . .
The Princess Patricia *was* . . .

The Princess Mary's *card* ...

Prince Rupert was the western terminus of the Grand Trunk Pacific Railway and an important north coast port. Here the *Princess Mary* and *Princess Beatrice* share the Government wharf.
—MCRAE PHOTO, PROVINCIAL ARCHIVES

The *Princess Patricia* was purchased to provide a fast day time service between Nanaimo and Vancouver. — LEONARD FRANK PHOTO, VANCOUVER PUBLIC LIBRARY

The *Princess Mary*'s card room featured rich hardwood panelling. — PROVINCIAL ARCHIVES

runs were not an express type of service. The ships had large dining rooms accommodating up to 150 persons at a sitting and 100 cafe seats. All 118 staterooms were provided with hot and cold water, electric heaters, lamps and outside windows. The single screw vessels had four cylinder triple expansion engines which proved capable of developing just over 18 knots on trials.

Perhaps the most unusual addition to the fleet was the turbine-powered *Princess Patricia*, which was acquired by the CPR in 1911. She was built in 1902 as the *Queen Alexandra* by the W. Denny & Bros. yards at Dumbarton, Scotland for service on the River Clyde. She was the second turbine-powered passenger vessel to enter service anywhere in the world and proved to be a speedy, reliable ship.

The development of the steam turbine for vessels was a most significant advance in marine engineering because of the high speed, vibration free, economical operation it allowed. On arriving on the Coast, the *Princess Patricia* was the first turbine-powered vessel in the Northwest. She created quite a sensation with her 21.6 knot top speed, permitting two-hour crossings of the Straits of Georgia. Her one weakness, which eventually contributed to her early retirement, was her lack of provision for carrying vehicles. In 1912, let alone in 1902 when she was built, vehicle accommodation was an insignificant function for any steamer.

The question has often been raised over which of the early Princess ships was fastest — the *Princess Victoria*, the *Princess Charlotte*, or the *Princess Patricia*. As often happens in such a controversy, fact and fancy often become inextricably intertwined. All three ships claimed record runs and undoubtedly all were fast, each being capable of well over 20 knots. Tidal conditions, winds, and loads, not to mention the skill of captain and crew, were all factors not to be ignored. When the three ships were converted to oil just before World War I, all achieved improved performance, but the *Princess Victoria* and *Princess Patricia* seem to have come out the best. The *Charlotte* never really lived up to expectations. While she had a design speed greater than the *Victoria*'s, she had difficulty making it in trials. It seems that she was under-boilered and while certainly fast, she lacked the reserves of power held by the *Victoria*. However, officially, the *Charlotte* held the record and the CPR made no attempt to better her performances with the *Victoria* although it was highly probable that she could have. It seems that the CPR wanted its newest ship to be speedier. It is difficult to say convincingly whether the *Victoria* or the *Patricia* was faster but perhaps it is just as well, for it is doubtful if many minds would be changed in any case. In later years the performance of all three of the early speedsters was overshadowed by the 22.5 knot sister Princesses, the *Kathleen* and the *Marguerite*, built in 1925, which thereafter decisively dominated the Triangle Route.

The *Princesses Maquinna, Mary,* and *Sophia* were all solidly built and well appointed coastal steamers designed for carrying

Few vessels are as fondly remembered on the coast as the *Princess Maquinna*, shown here at Bamfield. She served the isolated west coast of Vancouver Island for four decades.
— B.C. GOVERNMENT PHOTOGRAPH

The builder's plate from the *Princess Maquinna* is now in the B.C. Provincial Museum.
— ROBERT D. TURNER

Barges like the *Transfer No. 3*, which was built by the B.C. Marine Railway at Esquimalt in 1911, were used to carry railway cars.
— PROVINCIAL ARCHIVES

The builder's plate . . .

Barges like the . . .

both passengers and freight to the isolated settlements served by the CPR's steamships. The *Sophia* was the largest, designed specially for the Vancouver to Prince Rupert and Vancouver to Alaska routes. The *Maquinna*, named in honour of the daughter of the famous Nootka Indian Chief Maquinna, and the *Mary* were smaller, for use primarily on the less heavily travelled routes. These two ships developed a reputation for service that survived long after their passing. The *Maquinna* became for many people inseparable from memories of Vancouver Island's west coast. Only two years after entering service the *Mary* was withdrawn to be lengthened by 40 feet. The work was done over a five month period at Esquimalt and gave the ship significantly greater passenger and cargo space.

The arrival of these new ships enabled the Company to retire the *Amur*, which was sold in 1911 to the Coastwise Steamship and Barge Company. Eventually renamed *Famous*, she continued in use in British Columbia waters until 1929, when she was dismantled. In addition to the *Amur*, the CPR was also able to replace the three vessels taken over from the E & N Railway in 1905. The *City of Nanaimo* was sold in 1912 to the Terminal Steam Navigation Company, which renamed her *Bowena*. She was subsequently purchased by the Union Steamship Company of Vancouver and renamed *Cheam* four years before being scrapped in 1926.

On April 10, 1911, the small steamer *Iriquois* (not the PSN vessel of rate war fame) foundered in a storm while on her regular route serving the Gulf Islands. To avoid leaving the residents of the Islands without any service, the CPR put the *City of Nanaimo* into operation and after her sale in 1912 used the *Joan* which by that time had been replaced on the Nanaimo-Vancouver run by the new *Princess Patricia*. Subsequently, the *Joan* was replaced by the *Otter* and was sold to the Terminal Steam Navigation Company in 1914. She was renamed *Ballena* and remained in service until November 1920 when she was scrapped. Also in 1914, the former E & N tug *Czar* was sold to G. F. Payne when the tug *Nitinat* was purchased by the CPR.

The general upgrading of the fleet also saw many of the ships converted to burn fuel oil instead of coal. There were many advantages to using oil on the Princesses. Firing was more constant and certain, enabling the ships to stay closer to schedule. The *Princess May* was the first Princess to be converted. As a coal burner, she could not always make her desired service speed as time was often lost when fires had to be cleaned and ashes handled. Sometimes this caused her to miss the stage of the tide necessary for her to make some of the passages on the Alaska run. After conversion, she could maintain an average speed with only two boilers in operation that was about equal to what she had done before with three when coal fired.

Oil fires also provided a more steady heat which was easier on the boilers and reduced maintenance. However, the most significant advantage was in reducing labour. On an oil

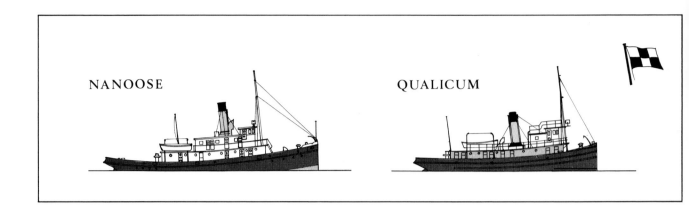

NANOOSE

QUALICUM

The tug Qualicum *was . . .*

The tug *Qualicum* was acquired for the railway car barge service to Vancouver Island. — CPR

The large salvage tug . . .

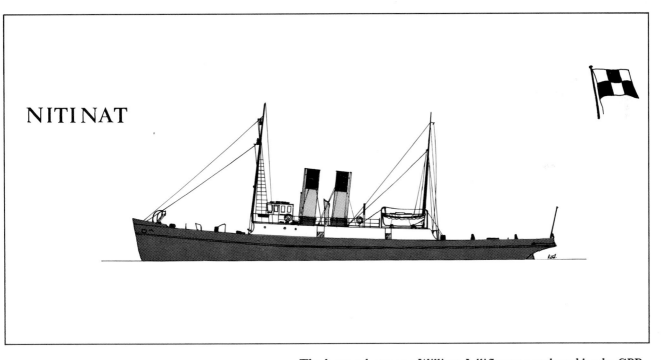

NITINAT

The large salvage tug *William Jolliffe* was purchased by the CPR and renamed *Nitinat*. The two-funnelled vessel was one of the most powerful tugs in British Columbia and participated in a number of salvage operations including the rescue of the stranded *Princess May* in 1910. — PROVINCIAL ARCHIVES

The *Princess Irene* was chartered to the British Admiralty for use
as a mine-layer. She blew up with heavy loss of life at Sheerness
Harbour in May 1915 after only three months of service. Note the
mine laying ports built into the ship's stern.
— JOE D. WILLIAMSON COLLECTION

Her builder's trials . . .

Her builder's trials demonstrated the fine
qualities of the *Princess Margaret*, but the
beautiful steamship was destined for war service
and never sailed on the Triangle Route
for which she was designed.
— PROVINCIAL ARCHIVES

burning ship, one man could do the work of up to 18 firemen and six to nine trimmers. Refueling was also simplified and much faster.

The *Princess Alice* was the first Princess built as an oil burner although she used coal on her voyage to the Pacific. Conversion work was soon carried out on the *Charlotte, Charmer, Adelaide, Victoria, Sophia, Mary* and eventually most ships in the fleet. To service the ships, a 55,000 barrel storage tank was built in Vancouver.

The large and magnificent *Princesses Irene* and *Margaret* never reached the West Coast for service on the Triangle Route as had been intended. They were ordered by the CPR on the 24th of May, 1913 in anticipation of increased traffic resulting from the Panama-Pacific Exposition to be held in 1915, and to accommodate the general boom in patronage being felt by the CPR. However, as the ships were nearing completion at the yards of W. Denny & Bros. at Dumbarton, Scotland, World War I broke out in Europe. The Royal Navy was in desperate need of fast vessels for mine-laying off the enemy coast, and on being completed the two CPR vessels were taken over on charter from the CPR by the Admiralty. With a design speed of 23 knots, the turbine-powered steamers were well suited for their wartime roles. They were each armed with two 4.7 inch guns and four smaller mounts and were outfitted to carry 400 mines.

The life of the *Princess Irene* as a naval auxiliary was short. On May 27, 1915, while in Sheerness Harbour, England the ship blew up and was a total loss. All but one of the crew of 274 officers and men and the 74 Sheerness Dockyard workers on board were killed by an explosion, whose cause was never fully explained. The *Princess Margaret* was more fortunate. She survived a number of hazardous operations during the war, once reportedly reaching a speed of 29 knots while escaping from a German squadron. After the war, she was purchased outright by the Admiralty and was employed in the Baltic in operations against the Bolshevic forces. In addition to mine-laying during this period, the *Princess Margaret* served as a hospital ship and refugee transport.

From late 1921 through to April 1923 the *Margaret* was extensively refitted as an Admiralty yacht at Portsmouth and in November 1923 was used to carry guests of the Admiralty for the Naval review. Finally in 1927 she was offered for sale. However, by this time the CPR had acquired replacement vessels that were better suited to the requirements of the Triangle Route as it had evolved by the mid-1920's and the services of the *Princess Margaret* were no longer required. On July 2, 1929, she was delivered to the Hughes Bolckow & Company yards at Blyth for scrapping.

Both the *Princess Irene* and the *Princess Margaret* would have made striking additions to the Princess fleet had they entered service on the Pacific coast. They were fast and were of a very attractive design. Their cruiser sterns and greater length made them look faster and more rakish than their

When World War I began in 1914, Canada quickly mobilized.
Many troops were trained on Vancouver Island and then moved
to the mainland on the Princess ships. It was a time of excitement, patriotism, fear and sorrow. In the upper view, the *Princess
Charlotte* is nearly fully loaded. — PROVINCIAL ARCHIVES

On the right, rain is falling as the *Princess
Victoria* is loaded. — PROVINCIAL ARCHIVES

If crowding . . .

The *Princess Mary* along with nearly all of the larger ships in the fleet saw service in troop movements. A long whistle blast, a last wave — a war ahead. — PROVINCIAL ARCHIVES

If crowding is any indication, troops travelling on the *Princess Patricia* had a more comfortable passage than those on the larger, more fully loaded *Princess Victoria*.
— BOTH PROVINCIAL ARCHIVES

Victorians watch the *Princess Sophia* back from her berth and leave for Vancouver.
— PROVINCIAL ARCHIVES

Troops of the 30th Battalion file between the spectators towards the docks.
— PROVINCIAL ARCHIVES

Victorians watch . . .
Troops of the 30th . . .

The classic steam powered tug *Dola*, shown in a wartime coat of grey paint, was used by the CPR on its barge service between Vancouver and Ladysmith from 1917 to 1933. By the time this photograph was taken in the 1940's, the hull of the veteran tug was showing signs of many hard years at sea. — JOE D. WILLIAMSON

eventual replacements, the *Princesses Kathleen* and *Marguerite*, both built in 1925. The *Irene* and *Margaret* were among the largest ships ever built for the CPR's B.C. Coast Service. They were exceeded in length only by the *Princess of Vancouver* built in 1955.

The war also affected many of the other ships in the CPR Coast Service, although far less dramatically than it did the fortunes of the *Margaret* and *Irene*. Many CPR employees left the Princesses to join the armed forces fighting in Europe and the ships themselves provided an important link in the movement of military personnel from their training grounds near Victoria to the mainland, where troop trains took them east for departure to Europe. The troops marched down to the docks from the Willows camps to board the waiting Princesses as crowds lined the streets to cheer them on. Often three or more steamers at a time would be loaded until it appeared the decks would overflow. These were times of excitement charged with patriotic feeling and inner fear, for all present knew that many boarding the liners might never return. Passchendaele, Vimy, Flanders and other scenes of lasting horror would intervene before the Armistice of November 1918, long years later.

The Island Princess, *Wrecks, and the Grand Trunk Pacific Steamships*

In 1916, the *Queen City* was scrapped in Victoria and in the following year, another tug, the *Dola*, was acquired. One further addition was made the next year. This was the small steamer, *Island Princess*, formerly known as the *Daily*. This 116 by 25 foot, wooden-hulled vessel from Puget Sound was purchased for operation from Victoria and Vancouver to the Gulf Islands. She was in fact the ninth Princess to be acquired by the CPR since 1910, but compared to the other new vessels she was overshadowed and many people were probably not aware of her existence. Her real importance lay in the improved service she provided to the Gulf Islands.

During this period of rapid change in the composition of the CPR fleet, two significant incidents occurred involving the Princesses. On May 5, 1910, the *Princess May*, while steaming at about 10 knots down the Lynn Canal, in heavy fog, ran hard aground on a reef off the north end of Sentinel Island, Alaska. While proceeding cautiously because of the poor visibility, the vessel still had sufficient momentum to be carried well up over the rocks which were submerged by the high tide. The wireless operator was able to send the following message before power was lost: "S.S. *Princess May* sinking Sentinel Island; send help."

The 80 passengers and 68-man crew as well as the mails and a gold shipment were all landed safely on Sentinel Island. As the tide receded, the ship was left stranded with her bow high out of the water above the rocks. The position was so unusual that photographs of the stranded ship were sold all along the coast. The passengers and crew were taken to Juneau on the *Princess Ena* and other rescue vessels which arrived on the scene.

The classic steam powered . . .

The Island Princess *was . . .*

When sold by . . .

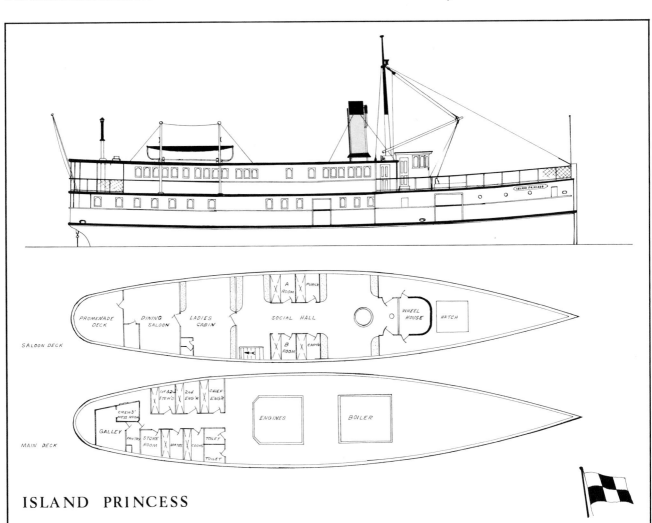

ISLAND PRINCESS

The *Island Princess* was the smallest of the CPR's Princess ships. She was purchased by Captain Troup for the summer service to the Gulf Islands. — CPR

When sold by the Company in 1930 she was renamed *Cy Peck* and rebuilt to carry automobiles. — B.C. GOVERNMENT PHOTOGRAPH

The stranding of the *Princess May* on August 5, 1910 on Sentinal Island produced what must be the most spectacular and famous shipwreck photograph in the history of the Pacific coast. She was salvaged by Captain W. H. Logan with the Seattle based salvage tug *Santa Cruz*. Sliding ways were built and much rock blasted away. One hundred and twenty plates were damaged in the wreck, with the largest hole being about 50 feet long and 18 inches wide. Several attempts were made to pull her free but it was not until high tide on September 3rd that the *Santa Cruz* and the tug *William Jolliffe* were able to refloat the ship. Within 30 hours of the salvage, one of the heaviest gales of the season occurred. The refloating of the *Princess May* was the 32nd successful salvage job performed by Captain Logan. — PROVINCIAL ARCHIVES

With her engine rooms flooded, the *May* was helpless, but fortunately the weather remained calm and the salvage tug *William Jolliffe* and the steamer *Santa Cruz* were eventually able to free the Princess and tow her to port. The cost of salvaging the *May* and carrying out the necessary repairs was $115,000.

In 1914 the *Princess Victoria* was involved in a more serious incident that led to the tragic loss of the Admiral Line's steamship *Admiral Sampson* and 16 of her passengers and crew. As in so many other marine accidents, fog was to blame for the collision between the *Princess* and the *Admiral*, which occurred in the early morning hours of August 26th off Point No Point north of Seattle. The *Princess Victoria* was proceeding southbound from Victoria to Seattle, while the *Admiral Sampson* had just sailed from Seattle, bound for Alaska.

Both ships were sounding fog signals, but neither could ascertain the exact position of the other vessel. They collided while both liners were still underway, though at reduced speeds. The bow of the *Princess Victoria* nearly cut the *Admiral Sampson* in half. Despite the efforts of Captain Hickey of the CPR vessel to hold the crippled *Admiral* afloat by keeping the ships together, she sank within 15 minutes. Ten members of the *Admiral*'s crew, including her master, Captain Zimo Moore, were lost while attempting to save the passengers, of whom six died. Canadian and American investigations into the collision differed in their findings. Canadian authorities attached no blame to the *Princess Victoria*, while their U.S. counterparts found both captains negligent for not stopping their steamers until the relative positions of the ships could be established.

Coincidental with the CPR's shipbuilding program was the arrival on the Pacific coast of the first of the Grand Trunk Pacific Railway's steamers, which were to provide connecting service between Seattle, Victoria and Vancouver and the railway's terminus at Prince Rupert. The first vessel to enter GTP service was the *Prince Albert*, which commenced sailings from Prince Rupert to Victoria and Vancouver early in 1910. The *Prince Albert* was a 841 ton, steel-hulled vessel built at Hull, England in 1892 as the *Bruno*. She was soon followed by the slightly larger steamship *Prince John* (formerly *Amethyst*), built in England in 1910. This vessel provided a GTP service to the Queen Charlotte Islands from Prince Rupert.

By far the most significant vessels acquired by the Grand Trunk Pacific were the fast, new, three-funneled *Prince Rupert* and *Prince George*. These two ships, whose construction had been announced at the time of the rate war between the CPR and the PSN, were equal to the promises of their owners. The 3,380 ton steamships were licensed to carry 1,500 passengers and had stateroom accommodations for 220. Both ships exceeded 18 knots on trials and could cruise comfortably at 16 knots. They were solidly built with double bottoms and were subdivided by watertight bulkheads into nine compartments. The *Prince Rupert* and *Prince George* began a once weekly

The Grand Trunk Pacific Railway entered the steamship business with a fleet of Prince ships. Their two most striking ships were the *Prince George* of 3,372 tons and the nearly identical *Prince Rupert*. The two large Princes had the potential of providing serious competition for the CPR's Princesses. They were comparable to the CPR ships in size, speed and accommodation. However, they did not seriously affect the CPR's hold on the Triangle Route. On the run to Prince Rupert they held their own against the CPR's smaller steamships. — LEONARD FRANK PHOTO, VANCOUVER PUBLIC LIBRARY

This exceptional view . . .
In this scene . . .

service from a newly constructed terminal at Seattle to Victoria, Vancouver, Prince Rupert and Granby Bay (Anyox). Running only once a week, they presented little serious competition for the CPR's Triangle Route, but the potential was there for the GTP to make significant inroads into the CPR's business. However, for a number of reasons, including the demands of World War I on the coastal ships and the eventual bankruptcy of the GTP, this company and later the Canadian National Railways, which absorbed it in 1920, was never able to successfully compete with the CPR, at least in the southern coastal waters.

Loss of the Princess Sophia

Nearly 18 years had passed since the tragic loss of the steamer *Islander* off the coast of Douglas Island, south of Juneau, Alaska. Probably few if any of the 269 passengers who boarded the sturdy *Princess Sophia* at Skagway, Alaska on October 23, 1918 thought about the *Islander* as baggage was loaded and last goodbyes were waved. On board were the crews of many ice-bound river steamers, miners, trappers, businessmen and a few late season tourists. Fifty women and children were noted on the ship's passenger list.

Meanwhile, Captain Louis P. Locke, a veteran CPR officer, and his crew of 73 were making last minute preparations for the *Sophia*'s departure. Fifty horses were loaded, as freight and mail were taken on board. In addition, there was a large shipment of Christmas parcels destined for soldiers from the Yukon fighting in France. Just before 11:00 p.m. the *Princess Sophia* slipped away from the Skagway docks and steamed out of the harbour.

As the *Sophia* proceeded down the Lynn Canal, the weather quickly deteriorated. This was a fairly common occurrence in the winter months and a storm in Alaskan waters was something to be remembered. Soon heavy snow squalls swirled around the liner cutting visibility to nearly zero. It was impossible to ascertain exactly where the ship was within the narrow confines of the fjord. Captain Locke guided his ship past Point Sherman, attempting to estimate his position carefully before the *Sophia* had to turn at Eldred Rock prior to making the difficult passage around Vanderbuilt Reef. In fair weather the two and one half mile wide channel presented few difficulties to an experienced navigator like Captain Locke. However, by 3:00 a.m., on the morning of the 24th, the weather had become so foul that the ship had drifted considerably off course and no safe anchorage was available. A strong northwest gale was blowing and snow hid every landmark.

Suddenly, at 3:10 a.m., the steamer ground to a sickening halt, stuck fast on Vanderbuilt Reef. Passengers were thrown from their berths and dishes shattered in the dining room as the ship's propeller thrashed helplessly. Not surprisingly, there were a few minutes of panic. Captain Locke ordered that the lifeboats be made ready for abandoning the ship and life jackets were distributed. A passenger describing the scene in a letter

This exceptional view of Victoria Harbour shows the CPR docks at left with the *Princesses Alice, Adelaide,* and *Beatrice,* the *Otter,* and the *Princess Victoria.* On the right are the Grand Trunk docks with both the *Prince George* and *Prince Rupert* in port. In the distance the *City of Nanaimo* is heading out to sea. — PROVINCIAL ARCHIVES

In this scene from the war years the *Princess Sophia* is at Bellingham, Washington with a large excursion crowd. — JOE D. WILLIAMSON

home noted: "Two women fainted and one of them got herself into a black evening dress and didn't worry about who saw her putting it on. Some of the men, too, kept life preservers on for an hour or so and seemed to think there was no chance for us." However, reports soon reached the bridge that the *Sophia* was held fast and was not shipping water.

With the storm still raging, the Captain decided it was safer to stay with the ship as long as her situation remained stable. Since the liner was two miles from shore, the prudent officer knew that his passengers and crew would stand little chance of survival in the rough sea should they take to the boats. The passengers settled down to wait for the morning, rescue, and whatever the night held in store. There was no other alternative.

By dawn the storm had slackened somewhat and the *Sophia* was still held fast. The morning high tide, which it was hoped would free the ship, passed at 6:00 and she remained totally immobilized. The barometer showed a rising trend indicating a probable improvement in the weather, so that Captain Locke, with justification, felt some optimism for the future of his ship and the 343 people onboard. If the steamer could survive the stress of the low tide at noon, perhaps she might be floated off at 4:00 p.m., the next high tide. Meanwhile, ships were answering the *Sophia*'s distress calls by radio and should arrive by evening. As the winds were still very high, it still seemed wiser to stay with the liner, since the passengers were relatively safe, warm, and dry.

As noon approached, the Captain and his officers became increasingly concerned about the approaching low tide. The *Sophia* was aground on the starboard bow and they feared that as the water supporting the stern receded, the ship might settle on the port side and at the stern causing her to capsize. Instead, the waves pounded her bow around and worked the keel into a groove in the reef, supporting the ship forward and on both sides. This left the stern exposed to the wind and waves, which gradually forced the ship further onto the reef. Still her double hull held tight and the *Sophia* remained dry.

By the afternoon high tide, it was no longer possible to float the ship free. Unless help arrived — and this might well have necessitated several tugs — to aid the steamer in getting off the reef, her last chance of escape had passed. To make matters worse, the winds had again strengthened, blowing with increased force from the north, down the narrow fjord. The *Sophia* received an increased pounding from the waves, even higher with the rising tides. Darkness quickly enveloped the *Princess*.

At 6:20 p.m. the steamer *King & Winge* arrived and at 8:00 she was joined by the lighthouse tender *Cedar*, followed later by other small ships. At least there were now several rescue vessels standing by. Wireless reports of the grounding had meanwhile reached CPR officials in Victoria. They remained optimistic. Eight years before, under somewhat similar conditions, the *Princess May* had been hard aground on Sentinel

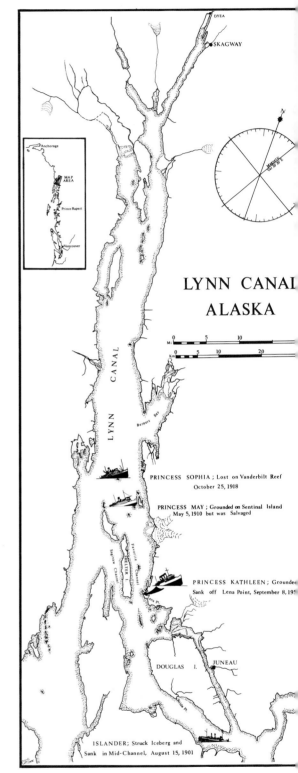

LYNN CANAL
ALASKA

PRINCESS SOPHIA ; Lost on Vanderbilt Reef
October 25, 1918

PRINCESS MAY ; Grounded on Sentinal Island
May 5, 1910 but was Salvaged

PRINCESS KATHLEEN ; Grounded
Sank off Lena Point, September 8, 195

ISLANDER; Struck Iceberg and
Sank in Mid-Channel, August 15, 1901

Stranded on Vanderbuilt ...

Stranded on Vanderbuilt Reef, the *Princess Sophia* was doomed. She was carried over the reef that night with all on board.
— BOTH PROVINCIAL ARCHIVES

Island and had survived without injury to any of the passengers. Furthermore, Captain Locke was a highly capable master, the ship seemed secure and other vessels were at the scene. Captain Troup immediately dispatched the *Princess Alice* from Vancouver, ordering her to steam to the *Princess Sophia* as quickly as possible and rescue the passengers at the earliest opportunity. As soon as it became apparent that the *Sophia* could not be floated off the reef, he also directed the salvage vessel *Tees* to sail to her assistance.

At 8:30 p.m., one of the main steam pipes on the *Sophia* broke and light and heat were lost. Still, the ship was in no immediate danger and Captain Locke instructed the two rescue ships to anchor for the night, but to stand by. Hopefully, the weather would soon moderate. By the morning of the 25th, power had been restored to the *Sophia* but winds were now of gale force, making the transfer of passengers impossible. Boats could not be launched safely and the rescue vessels had to stand away for their own safety. The ship had been stranded for over 24 hours.

The plight of the *Sophia* was well appreciated by her passengers. In his diary, John Maskell of Dawson wrote: "This morning we are surrounded by a number of small boats, but it is too rough to transfer the passengers. In the realization that we are surrounded by grave danger, I make this my last will ... "

The storm had risen sufficiently to prompt Captain Locke to send the nearby vessels to shelter since they too were endangered by the worsening weather. As the day wore on, the *Sophia* was gradually pushed higher on the reef with the rising afternoon tide, which was to peak at 5:47 p.m. By late afternoon, darkness, blowing snow, and 50 knot winds obscured the stranded *Princess*. She was never seen again.

At 4:50 the first indication of impending disaster was received on board the *Cedar*. It read: "Taking water and foundering. For God's sake come and save us." The *Cedar* replied: "Coming full speed, but cannot see on account of thick snows and taking heavy seas." For half an hour the *Sophia*'s radio operator kept in touch with the *Cedar* until the signal became almost too weak to receive. The *Cedar* radioed the operator on the *Sophia* to save his battery and he replied: "All right, but for God's sake hurry. Water coming in the room." Not long after, the final pathetic message was received on the *Cedar*: "Just time to say goodbye. We are foundering."

By the time the little *Cedar* had reached the vicinity of the reef there was no sign of the ill-fated steamer, except for one of her masts protruding from the water. The *Cedar* and the other rescue vessels searched for survivors, but none was found, save an Irish setter. As the search proceeded, 179 bodies were recovered, many covered with oil from the steamer's ruptured fuel tanks. Others were found on shore, where exposure had claimed them. All around the reef, hundreds of sea birds were found dead in the oil slick that spread from the wreck.

By the time Captain Slater brought the *Princess Alice* into

Juneau Harbour at the end of her emergency run from Victoria, there was little that could be done but return the bodies of the victims to Vancouver and Victoria. The *Sophia* and her passengers and crew were mourned along the entire Coast, but most of all in Victoria, her home port. The *Alice* loaded 156 caskets and steamed back to Vancouver, "A veritable floating hearse," commented her master. She arrived in Vancouver just as word of the Armistice ending the horror of World War I was received. Few British Columbians felt like celebrating. They remembered sadly how the *Sophia* had earlier sailed from Victoria, her decks overcrowded with troops leaving home for the war.

The *Tees*, which had been converted to a salvage vessel, arrived on the scene with a crew of divers and after the weather had moderated it was possible to examine the wreck. The divers were able to recover about $100,000 in gold from the purser's safe and the trunks of a number of the *Sophia*'s passengers. However, salvage of the ill-fated ship was impractical.

No one was officially blamed for the loss of the *Sophia* or the failure to rescue her passengers and crew. With experience on the CPR steamers *Amur*, *Princess Beatrice*, *Princess Royal*, *Charmer*, *Tees*, *Princess Alice* and *Princess Sophia*, Captain Locke had a record beyond reproach. While it might have been possible to remove some of the passengers on the 24th, undoubtedly there would have been some loss of life. With indications of better weather and his ship holding fast, his decision not to abandon ship at the time was certainly justified.

Governor Thomas Riggs of Alaska, completely exonerating Captain Locke, stated, " . . . everything possible had been done for the safety of the passengers that could be done, not only by the captain of the *Princess Sophia*, but by the captains of all vessels in the vicinity. The accident, or loss of life is no more due to any fault of these men than was the damage done in the recent flood at Juneau."

No ship on the CPR's coastal routes ever carried the name *Princess Sophia* after that tragic moment of 5:00 p.m., Friday, October 24, 1918. For 15 years afterwards legal battles were fought as relatives of the *Sophia*'s passengers sought damages from the CPR. The arguments finally reached the United States Supreme Court, where, as in other inquiries into the tragedy, it was determined that the CPR was not liable.

In early August 1919, the *Princess Ena*, the small coal-fired coastal freighter which had been built for the CPR in 1908, came close to ending her rather unglamourous career on the bottom of Seymour Narrows. The tides swirled quickly through the Narrows and the *Ena* was not the first ship to brush with Ripple Rock, the jagged pinnacle of a reef that blocked the centre of the channel to navigation. Several ships had come to grief on Ripple Rock, and Seymour Narrows became known as one of the most treacherous passages on the Coast.

The Princess Ena *and Ripple Rock*

118

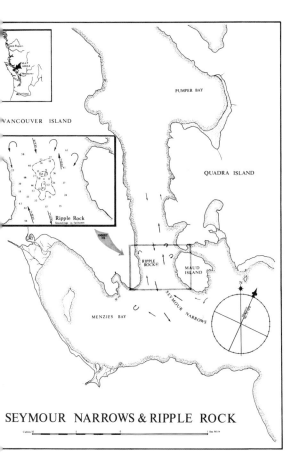

SEYMOUR NARROWS & RIPPLE ROCK

The CPR freighter, heavily laden with a cargo of coal, was steaming north through the Narrows bound for Prince Rupert at 6:30 on the morning of the 6th. As often happens in marine mishaps, the ship was only slightly off course, but the error was sufficient for the steamer to hit the rock with a glancing blow. The ship lurched over and water began to rush into the shaft tunnel and engine room. Fortunately, the engine room crew was able to close the watertight doors, preventing complete flooding of the machinery. Had that happened, there would have been no hope for the ship. The fires would have been put out and all power to the engines and generators would have been lost. Having cleared the rock and with the flooding under control, the *Ena* seemed stable. However, to be on the safe side the lifeboats were swung out in readiness. The vessel was able to make her way through the Narrows, and into Plumper Bay, where she was anchored. There, the engine room was pumped dry but water continued to flow into the afterhold. In consequence, the *Ena* was moved to Menzies Bay, where she could be beached at the receding tide.

Meanwhile, the salvage vessel *Tees* was dispatched from Victoria and reached the *Ena* shortly after the freighter had been grounded safely at Menzies Bay. The *Tees* was brought alongside the *Ena* and heavy portable steam pumps, standard salvage apparatus, were swung on board the crippled ship. At the same time, a diver inspected the damage and found a six foot hole on either side of the keel. The ship had settled over part of the hole, making it inaccessible to the divers, and it was therefore necessary to await high tide before patches could be applied. The operation took all of the next day. Finally at 6:30 p.m., the *Ena* was able to steam for Victoria, arriving early the following afternoon. The vessel was taken directly to the Victoria Machinery Depot where repairs were carried out.

Ripple Rock remained a potential death trap for ships until 1958, when its top was blown off by carefully planted explosive charges after an extensive mining and drilling operation. Finally, one of the worst hazards to shipping on the entire coast was eliminated.

The stately *Princess Louise* marked the beginning of the CPR's post-World War I construction program. She was built in North Vancouver in 1921 to replace the *Princess Sophia* on the Alaska route. She is the oldest surviving Princess, now preserved as a restaurant vessel in Long Beach, California. — CPR

CHAPTER V

THE PRINCESSES
ON THE COAST

New Construction on the Coast

THE LOSS of the *Princess Sophia* had deprived the CPR's B.C. Coast Service of one of its newest steamers at a time when acquiring a replacement vessel was next to impossible. Wartime construction had absorbed all of the shipbuilding efforts in the English and Scottish yards where the Company had traditionally had its ships built. Furthermore it was apparent that it would be several years after the Armistice before the backlog of orders could be cleared, and no firms in Great Britain were prepared to guarantee a delivery date satisfactory to the CPR. In consequence, the Company decided to have a replacement vessel built by a British Columbia shipbuilder, the Wallace Shipbuilding and Drydock Company of North Vancouver. This firm was given a contract to build and outfit a 4,032 ton steamer for service on the CPR's Vancouver to Alaska routes.

The vessel was duly built and on the afternoon of August 29, 1921, was christened by Mrs. Troup the *Princess Louise* to commemorate the old sidewheel paddle steamer of the Canadian Pacific Navigation Company, the first of the ships to bear the title Princess. Vancouver and all of British Columbia were proud of the *Princess Louise*, since she was very much a local product. Indeed, it was the hope of the local shipyards that the completion of this fine steamship would demonstrate to the CPR that the Company did not need to go to yards in Great Britain to obtain new vessels of high quality.

This was not an unreasonable hope, since the *Princess Louise* was, at the time of her launch, the largest ship in terms of displacement in the entire Princess fleet. Even the triple expansion engines were built locally and a large proportion of the ship's fittings, panelling, and furnishings were also manufactured in the province. On November 28th, the *Louise* was nearly ready for delivery to the CPR and sailed from the builder's yards to Esquimalt for drydocking to permit painting and last minute inspections before undergoing sea trials on November 30th.

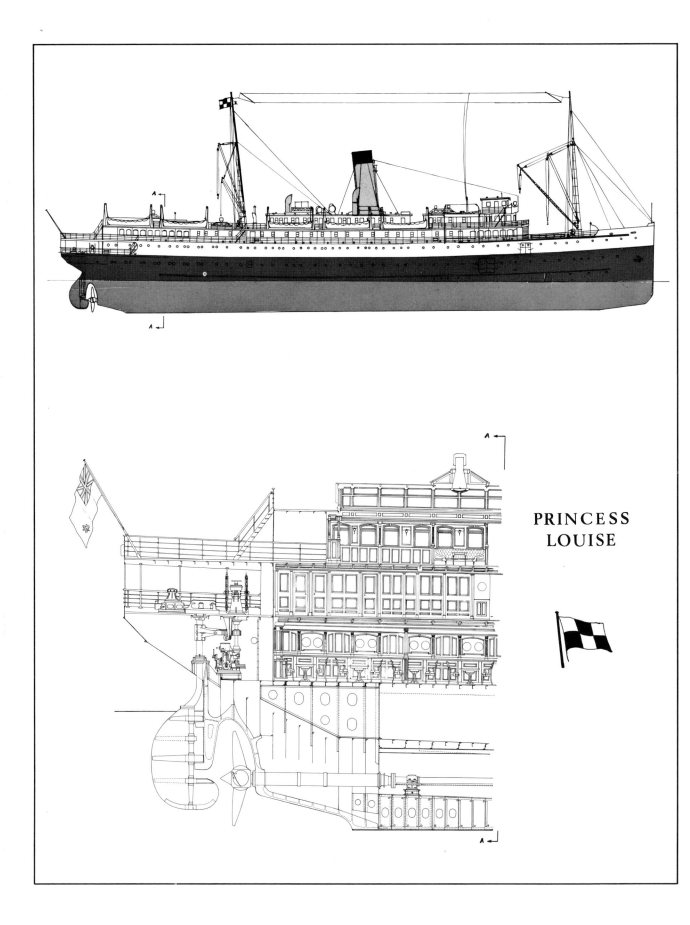

PRINCESS
LOUISE

The Wallace Shipyards . . .

The Wallace Shipyards of North Vancouver were justly proud of their work on the *Princess Louise*. This series of photos, taken for the CPR by the Dominion Photo Company, reflects the interior decor of the ship. The *Louise* was typical of the Princesses of this period. Her dining room seated 125 people, who were served on linen table cloths with polished silver. Her social halls and staircases were ornate and elegant.

A Lounge
Luxury

Economy

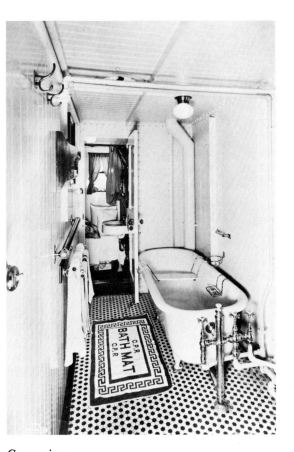

Convenience

Overnight accommodation on the *Princess Louise* provided 210 beds and 26 single berths in a variety of types of staterooms. The most expensive offered eiderdowns on the beds. The economical rooms had upper and lower berths. For the more affluent, baths adjoined the staterooms. The engine rooms were seldom seen by the public, but were kept spotless by the engineering crews.

— ALL PROVINCIAL ARCHIVES

The new ship performed beautifully on her trials, greatly impressing all on board with her design and construction. She exceeded her design speed of 16 knots on both occasions when she steamed the measured mile. The first run was completed with an average speed of 16.9 knots, while the second pass over the course averaged 16.2 knots. Later that day, in the course of a three-hour cruise in the Strait of Juan de Fuca with guests and officials of both the Company and the builders onboard, she reached an even 17 knots. This demonstration prompted Captain Troup to comment that it was "an ideal performance" and that the new vessel "handled beautifully and came up to expectations in every respect." The chief engineer, James Petticrew, observed that there "never was a trial trip better," and added that there was "no vibration at all, never a ship better." He concluded by commenting that the engines were "a masterpiece." Vibration free operation was a goal to strive for in the design of a ship, since it made such a difference to the comfort of the passengers.

The success of the *Princess Louise* was in every way a tribute to the craftsmanship of the Wallace yards (later known as Burrard Drydock Ltd.). The *Louise* was to be a most reliable and seaworthy vessel throughout the next 40 years of almost continuous service. There was great optimism at the time that more such contracts would come to the west coast shipyards, and it was even speculated that an Empress liner might be built in Vancouver for the CPR. However, such was not to be the case. During the next 40 years the only other CPR vessel to be built on the B.C. coast was the small, wooden-hulled *Motor Princess*, built by Yarrows Ltd. at Esquimalt. For the next major additions to the Princess fleet, the *Princesses Kathleen* and *Marguerite*, the CPR once again returned to shipyards in Great Britain. This must have come as a great disappointment to the local shipbuilders who had proven their abilities so well with the *Princess Louise*. However, it must be remembered that steel and construction costs in Great Britain were very competitive and that the CPR was a company in some respects bound in tradition. Furthermore, much of the Company's capital came from shareholders in Great Britain.

By the early 1920's, automobile ownership on the Coast was increasing to a point where the ships of the Princess fleet were finding it difficult to accommodate all the cars being shipped between the mainland and Vancouver Island. Looking to the future, Troup decided to order a vessel designed specifically for ferrying automobiles between Bellingham, Washington and Sidney, 18 miles north of Victoria. In designing the new ship, Captain Troup worked closely with Yarrows at Esquimalt. The basic concept was for a 14 knot vessel capable of carrying about 45 automobiles, with comfortable accommodations for passengers. These requirements presented some difficulties in balancing high engine power and economy of operation against the wide beam necessitated by the large amount of space required for vehicles. The problems were resolved by testing

Captain Troup saw the *Motor Princess* as an experiment but her
outstanding features — diesel power and large high clearance car
deck for vehicle accommodation — made her a successful
addition to the fleet and her design influenced later acquisitions
of new vessels and the conversion of the *Princess Victoria*.
— JOHN NEWMAN

Loading vehicles onto the *Motor Princess* was
much simpler than on the larger ships in the fleet.
— BOTH PROVINCIAL ARCHIVES

Loading vehicles . . .

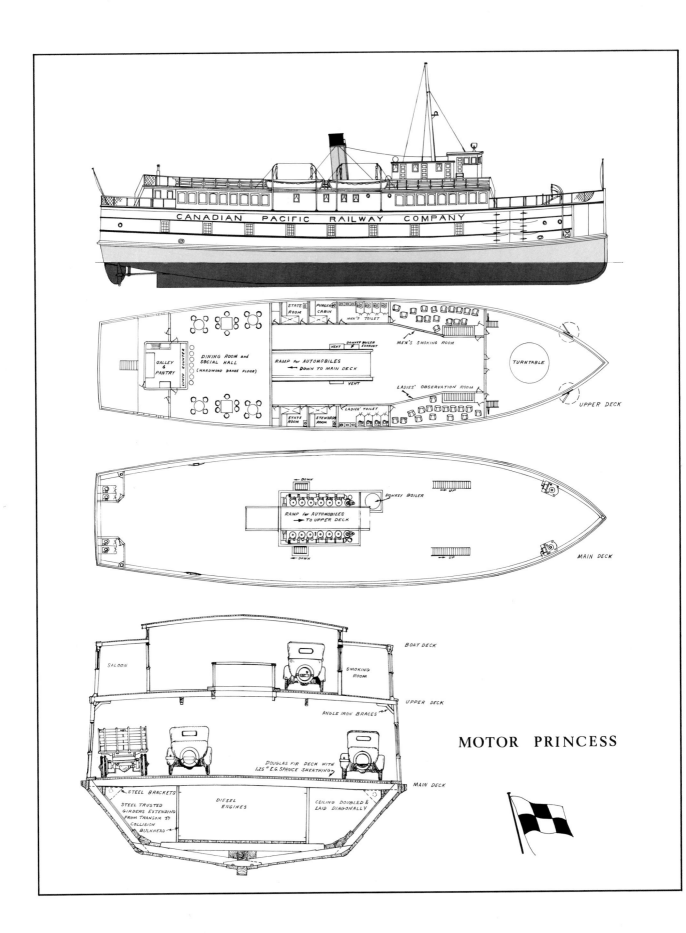

CANADIAN PACIFIC RAILWAY COMPANY

STATE ROOM · PURSER'S CABIN

MEN'S TOILET

DINING ROOM and SOCIAL HALL
(HARDWOOD DANCE FLOOR)

GALLEY & PANTRY

LUNCH COUNTER

RAMP for AUTOMOBILES
◄— DOWN to MAIN DECK

VENT · DONKEY BOILER EXHAUST

VENT

MEN'S SMOKING ROOM

TURNTABLE

LADIES' OBSERVATION ROOM

STATE ROOM · STEWARDS ROOM · LADIES' TOILET

UPPER DECK

DOWN · UP

RAMP for AUTOMOBILES
◄— TO UPPER DECK

DONKEY BOILER

DOWN · UP

MAIN DECK

BOAT DECK

SALOON

SMOKING ROOM

UPPER DECK

ANGLE IRON BRACES

DOUGLAS FIR DECK WITH
1.25" E.G. SPRUCE SHEATHING

MAIN DECK

STEEL BRACKETS

STEEL TRUSTED GIRDERS EXTENDING FROM TRANSOM TO COLLISION BULKHEAD

DIESEL ENGINES

CEILING DOUBLED & LAID DIAGONALLY

MOTOR PRINCESS

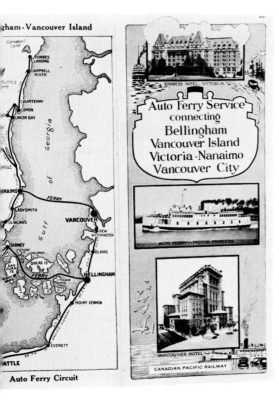

models at the William Froude Tank of the National Physical Laboratory at Teddington, England.

Finally, it was decided that the ship would be a diesel-powered, wooden-hulled vessel 165 feet long with a beam of 43.5 feet and a depth of 9.0 feet. It was found that diesel engines provided a greater power output for the space and weight available than various steam propulsion systems would have in a vessel of this size. Automobiles were carried on the main deck and on the forward end of the upper deck. An inclined ramp was designed to connect the two car decks.

Yarrows Ltd. was given the contract to build the ship at its Esquimalt yards. The vessel, to be appropriately named the *Motor Princess*, was launched on April 7, 1923. Ninety-seven days after her construction began, she was ready for service. On trials, the first diesel-powered vessel in the CPR's fleet attained a speed of 14.5 knots, with her two McIntosh Seymour six-cylinder diesels turning in an entirely satisfactory performance. Naturally, emphasis was on automobile facilities, but passengers were far from neglected. Though her lounge space was limited compared to the spacious equivalent quarters on the larger ships in the fleet, the *Motor Princess* was nonetheless well appointed. On both sides of the upper deck, carpeted lounges were provided with large windows for viewing the scenic Gulf Islands. In addition, the after two-fifths of the upper deck were devoted to a combination dining room and social hall with hardwood flooring. Two staterooms were also provided on the compact ship, and ample open deck space was available for leisurely strolls and relaxing in the sun during the summer months.

To some, the *Motor Princess* was the ugly misfit of the Princess fleet. Comparatively stubby, she lacked the grace and speed of her larger contemporaries. In addition, fumes from her diesel engines could be obnoxious. However, the *Motor Princess*, like many of the ships in the fleet, had a special charm and personality that made her memorable to many travellers.

Initially, Troup considered the vessel an experiment. He felt that a few years service would determine if larger, more costly ships would be warranted. However, like so many temporary measures, the *Motor Princess* became a permanent institution. The depression and World War II intervened to forestall any new construction of automobile ferries to replace her on her route. The influence of automobiles was to effect virtually all subsequent CPR coastal ship designs as more and more space had to be allocated for vehicles on the vessels.

The *Motor Princess* was used for only three years on the Bellingham to Sidney run for which she was built. Very effective competition from the Puget Sound Navigation Company vessels which operated between Anacortes, Washington and Sidney, coupled with a decline in traffic prompted Troup to reassign the vessel to the Nanaimo-Vancouver run to augment the service provided by the *Princess Patricia* which had minimal provisions for automobiles. When the *Princess Elaine* was built for this service to replace the aging *Princess Patricia*, a new route was established using the *Motor Princess*. Beginning in 1929, she sailed between Sidney and Steveston at the mouth of the Fraser River, providing a fast, efficient automobile ferry service from southern Vancouver Island to the B.C. mainland.

In 1923, the CPR began construction of a new terminal building in Victoria for its Coast Service. The imposing structure was designed by the architect F. M. Rattenbury, who had also designed the British Columbia Legislative Buildings and the CPR's Empress Hotel. The new $200,000 four-storey building featured cast concrete columns on the exterior and a large waiting room and ticket sales area. It replaced the inadequate wooden frame structure that had provided office space for the Victoria-based operations for many years.

Rattenbury's building remained in use by the CPR until the late 1960's, when the Coast Service moved to a smaller structure built to serve the more limited needs of the *Princess Marguerite* (the second vessel of this name), which was operating to Port Angeles and Seattle, and by that time the only CPR vessel sailing from Victoria. Fortunately, the outward appearance of the building was not materially altered, and it still complements the Empress Hotel and the Legislative Buildings as the most outstanding structures on Victoria's Inner Harbour.

Architect F. M. Rattenbury . . .

The Princesses Kathleen *and* Marguerite

By 1923, the best year on record for the Triangle Route, the backlog of orders in the shipyards in Great Britain had been filled and the CPR was able to place an order with John Brown and Company, at Clydebank, Scotland for the construction of two new steamships for the Triangle Route. These two vessels were to provide replacements for the *Princess Irene* and *Princess Margaret*, which had been taken over by the British Admiralty in 1914.

The first of the sister ships, the *Princess Kathleen*, was launched in late September 1924. She was followed two months later by the *Princess Marguerite*. The new ships were named after the daughter of Lord Thomas Shaughnessy, a former president of the CPR. Both vessels were completed the following year in time to take over the Triangle Route from the *Princess Victoria* and *Princess Charlotte* for the busy summer season. This freed the *Charlotte* for the Alaska cruise service where a brisk business was developing.

The new Princesses were in every way impressive, with striking lines, high speed and luxurious accommodations. Like the *Victoria* and *Charlotte* they were three-funneled ships, but many improvements were evident in their design. The vessels' twin screws were driven by compound steam turbines which were capable of producing higher speeds than the older design compound reciprocating engines of their predecessors. Significantly, the turbines were also more efficient when running in sustained high speed service.

The *Kathleen* and *Marguerite* were both licensed to carry

Architect F. M. Rattenbury was commissioned to design a new headquarters for the CPR's Coast Service in Victoria. The product of his efforts was the striking structure above. — PROVINCIAL ARCHIVES. The Building was illuminated at night to complement the adjacent Parliament Buildings, which were also a Rattenbury design.
— CHARLES F. TURNER PHOTO, AUTHOR'S COLLECTION

The *Princess Kathleen* and the *Princess Marguerite* were built to replace the *Princess Margaret* and *Irene*. The 5,878 ton ships were built at the John Brown and Company yards at Clydebank, Scotland in 1925. This is the *Princess Kathleen*.
— PROVINCIAL ARCHIVES

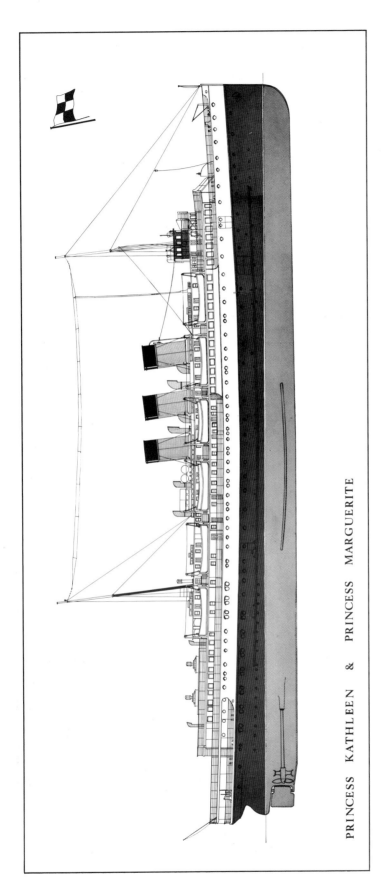

PRINCESS KATHLEEN & PRINCESS MARGUERITE

The Princess Marguerite . . .

The *Princess Marguerite* was nearly ready for launching in this
scene at the John Brown yards. — PROVINCIAL ARCHIVES

The *Princess Kathleen* was every bit as elegant as her predecessors. This view is of her 168-seat dining room.
— PROVINCIAL ARCHIVES

The Princess Kathleen . . .

133

Upon their arrival on the Pacific coast, the new steamships took over the Triangle Route from the *Princesses Charlotte* and *Victoria*. The *Kathleen* and *Marguerite* were striking ships and became very popular with the public. The *Kathleen* is shown above in a classic view by Leonard Frank.
— VANCOUVER PUBLIC LIBRARY

The *Princess Marguerite* is shown at Vancouver's Pier D with the *Princess Adelaide* in the background. — PROVINCIAL ARCHIVES

Upon their arrival ...
The Princess Marguerite *is ...*

The smoking lounge . . .
Also, a deluxe . . .

1,500 passengers and 290 berths were provided in 136 state-rooms.* Large observation lounges were situated fore and aft. They even carried grand pianos. Space was also provided for approximately 30 automobiles. This was a feature not present in the designs of the *Margaret* or *Irene* and the lack of vehicle accommodation would have been a severe disadvantage had these two vessels reached the Pacific.

The 5,875 ton steamships had an overall length of 368 feet, nine inches and a breadth of 60 feet. On trials, both vessels exceeded 22 knots with the *Marguerite* managing to work up to just over 22.5 knots. Both ships became known for their speed, taking away the records from the older CPR Princesses.

The *Princess Kathleen* and *Princess Marguerite* rapidly became established institutions on the Coast, with a large following of loyal patrons. They were a source of pride, not only to their owners and CPR employees, but also to the travelling public and residents of the cities served by the ships. Their speed and elegance made them truly incomparable on the Northwest Coast, where they dominated the Triangle Route until World War II. Initially they were relieved in the winter by the older vessels, but as traffic increased they remained on the route all year long, with only occasional days off for maintenance.

In 1925, to accommodate the two new large Princesses, the CPR moved its Seattle loading facilities from the Colman Dock to the Bell Street Terminal, where more modern facilities were provided. Not long before, the CPR had opened its new Pier B-C in Vancouver to accommodate new larger Empress liners used in the Company's trans-Pacific services. In the 1920's, the Princesses used Pier D in Vancouver, built just prior to World War I, while in later years operations were shifted to the more modern facilities at Pier B-C after the older structure was destroyed by fire.

*These figures represent the accommodations available at the time the ships were built. Later CPR figures (1942) show the licensed capacity to be 1,800, with 234 berths available in 123 staterooms.

Changes in Operations and the Retirement of Troup

The smoking lounge — aft on the *Princess Kathleen.* — PROVINCIAL ARCHIVES

Also, a deluxe cabin is shown in the second picture on this page. — PROVINCIAL ARCHIVES

The CPR was never slow to capitalize on the profit potential of the tourist trade, and since its earliest operations on the Pacific coast had operated many excursions and special sailings for sightseers. Much of the heavy summer traffic on the Triangle Route and from Vancouver to Alaska was a direct result of the Company's promotional efforts. In an attempt to open a new market, the Company announced that the *Princess Mary* would operate on a week-long "Around Vancouver Island" cruise leaving Victoria on July 3, 1926. For a fare of $60.00, which included berth and meals, the passenger was promised 1,000 miles of "delightful voyaging" and a chance to visit such exotic and remote coastal villages as Clayoquot, Matilda Creek, CeePeeCee and Kyuquot.

While the *Princess Mary* normally provided accommodation in berths for 160 passengers, the Company limited ticket sales to 125 to avoid overcrowding. Passengers could begin the cruise from Vancouver, Victoria, or Seattle by a scheduling arrangement that permitted Seattle travellers to join the cruise at Victoria via the *Princess Kathleen*, which was operating on the Triangle Route. Returning, they would catch the *Princess Marguerite*'s 4:30 p.m. sailing from Victoria to Seattle. Connections could also be made by passengers travelling from Vancouver. The cruise was well received, and excursions to the West Coast were perennially popular. The *Princess Maquinna* was the most frequently used vessel on such trips, since she was normally assigned to the Vancouver Island west coast route. This service was itself popular with tourists and the CPR advertised it as an alternate attraction to the Alaskan cruises. But the Company felt obliged to add the following warning:

The only drawback is the fact that the steamer is quite often, and sometimes for several hours at a time, in the open Pacific, and even in pleasant weather the ground swell that is always present results in attacks of seasickness with those who are poor sailors. The majority of passengers, however, are not affected, and most of the small minority look upon it as an experience to be talked about on their return home.

By the late 1920's, the CPR's services to the southern Gulf Islands — North and South Pender, Mayne, Galiano and Saltspring — were proving so successful that Troup felt justified in replacing his smallest passenger steamer, the *Island Princess*, with the larger, more luxurious, albeit very old, *Charmer*. The *Charmer* had been rebuilt to enable her to carry automobiles more conveniently and it was anticipated that tourist traffic would increase with the improved service.

The new schedule made it practical for people to travel between the mainland and Vancouver Island via the Gulf Islands on a very pleasant route, making stopovers of a day or two on the various islands. This new service began early in May 1927 and proved sufficiently successful to prompt the Company to sell the *Island Princess* to the Gulf Islands Ferry Company in 1930. The vessel was subsequently dieselized and renamed *Cy Peck*. She continued in service into the 1960's, eventually coming under B.C. Ferries ownership before being sold for use as a fish packer, the ultimate fate of many Northwest Coast ships. In 1975, however, the little ship was purchased by two Saltspring Island residents who returned the former ferry to Ganges where she was permanently moored.

At the same time the decision was reached to improve the service to the Gulf Islands, the CPR also decided to increase the number of its sailings to the west coast of Vancouver Island by having the *Princess Mary* make one trip a week from Victoria to Port Alice and various other ports on the north end of the Island. The *Princess Maquinna* was then better able to serve the settlements south of Hecate on Esperanza Inlet, which included Port Alberni, Bamfield and other usual ports of call. The *Princess Royal* was meanwhile being converted to burn oil and upon completion of the work was

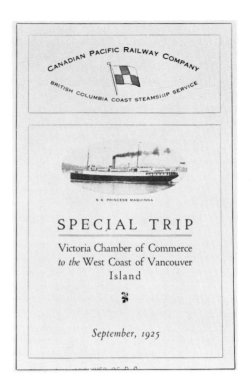

CANADIAN PACIFIC RAILWAY COMPANY
BRITISH COLUMBIA COAST STEAMSHIP SERVICE

S.S. PRINCESS MAQUINNA

SPECIAL TRIP

Victoria Chamber of Commerce
to the West Coast of Vancouver
Island

September, 1925

The menus offered . . .

LUNCHEON

HORS D'OEUVRES
Sweet Pickles   Anchovy Toast   Chow Chow

SOUP
Clam Chowder

FISH
Fried Soles and Tartar Sauce

SALADS
Lettuce   Sliced Cucumber   Pickled Beetroot

HOT DISHES
Baked Pork Sausage, Mashed Potatoes
Braised Ox Tail a la Jardiniere
Grilled Loin Steak, Fried Onions

COLD
Roast Ribs Beef   Roast Leg Mutton
Boiled Ham   Head Cheese

VEGETABLES
Baked Jacket and Boiled Potatoes
Stewed Turnips

SWEETS
Queen Pudding
Pear Pie   Compote Apricots
Imperial Canadian and Kraft Cheese
Crackers
Tea   Coffee

The menus offered on the Princesses were always excellent. A memorable dinner was steamed salmon with white sauce served with new potatoes, fresh peas and carrots. The prices were reasonable and the service excellent.
— BOTH PROVINCIAL ARCHIVES

Friendly Cove on Nootka Island was a stop for the ships on the Vancouver Island west coast route. In this Leonard Frank scene the *Princess Mary* is tied up at the dock.
— VANCOUVER PUBLIC LIBRARY

The *Princess Maquinna* was the regular steamer on the route along Vancouver Island's Pacific coast. Here, she is calling at the McTavish Cannery in 1921. — PROVINCIAL ARCHIVES

Friendly Cove . . .
The Princess Maquinna *was* . . .

FIVE-DAY CRUISES

ALONG THE WEST COAST OF VANCOUVER ISLAND

(July and August)

S.S. PRINCESS MARY

Leaves VICTORIA every Saturday for Clayoquot, Nootka, Esperanza Inlet, Cachelot and Port Alice.

Return Fare $35.50

S.S. PRINCESS MAQUINNA

Leaves Victoria every Wednesday for Barkley Sound ports, Port Alberni, Ucluelet, Clayoquot, Matilda Creek, Sydney Inlet, Nootka and Esperanza Inlets ports.

(Meals and Berth included except at Port Alice.)

Return Fare $28.00

Schedules and full information may be obtained from any Canadian Pacific Agent.

PACIFIC COAST AGENCIES

W. McILROY, Gen. Agt., 621 So. Grand Ave., Los Angles, Cal.
F. L. NASON, Gen. Agt., 675 Market St. San Francisco, Cal.
W. H. DEACON, Gen. Agt., 55 Third St. Portland, Ore.
E. L. SHEEHAN, Gen. Agt., 1320 - Fourth Ave., Seattle, Wash.
L. D. CHETHAM, Dist. Pass. Agt., 1102 Government St.
Victoria, B. C.
W. McGIRR, 173 Commercial St., Nanaimo, B. C.
GEO. BROWN, Agent, C. P. R. Wharf, Nanaimo, B. C.
F. H. DALY, Dist. Pass. Agt., 434 Hastings St. W.
Vancouver, B. C.
C. MILLARD, Ticket Agent, C. P. R. Depot, Vancouver, B. C.
W. S. STEWART, Ticket Agt., Hotel Vancouver, Vancouver, B.C.
S. G. LEMMON, Ticket Agent, Pier "D", Vancouver, B. C.
ED. GOULET, Agent, C. P. R. Station, New Westminster, B. C.

H. W. SCHOFIELD,
Dist. Pass'r. Agent,
Vancouver, B. C.

C. H. BOWES,
Asst. Gen'l. Pass'r. Agent,
Vancouver, B. C.

N. R. DES BRISAY,
Gen. Pass'r. Agent
Vancouver, B. C.

The CPR's advertising literature for vacation cruises sometimes featured a romanticized view of life on Vancouver Island as this brochure from the 1920's attests. Often the pamphlets were extensively illustrated with views of scenery, wildlife, native Indian carvings, and the isolated communities visited by the steamships. — PROVINCIAL ARCHIVES

The tug Kyuquot . . .

The tug *Kyuquot* (originally the *St. Florence*) was acquired by the CPR in 1924 for the railway car barge service to the E & N Railway on Vancouver Island. — CPR

assigned to the Vancouver-Powell River route on a tri-weekly service.

To better provide for automobile traffic on the vessel, the vertical clearance between the *Royal*'s decks was increased from five feet, six inches to six feet, four inches. Loading vehicles onto the older vessels was often a real challenge. Sometimes owners were required to deflate the tires and lower the folding tops of their cars before they could squeeze into the restricted space between the ship's low decks.

The year 1928 was an important one for the B.C. Coast Service. Of greatest significance was the retirement of Captain James W. Troup, at age 73, from the position of superintendent of the CPR's Pacific coast steamship operations. Troup left an indelible mark on the history of North Pacific coast shipping and was, more than any other individual, responsible for the success of the CPR's fleet of Princess steamers. He retired at the peak of his fleet's prosperity. A new steamship had just arrived on the Coast from the builders and the magnificent sister ships, the *Princess Kathleen* and *Princess Marguerite* had already established an unchallenged reputation for excellent service. People all along the Coast were lavish in their praise of Troup. He was saluted by British Columbia's Premier McLean and the newspapers carried lengthy accounts of his outstanding career.

In its lead editorial on August 18, 1928, the day Troup announced his retirement, the *Victoria Daily Times* noted:

To his initiative and boldness may be ascribed the splendid fleet of vessels operated by the company out of Victoria and Vancouver. Because his judgement and vision always have been justified by the result and because these qualities went hand in hand with unwearying zeal, loyalty and enthusiasm, he had in the fullest measure the confidence of the directorate of the Canadian Pacific Railway Company, and his recommendations were unvaryingly approved. One of the most convincing commentaries on the relations between him and his company is in the fact that he is eight years in age beyond the limit set in the company's rules for the retirement of its officials. It is not easy for those who know Captain Troup and who are struck by his physical and mental vigor and youthful appearance to realize that this is a correct statement of the case.

James Troup died on November 30, 1931, at age 76 years.

Troup was succeeded in the position of superintendent by Captain C. D. Neroutsos, a veteran of many years' service with the CPR's B.C. Coast Service and formerly Troup's assistant. It is interesting to note that Captain Troup retired just one year and two months after his old rival of the rate war days, Joshua Green of the Puget Sound Navigation Company. Green had by the late 1920's acquired the controlling interest in the Peoples' Savings Bank, of Seattle and sold a large proportion of his PSN stock to Captain Alexander Peabody, who became vice-president of that company. Green was to enjoy many more years of active life. He died at Seattle in 1975 not long after celebrating his 105th birthday.

Before his retirement, Troup was able to see his newest

steamship, the *Princess Elaine*, begin operations for the Coast Service. Designed especially for the Vancouver to Nanaimo day run, she had only six staterooms. However, in recognition of the potential of automobile traffic, the new *Princess* had room for 60 vehicles on her car deck. The vertical clearance was nine feet, ten inches, allowing nearly any vehicle of the period to be loaded without difficulty.

The *Elaine* was a triple screw, turbine steamer of 2,027 tons and was capable of nearly 20 knots, permitting her to make the Vancouver-Nanaimo crossing in two hours and fifteen minutes. In May 1928, in time for the heavy summer crowds, the new steamer made her first sailings on the route, which was to be her major assignment for nearly all her active life. The *Princess Patricia*, on the route since 1912, was withdrawn and used as a relief vessel and for excursion services. The provisions for automobiles on the *Princess Elaine* also made it possible to take the *Motor Princess* off the Vancouver-Nanaimo run and place her on the new service, inaugurated in 1929, between Steveston and Sidney. This route provided a fast service for passengers with vehicles and was the forerunner of the rapid automobile ferry operations between the southern end of Vancouver Island and the British Columbia mainland that would be developed in the late 1950's and early 1960's.

Early in 1929, another new ship for the CPR's coastal fleet arrived in Victoria. This vessel was the *Princess Norah*, built by the Fairfield yards at Govan, Scotland for the service to the west coast of Vancouver Island. This fine new cargo liner was a beautiful ship with very pleasing lines. Of 2,731 gross tons, she measured just over 250 feet in length and 48 feet in breadth. Accommodations were provided for 700 day passengers and 179 berths in 61 staterooms were available for overnight travellers. A particularly interesting feature of her design that made her especially well suited to the coastal trade was the incorporation of a rudder in her bow. This mechanism made her extremely manoeuverable in the confined waters of the coastal inlets and fjords of the B.C. and Alaska coasts.

It was originally intended that the *Norah* replace the smaller *Princess Maquinna*, which by 1928 was 16 years old. However, this never really happened, although the *Norah* did spend a large portion of her career on the west coast of the Island, particularly during the busier summer season. The *Maquinna* usually returned to this service in the winters when traffic was lighter and insufficient to warrant the operation of the larger vessel. In fact, the *Maquinna* remained the old stalwart of the service into the early 1950's. During the winter months, the *Norah* often took over the Alaska or Prince Rupert runs.

The arrival of the *Norah* made it possible to retire the obsolete wooden-hulled 25-year-old *Princess Beatrice*. She was sold for scrapping to the Vancouver firm of B. L. Johnson, Walton and Company, which stripped the ship of her machinery and sold the hull for use as a floating cannery. The *Princess Victoria*, although of similar vintage to the *Beatrice*, had a far different future in store, largely because she had a steel hull,

Captain Cyril D. Neroutsos, ...

Captain Cyril D. Neroutsos, pictured left with Captain Edward Gillam, succeeded Captain Troup as Manager of the CPR's B.C. Coast Steamship Service in 1928. Captain Gillam was Master of the *Princess Maquinna* and a veteran of 20 years on the Vancouver Island west coast route. — CARL F. TIMMS PHOTO, PROVINCIAL ARCHIVES

The *Princess Elaine* was launched at Clydebank, Scotland on October 26, 1927. She was built to replace the *Princess Patricia* on the Vancouver-Nanaimo route. — PROVINCIAL ARCHIVES

PRINCESS
ELAINE

The Princess Elaine *was . . .*

After she went into service, the *Princess Elaine* soon became an
institution on the coast. She lacked the grace and comfort of the
larger vessels and was prone to vibration. She had only six
staterooms since she was designed for daylight service across
Georgia Strait. She is shown in April 1938 passing under the
Lion's Gate Bridge which was being built across the First Narrows
in Vancouver. — LEONARD FRANK, VANCOUVER PUBLIC LIBRARY

which was still in excellent condition. As she was nearing the end of the normal useful life of a ship, it was almost certain that she would be replaced. However, the Company decided instead to rebuild and convert her into an automobile ferry to augment the Victoria to Seattle summer service, where traffic was growing steadily.

Unlike many such conversions that were applied to older steamships, the rebuilding of the *Princess Victoria* did not totally destroy her lines. In September 1929, the *Victoria* was stripped of her interior fittings at the CPR's Belleville Street dock in Victoria and then turned over to Yarrows Ltd. of Esquimalt for conversion. In addition to changing her dining room and stateroom layout, her hull was sponsoned to widen the ship, increasing her beam by 18 feet. These alterations made it possible for 60 automobiles to be accommodated. The number of staterooms was reduced from 76 to 48, with a consequent decrease in the number of berths from 152 to 92.

After completion of the work, the *Princess Victoria* was no longer the sleek liner that created such a sensation on the Coast when she arrived, but she was still well proportioned, and had become a more efficient vessel. Her trials indicated that her speed had not been significantly affected by the changes, since she could still easily make 19 knots. Externally, the conversion made her look bulkier in the stern and some passengers claimed she did not ride as well as before. However, the rebuilding added another 20 years to the life of the *Princess*. The CPR was never to regret modernizing her, as she proved invaluable in later years in a variety of intercity services, both as scheduled vessel and in relief duties. She was also popular for excursions. With the loss of the *Princess Kathleen* and *Princess Marguerite* to war service in 1941, the *Victoria* filled in admirably for these newer steamships that had been built to replace her on the demanding Triangle Route.

Indicative of the increase in vehicle traffic between Puget Sound ports and Vancouver Island was the creation of the Edmonds-Victoria Ferry Company in 1928. This U.S. company purchased the large steel-hulled ship *Alabama* from the Baltimore Steam Packet Company and brought the vessel to the West Coast. The 35-year-old ship was renamed *City of Victoria* for service to Vancouver Island. The Company operated the well proportioned 1,938 ton steamer that summer season, and the following year chartered her to the Independent Ferry Company, which continued the service. However, with the introduction of the rebuilt *Princess Victoria* to the Victoria-Seattle run, coupled with the depression of 1929, the venture proved unprofitable. The *City of Victoria* was laid up and remained inactive until 1939, when she was sold to satisfy creditors, as claims totaling $343,000 had accumulated against her. She was eventually acquired by the Puget Sound Bridge and Dredging Company and converted to a barracks to accommodate workers building the Naval air base at Sitka, Alaska. Afterwards, she returned to Puget Sound and was scrapped in 1948.

Bamfield, at the entrance to Barkley Sound, was one of the larger communities served by the Princesses on Vancouver Island's west coast. In the scene above, the *Princess Norah* is on her inaugural cruise. She was designed specifically for navigating in confined waters and featured a rudder in the bow. — CPR

PRINCESS
NORAH

The cruise from Victoria . . .

The cruise from Victoria along the Pacific coast
of Vancouver Island was thought by many to be
as scenic as the route to Alaska. Here is the *Norah*
on the Alberni Canal.
— B.C. GOVERNMENT PHOTOGRAPH

The Alberni Canal and the *Princess Norah.*
— B.C. GOVERNMENT PHOTOGRAPH

Quatsino Narrows taken from the bridge of the *Norah.* — B.C. GOVERNMENT PHOTOGRAPH

The Alberni Canal . . .
Quatsino Narrows . . .

After over a quarter century of service, the *Princess Victoria* was rebuilt to carry about 50 automobiles. She is shown here about 1930 at Vancouver's Pier D just after her conversion. In the background is the *Princess Elaine.*
— LEONARD FRANK PHOTO,
VANCOUVER PUBLIC LIBRARY

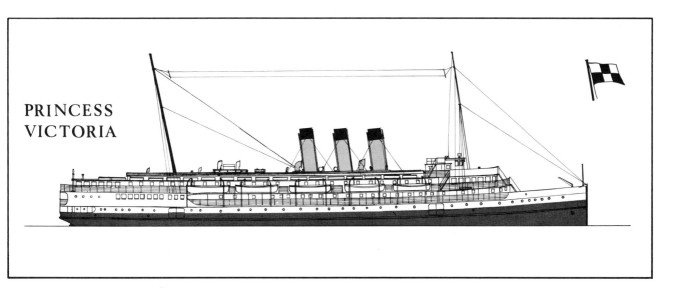

PRINCESS
VICTORIA

After over a quarter century . . .

WEST COAST VANCOUVER ISLAND
VICTORIA - NOOTKA - PORT ALICE AND WAY PORTS
STEAMSHIP "PRINCESS NORAH"

Read Down 1st 11th 21st	Ports of Call	Read Up 8th 18th 28th
Lv. — Leave Victoria, B.C., 11 p.m.	VICTORIA Ar. 1 p.m.	Ar. — 8 18 28
2 12 22	Port Renfrew	8 18 28
2 12 22	⊙⊙Carmanah	8 18 28
2 12 22	⊙Clo-oose	8 18 28
2 12 22	Bamfield	8 18 28
2 12 22	⊙Sarita Bay	8 18 28
2 12 22	⊙McCallum Bay	8 18 28
2 12 22	⊙Kildonan	8 18 28
2 12 22	⊙Green Cove	7 17 27
2 12 22	⊙Nahmint	7 17 27
2 12 22	⊙Franklin River	7 17 27
2 12 22	⊙Underwood Cove	7 17 27
3 13 23	⊙Port Alberni	7 17 27
3 13 23	⊙Ecoole	7 17 27
3 13 23	⊙Davis Island	7 17 27
3 13 23	⊙Sechart	7 17 27
3 13 23	⊙Lucky Creek	7 17 27
3 13 23	Ucluelet	7 17 27
3 13 23	⊙Port Albion (Ucluelet Arm)	7 17 27
3 13 23	Tofino	7 17 27
3 13 23	⊙Clayoquot	7 17 27
3 13 23	⊙Kakawis	7 17 27
3 13 23	⊙Ahousat	7 17 27
3 13 23	⊙Matilda Creek (Watson's)	7 17 27
3 13 23	⊙Matilda Creek (Gibson's)	7 17 27
3 13 23	⊙Riley's Cove	7 17 27
3 13 23	⊙Hesquiat	7 17 27
4 14 24	Nootka Cannery	6 16 26
4 14 24	⊙Ceepeecee	6 16 26
4 14 24	⊙McBride Bay	6 16 26
4 14 24	⊙Tahsis	6 16 26
4 14 24	⊙Espinosa	6 16 26
4 14 24	⊙Queen's Cove	6 16 26
4 — —	Cachelot	— 16 26
4 14 24	⊙Easy Creek	6 16 26
4 14 24	⊙Chamiss Bay	6 16 26
4 14 24	⊙Caledonia	6 16 26
4 14 24	⊙Kyuquot Village	6 16 26
4 14 24	⊙Quatsino Cannery	6 16 26
5 15 25	⊙Koprino	6 16 26
5 15 25	⊙Quatsino Village	6 16 26
5 15 25	⊙Jeune Landing	6 16 26
5 15 25 Ar.	PORT ALICE Lv.	5 15 25

NOTE:—Where no date is shown steamship does not call.

⊙Call made when business offers.   ⊙Boat landing.
Ⓢ Call is made northbound each trip. The southbound call will be made if business offers.
Ⓗ Steamship will not sail northbound prior to 12:01 a.m. on advertised date.

6

POWELL RIVER - COMOX
STEAMSHIP "PRINCESS MARY"

	Tuesday	Thursday	Saturday
Lv. Vancouver	11:45 p.m. Tue.	11:45 p.m. Thu.	11:45 p.m. Sat.
Ar. Powell River	6:30 a.m. Wed.	6:30 a.m. Fri.	6:30 a.m. Sun.
Lv. Powell River	8:00 a.m. Wed.	8:00 a.m. Fri.	8:00 a.m. Sun.
Ar. Hornby Island	10:00 a.m. Wed.		10:00 a.m. Sun.
Ar. Denman Island	10:00 a.m. Wed.		
Ar. Union Bay	a.m. Wed.	a.m. Fri.	a.m. Sun.
Ar. Comox	p.m. Wed.	p.m. Fri.	p.m. Sun.
Lv. Comox	2:30 p.m. Wed.	2:30 p.m. Fri.	6:00 p.m. Sun.
Ar. Powell River	p.m. Wed.	p.m. Fri.	p.m. Sun.
Lv. Powell River	11:15 p.m. Wed.	11:15 p.m. Fri.	11:15 p.m. Sun.
Ar. Vancouver	6:30 a.m. Thu.	6:30 a.m. Sat.	6:30 a.m. Mon.

Where no date shown steamship does not call.

MEAL SERVICE
Breakfasts, 35c. to 75c.; Children, 35c. to 40c.; Table d'Hote Luncheon 50c. and Dinner 75c.; Children 40c.; Afternoon Tea 35c.; Night Lunch, 50c.

ESQUIMALT AND NANAIMO RAILWAY
NORTHBOUND train for Royston and Courtenay leaves Union Bay at 3:58 p.m. daily except Sunday.

SOUTHBOUND train for Nanaimo, Victoria and intermediate points leaves Union Bay at 11:35 a.m. daily except Sunday.

OCEAN FALLS - PRINCE RUPERT
WEEKLY SERVICE
STEAMSHIP "PRINCESS ADELAIDE"

Northbound Read down			Southbound Read up
Wed. 8:00 p.m. Lv.	Vancouver	Ar.	7:30 a.m. Mon.
Thur. a.m.	Campbell River		p.m. Sun.
" a.m.	Englewood		a.m. "
" a.m.	Alert Bay		a.m. "
" p.m.	Port Hardy (Hardy Bay) ⊙		8:00 a.m. "
" p.m.Ⓢ	Namu ⊙		a.m. "
" p.m. Ar.	Ocean Falls	Lv.	10:00 p.m. Sat.
" p.m. Lv.	Ocean Falls	Ar.	p.m. "
Fri. a.m.	Walker Lake Cannery		a.m. "
" a.m.	Butedale		
" a.m.Ⓢ	Bishop Bay		
Fri. p.m. Ar.	Prince Rupert	Lv.	10:00 p.m. Fri.

⊙Steamship will not leave Port Hardy southbound earlier than 8:00 a.m.

ⓈCall will be made at Bishop Bay northbound only.

Note—Steamship will call at Powell River Northbound by Special Arrangement, for two or more passengers destined to Ocean Falls or North thereof.

Where no date shown steamship does not call.

5

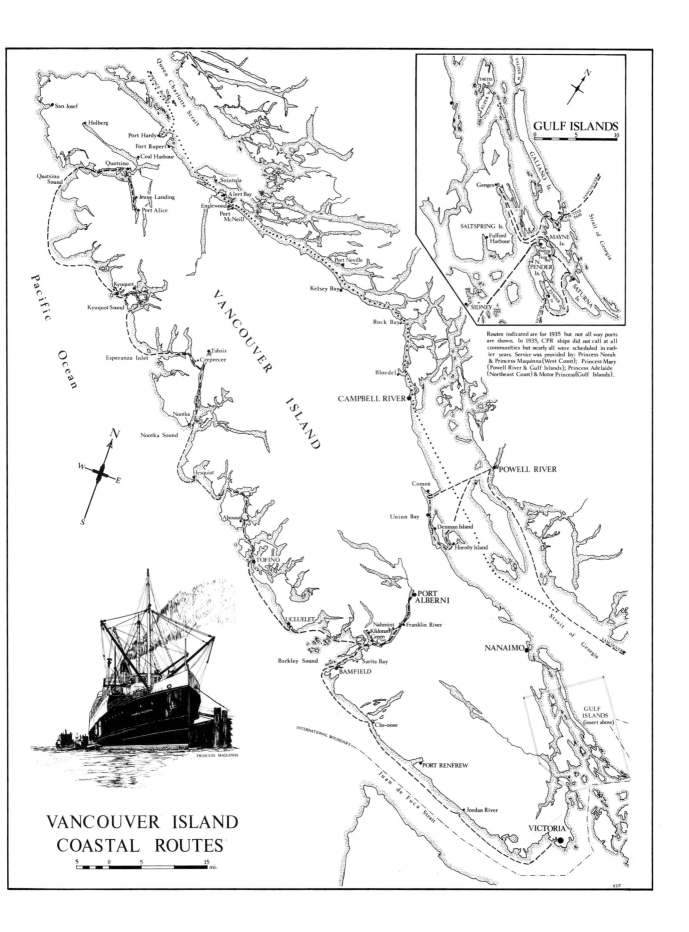

Queen Charlotte Strait

San Josef

Holberg

Port Hardy
Fort Rupert
Coal Harbour

Quatsino
Quatsino
Sound

Jeune Landing
Port Alice

Sointula
Alert Bay
Englewood
Port
McNeill

VANCOUVER ISLAND

Port Neville

Kelsey Bay

Kyuquot

Kyuquot Sound

Rock Bay

Pacific

Ocean

Tahsis
Ceepeecee

Esperanza Inlet

Bloedel

CAMPBELL RIVER

Nootka

Nootka Sound

N
W   E
S

POWELL RIVER

Comox

Hesquiat

Union Bay

Denman Island

Hornby Island

Ahousat

TOFINO

PORT
ALBERNI

UCLUELET

Nahmint   Franklin River
Kildonan
Green

NANAIMO

Barkley Sound   Sarita Bay

BAMFIELD

Strait of Georgia

GULF ISLANDS
(insert above)

INTERNATIONAL BOUNDARY

Clo-oose

PORT RENFREW

Juan de Fuca Strait

Jordan River

VICTORIA

PRINCESS MAQUINNA

VANCOUVER ISLAND
COASTAL ROUTES

5   0   5   15
                    mi.

GULF ISLANDS

N

0   5   10

THETIS Is.

Ganges

GALIANO Is.

SALTSPRING Is.

Strait of Georgia

Fulford
Harbour

MAYNE
Is.
Port
Washing
ton

N.
PENDER
Is.

SATURNA
Is.

SIDNEY

Routes indicated are for 1935 but not all way ports
are shown. In 1935, CPR ships did not call at all
communities but nearly all were scheduled in earlier years. Service was provided by: Princess Norah
& Princess Maquinna (West Coast); Princess Mary
(Powell River & Gulf Islands); Princess Adelaide
(Northeast Coast) & Motor Princess(Gulf Islands).

RDT

Seattle had grown . . .
The Seattle terminal . . .

The CPR's Atlantic Princesses

The Princess Helene . . .

In 1929, the CPR ordered another Princess ship. However, this vessel was intended for operation on the east coast of Canada, across the Bay of Fundy between St. John, New Brunswick and Digby, Nova Scotia. The 4,505 ton ship was named *Princess Helene* at her launching on May 12, 1930 at the W. Denny & Bros. shipyards at Dumbarton, Scotland. Following her fitting out and sea trials, she sailed for St. John, arriving in late August 1930. She became the first CPR Princess to operate on the east coast of Canada.

The *Helene* provided an important link across the Bay of Fundy, making it possible for passengers and freight shipments to avoid the much longer, time-consuming route around the head of the Bay. At Digby, the Dominion Atlantic Railway, a CPR subsidiary, provided trains to Yarmouth, Halifax and Truro.

The CPR took over the Bay of Fundy service two years after it leased the Dominion Atlantic Railway for 999 years on November 13, 1911. Before that time, the CPR and the DAR co-operated to provide connecting services in conjunction with the Dominion Atlantic's steel-hulled sidewheel steamer *Prince Rupert*. This 1,158 ton vessel had been acquired for the run in 1895 and continued in service until 1919. Other steamers, including the *Yarmouth, St. George* and *Empress*, were used in the service before the arrival of the *Princess Helene*. Until 1940, the CPR also operated ships across the Minas Basin between Parrsboro and Kingsport, Nova Scotia.

The *Princess Helene* remained on the Bay of Fundy until 1963, when she was replaced by the newer, larger steamship, the *Princess of Nanaimo*, which at that time was transferred from the Pacific coast. The *Helene* was then sold to Marvic Navigation Incorporated of Monrovia for service in the Mediterranean under the name *Helene*, later *Carina II*, and finally simply *Carina*.

The New Night Boats

Seattle had grown considerably in the years since the CPR Princesses began to sail from Elliott Bay. In this scene from about 1930, the *Princess Alice* is leaving her pier for Vancouver.
— JOE D. WILLIAMSON

The Seattle terminal of the CPR Princess ships is shown in the lower photo. — CPR

The *Princess Helene* operating between St. John, N.B. and Digby, N.S. — CPR

The 1929 depression that brought ruin to the operators of the *City of Victoria* inevitably had its effect on the CPR Princesses as well. Services were cut back and smaller steamers were more frequently substituted on the runs during the offpeak traffic periods. However, no runs were abandoned and the basic operations of the fleet had become so essential to the life of the communities on the Coast that the fleet passed through the hard years of the 1930's intact, except for the retirement of a few of the oldest ships already obsolete and due for disposal.

Before the collapse of the stock markets in October 1929, the Company had placed an order for two new 5,251 ton steamships with the Fairfield Shipbuilding and Engineering Company's yards at Govan, Scotland. These vessels were designed for the Vancouver-Victoria night service and were referred to as "floating hotels" because of the large number of staterooms incorporated into their design. The cost of each vessel was 210,000 pounds ($1,050,000). Fortunately, the depression did not prevent work on the ships from continuing and the *Prin-*

CANADIAN PACIFIC PRINCESS

A Travelogue and Guidebook to British Columbia-Puget Sound issued aboard Princess Steamers of the British Columbia Coast Steamship Service.
DISTRIBUTION FREE TO PASSENGERS.

Published Monthly by Pacific Publishers, Limited, 319 Pender Street West, Vancouver, B. C.
TRinity 1945.

Vol. 4   JULY, 1939   No. 41

Service Features On Board Night Steamers

"SS. PRINCESS MARGUERITE," "SS. PRINCESS KATHLEEN"
"SS. PRINCESS JOAN" and "SS. PRINCESS ELIZABETH"

Between

VANCOUVER — VICTORIA — SEATTLE

Our aim is to make our passengers comfortable. If your stateroom is not satisfactory ring for your steward, he will adjust your windows, turn on your heat, or provide extra bedclothes.

Stateroom doors should be kept locked, when not occupied.

Light lunches and Soda Fountain beverages served in the Coffee Room from 10:00 p.m. until midnight.

Combination Breakfasts from Thirty-five Cents to Seventy-five Cents, served in the main Dining Saloon, from 7 a.m.

Tea or Coffee with Toast, served to Staterooms, Twenty-five Cents.

The News Stand carries an assortment of toilet articles, magazines, b o o k s, chocolates, cigars and cigarettes.

The Wireless Operator will accept at current rates, messages for shore stations or other vessels.

Valuables should be checked at the Purser's Office.

Hot water bottles provided on request.

This steamer is equipped with free local telephone connection alongside the Pier at Victoria and Vancouver.

For Valet Service, clothes pressing, light tailoring or shoe shining, while you sleep, ring for the stateroom steward. For ladies' maid, please apply to the Stewardess.

Before going ashore ring your bell and stateroom steward will arrange taxi or baggage service.

SILENCE: We invite your assistance in discouraging loud talking in the staterooms to the annoyance of occupants in adjoining rooms.

Connections for electric razors are installed in all men's public washrooms on Victoria - Vancouver and Seattle steamers. Direct current only.

The Master-at-Arms is on duty all night on Victoria-Vancouver ships.

Suggestions for the betterment of the service are welcomed by the management.

When disembarking, please leave stateroom key in the door lock.

Advertising for some of the service features on the night boats was included in the CPR publication *Canadian Pacific Princess* which was distributed free to passengers. — AUTHOR'S COLLECTION

The last of the CPR's . . .

The last of the CPR's three-funneled coastal liners were the 5,251 ton sister Princesses, *Joan* and *Elizabeth*. They were the largest night boats on the north coast and might well have been called floating hotels. They were not fast and had limited open deck space but they had pleasing lines. They developed an excellent reputation for reliability on the Vancouver - Victoria night run and also in daytime use on the Triangle Route. The *Princess Elizabeth* is shown above passing Victoria's Ogden Point. — CPR

cess Elizabeth, named after Queen Elizabeth, wife of King George VI, was launched on January 16, 1930. Her sister ship, the *Princess Joan*, followed less than two months later, on March 4th. In May, the *Princess Elizabeth* was ready for trials and delivery to the CPR. Preceding the *Princess Joan* on the voyage to the Pacific coast by two weeks, she was able to complete the trip from the builder's to Victoria with only one minor incident.

Shortly after the *Elizabeth* left the builder's yards, her wireless set burnt out, forcing Captain C. C. M. Sainty to take the vessel to Falmouth, England, where repairs were carried out. A layover of four days was required to repair the damage to the Marconi equipment. With the job completed, the ship proceeded to Victoria, arriving on May 3, 1930.

Her arrival was greeted with great enthusiasm and excitement. While not as large as the sleek *Marguerite* and the *Kathleen*, the new vessel was nonetheless an impressive addition to the fleet. Displacing 5,251 tons, she was fully 2,500 tons heavier than the *Princesses Alice* and *Adelaide*, the last ships built especially for the night boat service. She was equal in every way to the high standard established by the CPR for its Coast Service. In all, 405 first class and 26 second class passengers could be accommodated in berths for the midnight boat service, while she was licensed to carry 1,000 day passengers. The ship's complement was 102 officers and men.

The staterooms, social halls, smoking lounge and observation rooms were situated on the Upper, Promenade and Boat ("E") Decks. While all the staterooms were well appointed, there was considerable variation in the type of accommodation provided. Not surprisingly, the location of rooms was very important. Staterooms on the Boat Deck, while pleasant inside, were accessible only from the open deck. Particularly in winter, leaving or entering the rooms could be a chilling experience. At the other extreme, staterooms located near the engine rooms or exhaust stacks could become uncomfortably hot.

On the Main Deck, space was provided for up to 70 automobiles. The beautifully decorated dining room on the Orlop Deck provided seating for over 100 passengers at a time. There was no better place to eat than in the dining rooms of the CPR's Princess ships. Throughout, the vessel was panelled with mahogany and other hardwoods.

Since the leisurely schedule of the night boats allowed a crossing time of seven hours, speed was not as critical a consideration in the design of the two new steamships as it had been in the specifications of the *Princesses Kathleen* and *Marguerite*. The *Joan* and the *Elizabeth* were driven by heavy duty quadruple expansion engines fed by four single-ended, oil-fired Scotch boilers with a working pressure of 250 pounds per square inch. The design called for a service speed of 16.5 knots, but both vessels are known to have done better. However, comfort and vibration-free operation rather than speed were the characteristics the naval architects strove for in building the last of the CPR's three-funneled "pocket" liners.

The *Princess Joan* is seen leaving Vancouver.
LEONARD FRANK PHOTO, VANCOUVER PUBLIC LIBRARY

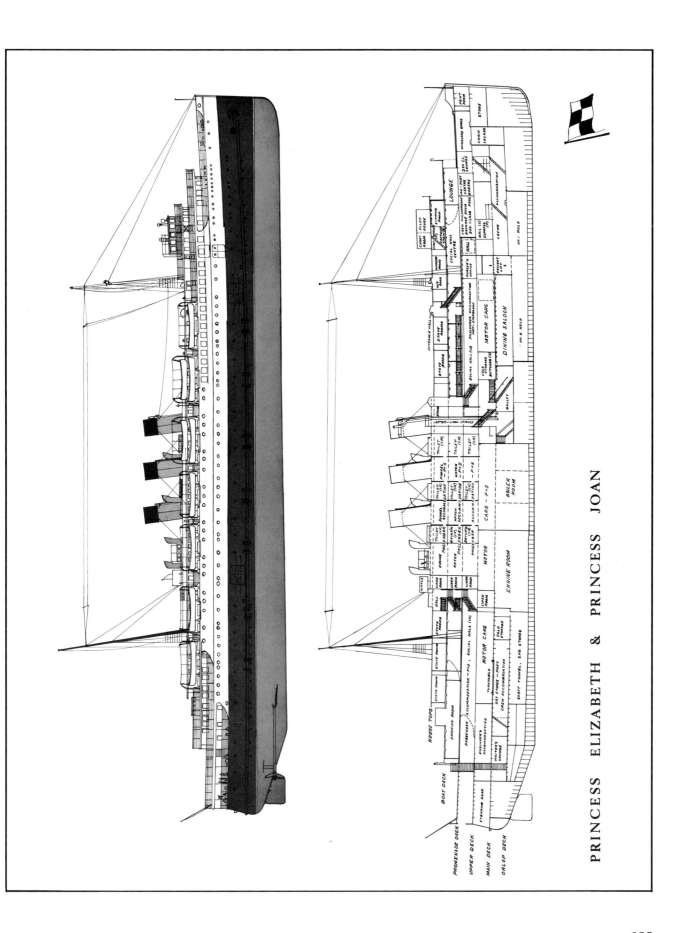

PRINCESS ELIZABETH & PRINCESS JOAN

In 1930, the Canadian National Railways, which had taken over the Grand Trunk Pacific Railway and its steamships in 1920, brought a trio of new three-funneled liners to the Coast. By this time, the *Prince Rupert* and *Prince George*, which had been operating on the B.C. coast since 1910, had discontinued service to Victoria and Seattle by terminating their runs up the north coast at Vancouver.

However, in the late 1920's, the CNR decided to go into direct competition with the CPR on the Triangle Route. For this purpose, the CNR had the fine, massive looking *Prince David*, *Prince Henry* and *Prince Robert* built at the Cammell, Laird and Company Limited shipyards at Birkenhead, England.

The 6,892 ton ships were over 366 feet long and had a breadth of just over 57 feet. They were turbine-powered and were capable of speeds of 24 knots. The three new Princes were built to Navy specifications so that in wartime they could be converted quickly to merchant cruisers. In passenger service, they seldom made use of their reserves of speed and power. On the Vancouver-Victoria-Seattle service, inaugurated by the *Prince David* in August 1930, only three of the ship's four boilers were used at any one time.

Of the three new ships, the *Prince Henry* was the first to arrive, being placed on the Vancouver-Prince Rupert route early in July 1930. She was followed shortly after by the *Prince David*, while the *Prince Robert* did not reach Vancouver until the following spring after spending the winter in cruise service from Atlantic coast ports to the West Indies.

The Vancouver-Victoria-Seattle service was maintained by the CNR until the spring of 1931 using the new vessels and the older *Prince Rupert* and *Prince George*. In May 1931, the newly arrived *Prince Robert* took over the run and the following month she was joined by the *Prince David*. These two ships then provided a double daily return service over the route. However, on July 31st, the *Prince Robert* ran aground near Port Townsend and had to be withdrawn. Despite its efforts to provide an efficient, attractive service, the CNR operation simply did not pay and after September 15, 1931 the Vancouver-Victoria-Seattle runs were suspended.

The *Prince Henry* and *Prince David* were moved to the East Coast for cruise services and the *Prince Robert* was used to augment the older Princes sailing north to Prince Rupert from Vancouver. When the war came in 1939, all three of the new Princes were taken over by the Canadian Navy and none was returned to passenger operations after the war.

The *Prince Rupert* remained in operation until the mid-1950's, when she was sold for scrap. Her sister ship, the *Prince George*, was destroyed by fire in 1945 and was replaced by a new vessel, also named *Prince George*, built in 1948. This vessel was the last of the CNR Princes in service. She operated on cruises to Alaska until the end of the 1974 season and was scheduled for retirement in fall 1975. However, a fire damaged her accommodations and she was put up for sale and her 1975

The CNR's Princes

The Prince Rupert *and . . .*
Competition returned . . .

season was cancelled. She was then purchased by the British Columbia government for a planned service to north coastal communities, but this operation did not materialize.

The Princesses in the 1930's

The early 1930's were marked by a decline in traffic which hastened the retirement of several of the oldest ships still in CPR service. In April 1932, Captain Neroutsos announced that the coastal freighter *Princess Ena* had been sold for use as a cannery station. The vessel had been laid up at Esquimalt for some time prior to the sale and had been superceded by the larger, more modern freighter *Nootka*, which the Company had acquired in 1926. In making the announcement, Neroutsos also disclosed that negotiations had been opened for sale of the *Princess Royal*, no longer needed since the *Princesses Alice* and *Adelaide* were available for a variety of duties following their replacement on the Vancouver-Victoria night service by the *Princesses Joan* and *Elizabeth*.

In 1933, the 46-year-old *Charmer* was relegated to providing accommodation for bathers at Newcastle Island, a resort just off the Nanaimo waterfront. This small island, once the site of large coal mines, was purchased by the CPR in 1930 with the hope that it could be developed into a tourist attraction for people living in Vancouver and Nanaimo. The following year, the *Charmer* was replaced by the *Princess Victoria*, which became a floating hotel for visitors to the Island. People renting the *Victoria*'s staterooms were permitted to use her galley to prepare their own meals. The *Charmer* was then of no further use to the Company and was scrapped in 1935 at Capital Iron and Metals at Victoria.

By that time the *Princess Royal* had been sold to the same firm for scrapping. Being of wooden construction, there was less salvageable metal in the *Royal* than in the *Charmer*. In mid-August 1934, after being stripped of her machinery, she was towed out to Albert Head not far from Victoria and burned. It was a Viking's funeral for the once elegant *Princess*. She had proven to be most versatile in her 27 year career with the CPR and undoubtedly repaid the Company many times over for its initial investment in the ship. The *Princess Royal* was a veteran of the Triangle Route, the Victoria-Vancouver and Seattle-Vancouver night boat runs, the Alaska and North Coast services, the Vancouver-Nanaimo ferry run and the routes to Powell River, Comox and the Gulf Islands. In fact, the only service she did not operate on was to the west coast of Vancouver Island.

In 1934, Captain Neroutsos retired as head of the B.C. Coast Steamship Service. His position was filled by Marine Superintendent Captain R. W. McMurray who had brought out both the *Kathleen* and *Marguerite* from Scotland to the Pacific. McMurray remained in charge of the Princesses until 1945 when he was appointed managing director of the CPR's Atlantic services.

Operations throughout the 1930's were generally uneventful

The *Prince Rupert* and *Prince George* both seemed destined for trouble during their long careers on the coast. The *Prince Rupert* is shown above in March 1931 after she sank in Esquimalt Harbour while she was being refitted. Apparently painters left a port open and the ship settled into 40 feet of water and took on a 50 degree list. Damages were estimated at $100,000.
— AUTHOR'S COLLECTION

Competition returned to the Triangle Route for a brief period during 1930 and 1931 when the Canadian National steamships *Prince Henry*, pictured here, *Prince Robert* and *Prince David* were brought to the Pacific. They were large, fast ships but the depression ended any hopes for them to pay their way. Only the *Prince Robert* was retained on the Pacific coast with the older former Grand Trunk Pacific steamships.
— AUTHOR'S COLLECTION

The freighter Nootka ...
In a classic CPR advertising ...

The Union Steamship Company . . .

The freighter *Nootka* was acquired by the CPR in 1926 for service on the B.C. coast. — CPR

In a classic CPR advertising photo, the *Princess Alice* is shown off the Oak Bay golf course just a few miles from the Company's Empress Hotel in Victoria. — CPR

The Union Steamship Company competed with the CPR for the freight and passenger business to the small coastal communities. The 1,369 ton *Camosun* is representative of their larger steamships. — LEONARD FRANK PHOTO, VANCOUVER PUBLIC LIBRARY

and were marred by only a few mishaps. In February 1935, two incidents occurred which demonstrated that even in the mid-1930's, fog was still the greatest enemy of coastal shipping. Along the south coast of British Columbia and around Vancouver Harbour in particular, heavy fogs are not infrequent in the winter months. On February 4th, a dense blanket of nearly impenetrable mist had closed in on the coast, decreasing visibility to nearly zero.

About 8:45 a.m., the West Vancouver ferry *No. 5*, a small vessel capable of carrying only a few passengers, was crossing the harbour mouth west of the First Narrows when, without warning, the bow of the *Princess Alice* loomed out of the fog and crashed into her. The *No. 5* remained afloat for only eight minutes, but it was long enough for the crew and six of the seven passengers to escape. One woman was caught in the wreckage and despite a desperate attempt to free her by Captain Darius Smith, she could not be saved before the little ferry sank.

Later the same day, at 7:30 p.m. the *Princess Charlotte*, proceeding to Vancouver inbound from Seattle and Victoria, was about one hour late due to the fog. At the same time, the Union Steamship Company's *Chelohsin* was sailing for Loughborough Inlet from Vancouver. Fortunately, the two vessels sighted each other in time and were able to swing away from their collision course, but not soon enough to prevent them from sideswiping each other. The damage was moderate and both steamers were able to proceed to port under their own steam.

Incidents such as these were common before the use of radar on merchant ships became widespread in the years following World War II. This device made it possible for navigators to track other ships in virtually any weather conditions. Radar was equally helpful in determining the positions of icebergs and exposed reefs. Since its introduction, the number of marine accidents due to faulty navigation and poor visibility has decreased significantly.

In 1935, veterans of the steamship operations all along the Pacific coast from Oregon to Alaska were saddened to hear that Captain John Irving, founder of the Canadian Pacific Navigation Company which developed into the CPR's B.C. Coast Service, had died in Vancouver on August 10th at the age of 83. Irving, a pioneer steamboat captain and enterprising businessman, had, like Troup, seen the Northwest Coast of North America develop from a little known frontier into a modern productive region. He had helped make early settlers' and businessmen's dreams of taming the West Coast come true by providing the transportation links that were so vital to economic development and stability. What had been the Canadian Pacific Navigation Company fleet had grown under CPR control to become one of the finest coastal steamship services in the world. So much change had occurred in the 35 years since the CPR takeover of the CPN that not one of the original vessels acquired by Irving was in service, and the new ships,

Both CNR and CPR vessels . . .
The CPR's shipping . . .

Sketch of *Princess Patricia.* — ROBERT D. TURNER

Both CNR and CPR vessels served the pulp mills at Ocean Falls. In this photograph one of the CNR Princes is docked next to the CPR freighter *Nootka.* — B.C. GOVERNMENT PHOTOGRAPH

The CPR's shipping operations in Vancouver centred on Pier B-C and Pier D. At Pier B-C is the trans-Pacific liner *Empress of Asia*, while the *Princess Joan* is berthed at Pier D in this 1934 view. To people on the coast, the Princesses always seemed like big ships, but when compared to the Empresses they looked small indeed. The Union Steamship Company's *Cardena* is visible on the right and behind her is the CNR's *Prince Robert.* — LEONARD FRANK PHOTO, VANCOUVER PUBLIC LIBRARY

The *Princess Patricia*, replaced on the Nanaimo - Vancouver run by the *Princess Elaine*, spent her last active years as a relief vessel and on excusions. The end came in 1937 when she was scrapped at Capital Iron and Metals in Victoria. — PROVINCIAL ARCHIVES

such as the *Princess Joan* and *Princess Elizabeth*, were dramatically different in design from the small sidewheelers and coastal steamers that had been so important in the days of Irving's CPN.

By January 1937, the CPR steamer *Princess Patricia* had reached the end of her long career on the B.C. coast. Since being relieved on the Vancouver-Nanaimo route by the *Princess Elaine*, the *Princess Pat* had been variously employed as a relief vessel and excursion steamer, operating out of Vancouver and Victoria. While structurally sound despite her age, she was not suited to the evolving role of the B.C. Coast Steamship Service in the late 1930's. She was particularly ill-equipped for carrying automobiles, being both too small physically and having very low clearance, which made loading and unloading extremely difficult. Many people regretted the scrapping of such a fine steamer, but the hard realities of economics left little room for sentiment and the *Princess Patricia* was sold to Capital Iron and Metals in Victoria on March 27, 1937 and subsequently dismantled. As a final tribute, Captain G. Goold of the *Empress of Asia* which was berthed in Victoria at the time, ordered a whistle salute to the *Princess* as she was towed by on her way to the ship breaker's yards.

After over a decade of heavy service on the Triangle Route and Victoria-Vancouver night services, the *Princesses Kathleen* and *Marguerite* continued to demonstrate their reliability and capacity for prolonged operation without major maintenance problems. Between April 17, 1937 and April 9, 1938 the *Princess Marguerite* steamed 91,983 nautical miles at average speeds ranging between 17 and 22 knots. On May 11th, after nearly four weeks on the Vancouver-Victoria night run, the *Marguerite* began sailing the Triangle Route. From that time until the following April, she was in continuous service with the exception of three days in September when her underwater surfaces were cleaned and repainted. The tight schedule on the Triangle Route allowed only two and a half hours in port at any one time for minor repairs and maintenance. Similarly, the *Kathleen* steamed 89,878 sea miles on the Triangle Route between March 24, 1937 and February 14, 1938 with only three days in drydock. During this time, the sleek *Princess* had consumed over 110,000 barrels of fuel oil, fuel consumption being greater at the higher speeds she maintained. Service records such as these were later to contribute to the sister ships being taken over by the Navy for service during World War II.

The sale of the *Princess Patricia* was the last major change in the fleet prior to World War II, as all other vessels were needed to maintain the various routes along the Coast. Thus, as the 1930's came to a close, the Company was left with a fleet of ships which included the *Princesses Joan, Elizabeth, Alice, Adelaide, Charlotte, Victoria, Kathleen, Marguerite, Maquinna, Mary, Norah, Louise* and *Elaine*, plus the *Motor Princess*, the freighter *Nootka* and several tugs and barges. No new vessels had been added since the arrival of the *Joan* and

Pier D caught fire on July 27, 1938 and was destroyed. The *Princess Charlotte* barely escaped disaster. — VANCOUVER MARITIME MUSEUM; SAM LEWIS PHOTO

Pier D caught fire . . .

Elizabeth in 1930. While all of the ships were still highly serviceable, nearly one half of them had reached or were approaching 30 years of age. It was apparent that before very long a number of new ships would be required. In 1938, plans were formulated for the construction of two vessels, but World War II intervened and eliminated any possibility of new construction until the end of the 1940's.

The 1920's and 1930's saw the Princesses at their peak of service and efficiency. Maintaining and operating the ships was an involved and complex process. Victoria, where the Coast Service's headquarters were located, was also the major maintenance base for the ships. There, the catering, stores, and engineering departments were situated. To illustrate the size of the operation, in July 1939 alone, the catering department's 565 employees prepared and served 115,386 meals to passengers and a further 142,116 to crew members. Provisioning the ships for the month cost over $51,000. Sales in the news service amounted to about $15,000 per month during the summer season.

During the late 1930's, the ships were steaming a total of nearly 650,000 miles per year and burning over 600,000 barrels of bunker oil annually. Fuel economy was very important and the Company saved a great deal by scheduling low speed operation. To illustrate these savings, the *Princess Victoria*'s consumption was 1.4 barrels per mile at 18 knots, 1.0 barrels at 16 knots and only .67 barrels at 14 knots.

Normally each ship was drydocked twice a year for cleaning and painting the underwater surfaces and in addition was withdrawn from service once annually for a longer period to permit a more general overhaul. During the yearly refitting, all machinery was repaired and serviced, the interiors were painted and decorated, and the boilers cleaned and inspected. All carpets, linens, mattresses and curtains were cleaned and the upholstery was repaired. The lifesaving gear required inspection and systematic replacement. Much of this work was carried out by the Coast Service's own staff in its carpenter, machine, paint and upholstery shops and at its sail and rigging lofts. The drydocking was usually done at Esquimalt but occasionally ships were repaired in Vancouver or Seattle. The annual budget for paint alone was approximately $20,000.

Throughout the 1930's, both the freight and the passenger businesses were brisk. All of the cargo liners were of necessity equipped for freight handling, but the intercity passenger vessels on the Triangle Route and other south coast runs also carried considerable quantities of cargo in their holds or on the automobile decks. This freight was loaded through the side shell doors of the ships and was usually handled on pallets or dollies. Many businessmen relied on this fast, reliable service for the delivery of small shipments of merchandise and supplies. Gradually, however, this business was lost to trucking services which became increasingly important after World War II.

During the busy summer season of June, July, and August, when nearly one half of the yearly passenger volume was

With systematic drydocking and maintenance, the CPR kept its ships in excellent condition. The *Princess Charlotte* and *Princess Joan* are shown, top right, at Esquimalt. The crews were expected to keep the ships clean and to carry out running repairs as a matter of routine. The boilers were scrubbed down with soft soap and soda, the plates scrubbed with sand and wire brushes and the furnaces kept painted. Minor repairs such as on bearings were done during the short in port layovers. During the 1930's the engineering crew members received about $75 per month plus room and board for their efforts. Usually the food was of the same good quality as that served to the passengers, but the hours were long and the days onshore few and far between. In the other view, the long, narrow picture on the left, workers are painting the *Princess Louise*.
— BOTH PROVINCIAL ARCHIVES

In a classic Victoria scene, the *Princess Alice* arrives in the Inner Harbour.
— PROVINCIAL ARCHIVES

With systematic drydocking . . .
In a classic Victoria . . .

carried, staff had to be increased and virtually all the ships were kept busy. The following table shows the fleet's summer and winter complement for 1938.

	Officers	Ratings	Total
Deck Department			
— summer	61	335	396
— winter	56	275	331
Engine Department			
— summer	84	184	268
— winter	63	144	207
Stewards Department			
— summer		565	
— winter		338	

In that year 878,290 passengers were carried which represented an increase of only 30,343 over 1929. However, over the same period, the number of vehicles carried increased by over 50 per cent from 40,440 to 63,531. These volumes were indicative of the general trends of traffic for the Coast Service. The rapid growth in automobile traffic continued the pattern established in the 1920's and which had been interrupted only briefly by the Depression when in 1932, a low year, only 27,886 vehicles were carried. The virtual stabilization in the number of passengers was prophetic of the decline in these types of services that began after the war.

World War II disrupted these trends and curtailed the growth of automobile traffic. Significantly, it provided a brief surge of high volume foot passenger travel that benefited all of the steamship lines on the Coast. However, after the war, the peacetime shift to automobile oriented travel revived and passenger volumes on the steamships declined; most noticeably on the once highly patronized night boats.

As the world slipped closer to war in 1939, many Canadians were cheered by a visit to Canada by King George VI and Queen Elizabeth. The Royal party travelled across the country by train and from Vancouver to Victoria on the CPR's *Princess Marguerite*. The ship was given the most thorough cleaning and inspection ever accorded a CPR Princess and the entire crew under Captain Clifford Fenton was dressed in new uniforms. With the Royal Standard flying from the foremast, she made a flawless crossing to Victoria. She was escorted by destroyers and was met by the *Princess Kathleen* carrying enthusiastic Victorians. For many CPR employees, the Royal visit was the highlight of their career and an event long remembered on the Coast. For the return to Vancouver, the King and Queen sailed on the CNR's *Prince Robert*.

In a scene repeated . . .
In contrast to . . .

In a scene repeated thousands of times in Victoria, Vancouver and Seattle, passengers disembark from the *Princess Kathleen*. This photograph was taken from the film "Island of Enchantment" which featured the CPR steamship arriving in Victoria. — NATIONAL FILM BOARD

In contrast to the crowded conditions shown above, passengers at the smaller ports of call usually experienced more relaxed arrivals and departures of the steamships. This view shows the *Princess Mary* during the 1940's.
— PROVINCIAL ARCHIVES

The War Years

The Princess Charlotte . . .

When war broke out in Europe in 1939 and Canada's involvement in the fighting deepened, the effects were soon felt on the B.C. coastal shipping lines. For the CPR's Princess ships, it meant increases in traffic as the economy geared up to meet the demands of the war. Fortunately, the fleet was well equipped, with enough ships to handle the growth in business. One service to be adversely affected by the war was the *Motor Princess*'s, whose automobile ferry operations were cut back because of the decreased use of private automobiles during the war years. As the war reached a critical stage in 1941, the British Admiralty became desperately short of fast vessels suitable for auxiliary services such as transporting troops. Consequently, in September 1941, the *Princesses Kathleen* and *Marguerite* were both taken over for war service by the Royal Navy. The removal of these two steamers from operation on the Triangle Route meant that their functions would have to be assumed by the *Princess Charlotte, Princess Alice,* and *Princess Victoria*.

On November 1, 1941, the direct night boat between Vancouver and Seattle was discontinued for the winter. Already declining patronage, combined with wartime economy measures prompted the temporary cancellation of the service. It was resumed during the summer of 1942, but after that season it was not reactivated until June 1947. The 1947 and 1948 summer operations marked the end of the night service on this leg of the Triangle Route. Declining revenues from the night boats, indicative of a trend in many similar operations across North America, finally made such services uneconomical. The vessels required large crews and their operating costs were high. To an increasing extent their revenues became dependent on the leisurely travel of tourists during the summer months.

As the war progressed, the ships of the Coast Steamship service were painted battleship grey and some were armed with anti-aircraft weapons. The once attractively painted steamships took on the drab appearance of armed merchant cruisers.

Fortunately, none of the vessels in operation on the West Coast were exposed to real danger as a result of enemy activity, although a sailing of the *Princess Norah* was delayed for two days in 1942 due to a submarine warning when the lighthouse at Estevan Point on the west coast of Vancouver Island was shelled by a Japanese submarine.

The Kathleen *and the* Marguerite *at War and the Princesses at Home*

The *Princess Charlotte* was repainted dark grey during the war years. — TED ROBSON PHOTOGRAPH

For the *Princess Kathleen* and *Princess Marguerite* in service as troop ships in the Mediterranean, it was an entirely different story. Initially, it was planned to use the two ships to supply aviation fuel and personnel to aircraft carriers. The *Marguerite* was converted for this purpose by Yarrows, Ltd. at Esquimalt and the *Kathleen* was rebuilt at the Victoria Machinery Depot.

The two ships sailed from Victoria on November 7, 1941, bound for Alexandria, Egypt via Honolulu and the South Pacific. Difficulties with the crew of British seamen developed en route and in Ceylon, replacements were found in the

167

Fatally hit during...
The Princess Kathleen *sailed...*

— AUTHOR'S COLLECTION

Fatally hit during war duties in the Mediterranean, the *Princess Marguerite* is engulfed in flames shortly before capsizing.
— PROVINCIAL ARCHIVES

The *Princess Kathleen* sailed to Malta during her war service as a troop transport.
— CPR COLLECTION

Chinese crew of the CPR liner *Empress of Russia*. On their arrival in Egypt, the ships were inspected by the British officials and found to be unsuitable for their intended role as aircraft carrier support ships. Instead, they were assigned duties as troop ships. The *Marguerite* evacuated British and Maltese administrators' families from Alexandria as the German offensive threatened that city. Afterwards she assisted in various troop movements in the eastern Mediterranean.

On August 17, 1942, with soldiers of the British Eighth Army onboard, bound for Cyprus, the *Marguerite* was torpedoed. The German submarine *U-82* had been able to penetrate her escort of three destroyers and the merchant cruiser *Antwerp* and hit the zig-zagging *Princess* with the fatal exposive. Fires spread rapidly throughout the ship and she sank only 40 minutes after the torpedo hit, but only 55 of the 1,200 men onboard were lost. The *U-82* escaped and fought in the Mediterranean for another six months before being sunk by Royal Air Force aircraft east of Cartagena on March 4, 1943.

The news of the sinking of the *Princess Marguerite* was not made public until January 1945 when the war in Europe was nearing an end. The *Princess Kathleen* was more fortunate than her ill-fated sister ship. In some 250,000 miles of wartime service, she was untouched by the Axis forces. She sailed both alone and in convoy to Malta during the German siege of the Island, carried invasion troops to Tobruk and to Italy, and witnessed the surrender of the Italian fleet in 1944. Later she was present at the surrender of the enemy forces on Rhodes and took onboard as a prisoner General Wager, the German commander. She also carried Jewish refugees to Palestine and transported thousands of Allied soldiers being reassigned as the war in the Mediterranean came to a close. Finally, in 1946, she was relinquished by the British Admiralty and returned to the CPR.

During the war years, the Princesses continued to provide a reliable service despite the strain imposed by heavy traffic and a shortage of vessels. Various scheduling and route adjustments were introduced to balance the use of the available ships with the traffic. Particularly during the holiday seasons it was not uncommon for passengers to be unable to find seats on the ships operating on the Triangle Route.

It was during this period that the *Princess Victoria*, by then known affectionately as the *"Vic"*, was once again able to demonstrate her speed. She was used primarily as the relief vessel on the Triangle Route and was regularly operated as a "second section" to provide an extra sailing during holidays. However, at least once when traffic was particularly heavy at Christmas, the *Vic* was assigned to operate as the third section on the Victoria to Vancouver afternoon run. She was the last of the three vessels to leave Victoria, but she was instructed to overtake and pass the other two Princesses and arrive in Vancouver first so that she could be unloaded and clear of the terminal before the other ships arrived.

Since there were important training facilities on Vancouver

Wartime saw the Princesses . . .

Wartime saw the Princesses take on coats of drab grey and some
ships were even fitted with anti-aircraft guns. On these facing
pages three of the ships are shown as they appeared in service on
the Triangle Route: the *Princesses Joan, Victoria,* and *Alice,*
photographed by JOHN NEWMAN.

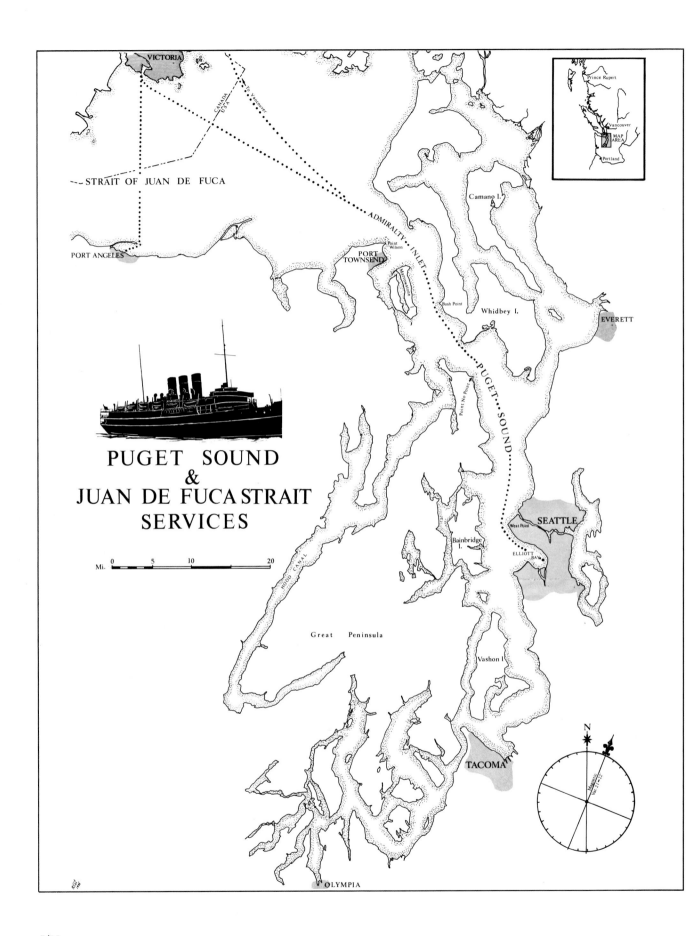

STRAIT OF JUAN DE FUCA

PUGET SOUND
&
JUAN DE FUCA STRAIT
SERVICES

Mi. 0   5   10   20

VICTORIA

PORT ANGELES

ADMIRALTY INLET

PORT
TOWNSEND

Point
Wilson

Bush Point

Whidbey I.

Camano I.

EVERETT

PUGET SOUND

Point No Point

West Point

SEATTLE

ELLIOTT
BAY

Bainbridge
I.

HOOD CANAL

Great   Peninsula

Vashon I.

TACOMA

OLYMPIA

N

Prince Rupert

Vancouver

MAP
AREA

Portland

Island and a major naval base at Esquimalt, servicemen often made up a large proportion of the passengers onboard. Returning to base from leave or going to new assignments often meant sailing on one of the Princess ships.

The usual hazards of operating on the rock-bound, stormy coast of British Columbia and Alaska did not ease during the war. On one day early in 1943, on the Alaska run, the *Princess Norah* ran into a severe storm. Mist rising off the water, reportedly ten times as thick as fog, closed over the ship and later gales up to 70 miles per hour were encountered. Waves broke over the steamer and the water, turning to ice, covered the rigging and nearly the entire superstructure. By the time the *Norah* reached port, an estimated 500 tons of ice had accumulated on the ship and the air temperature had dropped to −22° Fahrenheit. An automobile being carried on deck was frozen so tightly to the ship that it could not be freed and had to be returned to Vancouver. It was delivered on the next sailing north. Perhaps because of incidents such as this, the *Princess Norah* was the first ship in the fleet to be fitted with "hot glass" windows to improve visibility, although this was not until 1949 when Libby-Owens Ford Electropane glass was installed in the bridge.

The year 1943 was an unfortunate one for the *Princess Norah*. On April 21st, while relieving the *Princess Mary* on the Gulf Islands route, she ran hard aground on Zero Rock off Cordova Bay while on the way to James Island, not many miles from Victoria. The *Princess Alice* stood by and took aboard the *Norah*'s 18 passengers, who were transferred by lifeboat. The *Norah* was refloated and taken to drydock for repairs, which kept her out of commission for several weeks.

Later that year the *Princess Joan* was involved in a potentially even more hazardous accident when she rammed and sank the steamer *Squid* off Point Grey during the early morning hours of October 12th. The *Princess Joan* was on the Vancouver to Victoria night boat run with 400 passengers onboard, while the *Squid* was carrying 25 tons of explosives to Britannia Beach on Howe Sound. Fortunately, the *Squid*'s cargo was dynamite, a fairly stable exposive, and it did not ignite. If it had, the results might well have been catastrophic. As it turned out, the *Princess* took the five-man crew of the *Squid* onboard and proceeded to port without further incident.

In July 1945, Captain O. J. Williams became manager of the Coast Service. At age 43, he was the youngest man ever to take the position. He had joined the Company in 1924 as a third officer and had served as navigating officer on the delivery voyages of the *Kathleen, Marguerite, Elaine, Norah* and *Joan*. In 1940 he had been promoted to Marine Superintendent. He was to remain in charge of the fleet until his retirement in 1962.

The war years were hard on the Princesses. The older vessels were pressed into demanding services that hastened the end of their useful lives. At the same time, needed replacement programs had to be delayed for many years.

When the *Princess Kathleen* returned to the Triangle Route after
World War II, she was as fast, beautiful and popular as ever.
Here she is making over 20 knots steaming down Puget Sound.
— JOE D. WILLIAMSON

CHAPTER VI

THE POST-WAR YEARS

Resumption of
Peacetime Operations

THE PERIOD IMMEDIATELY following the end of World War II found the CPR in an unenviable position. The Company was facing continued increases in traffic as wartime austerity measures were removed, but had only an aging and inadequate fleet of ships at its disposal. The *Princess Marguerite*, the only war loss suffered by the CPR's Coast Service, would, at best, take several years to replace, and the *Princess Kathleen*, when released from military service, would need extensive renovation before she would be suitable for peacetime operation.

Thus, the heaviest services on the Victoria, Seattle and Vancouver routes would have to continue to fall on the *Princesses Victoria, Charlotte and Alice*. All were either nearing or well into their fourth decade of almost continuous service on the Pacific coast. Only the *Princesses Joan* and *Elizabeth* could be considered modern vessels, and even they had been in operation since 1930. They were also limited in their flexibility because of the large proportion of their passenger and deck space devoted to cabin accommodation for the night boat services.

On August 2, 1946, the *Princess Kathleen* returned to Victoria. Five years of hard war service had taken its toll on the once beautiful ship. Painted in dark battleship grey, where once she had been a gleaming white, the *Princess Kathleen*, or *"Kitty"* as she was fondly called, was every inch the wartime troop transport, with anti-aircraft gun tubs still adorning the bridge and the upper decks. Off the William Head quarantine station near Victoria, the *Kathleen* was met by the CPR tug *Kyuquot* with welcoming dignitaries, including Captain Williams, coastal superintendent for the CPR's steamships, and the mayor of Victoria, Percy George. One man who could not have helped being moved by the *Kathleen*'s arrival that day was Captain L. C. Barry, who had, five long years before, sailed the *Princess* off to war.

It was a moving scene as the *Kathleen* approached the CPR dock in Victoria's Inner Harbour, the warm summer sun welcoming her arrival. The *Princess Joan*, awaiting the night

By the end of World War II the *Princess Alice* was nearing her
35th year of service for the CPR. — JOHN NEWMAN

The Princess Charlotte *was . . .*

The *Princess Charlotte* was a fascinating subject for a small boy's curiosity as she steamed along the Victoria waterfront on a summer day in 1946.
— CHARLES F. TURNER, AUTHOR'S COLLECTION

boat sailing to Vancouver, gave three deep blasts of her whistle in greeting and was answered by the *Kathleen*. A cheering crowd of Victorians and tourists was on hand to greet the favourite of the Triangle Route and her wartime crew, under command of Captain Richard Leichester. He had been master of the *Princess Marguerite* when she had sailed from Victoria for the last time. More than a few of those present must have thought back to the pre-war years in that different world of the 1930's, when the two sister Princesses had flawlessly maintained the tradition of speed and elegance that had made the Triangle Route famous. Now only the *Kathleen* remained to serve it and some must have sensed that an era and a way of life were passing.

Returning with the *Princess Kathleen* was Sandy, a large yellow cat, the ship's mascot of 12 years. He was the only member of the *Kathleen*'s crew to have stayed with the ship from the time of her 1941 departure from Victoria until her return home. However, Sandy's record was not entirely unblemished. In Tripoli, he went absent without leave and was not returned to the ship until three months later, apparently none the worse for his experience.

With the *Kathleen* safely at home the job of refitting and conversion to return her to passenger service began. Under the supervision of the British Ministry of War Transport, careful surveys were made to determine the extent of the necessary work before bids were called from local shipyards. On October 1st, it was announced that the Victoria Machinery Depot would undertake the overhaul, estimated to cost approximately $1,500,000 to complete. The entire ship required a general cleanup and repainting, armour plating had to be removed and the engines overhauled. Finally and of greatest importance, the passenger accommodations had to be rebuilt to replace the dormitory arrangements used for the troops. Completion of the job was promised in time for the following summer when heavy traffic was expected on the Triangle Route.

While the *Kathleen* was being refitted, her engines were given their first major overhaul after 22 years of nearly continuous operation. Since entering service in 1925, the veteran steamship had sailed about 1,750,000 miles without breaking down, prompting Captain Williams to comment to the newspapers that the *Kathleen*'s engines were "the finest we have ever had on any of our ships."

The *Princess Kathleen*'s refitting was completed the following spring as promised and on June 22, 1947, she was placed on the familiar Triangle Route for which she had been built. With the matronly *Princess Charlotte*, the *Kathleen* maintained the Vancouver-Victoria-Seattle service. One vessel left Vancouver and Seattle each morning and arrived at the opposite terminal after a stop at Victoria, approximately 11 hours later. At this time, the night service between Vancouver and Seattle was provided only during the summer months. However, the *Princesses Joan* and *Elizabeth* continued the night boat operations between Victoria and Vancouver.

The Princess Kathleen . . .
Transformed . . .

At the same time, the *Princess Mary* served the Gulf Islands route and provided tri-weekly sailings to Comox, Powell River and Texada, Hornby and Denman Islands. The *Princess Adelaide* was assigned to the Vancouver-Prince Rupert weekly service, while the *Princess Maquinna* sailed to ports on the west coast of Vancouver Island as she had done in the past. The Alaska service was entrusted to the *Princesses Louise* and *Norah*. With the *Princess Elaine* making two daily sailings between Vancouver and Nanaimo, augmented by the *Princess Victoria* in the summer months, only the *Princess Alice* was in fulltime reserve as a relief vessel, while the *Victoria* was available for these duties in the winter. The little *Motor Princess* was used during the summer on the Sidney to Steveston automobile service as well as on a Sunday only Sidney to Vancouver sailing via the Gulf Islands.

The Second Princesses Patricia *and* Marguerite

The post-war years marked a resumption and acceleration of the modernization of the transportation industry in North America that had begun in the late 1930's. Trends towards increased private ownership of automobiles, improved highway systems, dieselization of railroads, streamlining of passenger equipment and increased and efficient intercity airline services had all been developing before the war. One of the net results of these various changes was a decline in the popularity of long distance day and night ferry operations. Travellers were increasingly interested in making maximum use of automobiles and at the same time limiting the amount of travel on connecting ferry services.

The era of the fast automobile ferry had come and the CPR was ill-equipped to handle the fundamental change required in services. Obsolete vessels, terminals, and facilities compounded the problem. The vessels on the key routes were in urgent need of replacement and the highest priority had to be given to the acquisition of new ships that could sustain the existing intercity operations.

Two new vessels were ordered after considerable agitation from the coast business community to have the CPR ferry services modernized. The two ships were pre-war in concept and reflected the design established with the *Princess Victoria* nearly half a century before and which had evolved with the construction of the *Princesses Charlotte, Margaret, Kathleen,* and *Elizabeth*. Intended as replacements for the *Kathleen* and *Charlotte* on the Triangle Route, the new 5,911 ton vessels had sleeping accommodations for 90 passengers in 49 cabins and could carry 2,000 day passengers each. In addition, each vessel could accommodate 50 to 60 automobiles on the main deck.

While their decor was influenced by the styles of the mid-1940's, the traditional use of heavy wood panelling, tapestries and luxurious appointments still dominated the design of the ships. They were fast, with a speed of 23.5 knots, and featured a turbo-electric system of propulsion that was quiet and effi-

The *Princess Kathleen* was home, the years of hard war service behind her. — CPR

Transformed after an extensive refit, the 22-year-old steamship returned to service on the Triangle Route in June 1947. — JOHN NEWMAN

After the destruction of . . .

The first new ships . . .

After the destruction of Pier D in Vancouver the Princesses moved to Pier B-C. In these views, from the later 1940's, the *Princess Victoria, Princess Elizabeth,* and *Princess Louise* are in port. — BOTH CPR

The first new ships built for the Coast Service after the war were the *Princess Marguerite,* shown here at her launch on May 26, 1948, and her sister ship, the *Princess Patricia.* — CPR

cient. With twin funnels, a well-proportioned superstructure and cruiser sterns, they were beautiful ships and a credit to the CPR. Appropriately, the sister ships were named *Princess Marguerite* after the vessel lost in the war in 1942, and *Princess Patricia* after the turbine-powered ship once used on the Vancouver-Nanaimo service.

Both of the new *Princesses* were built by the Fairfield Company Limited at Govan, Scotland and were ready for delivery to the CPR early in 1949 following their trials. The *Princess Marguerite* was completed first and sailed for Victoria on February 15th under the command of Captain Thompson of the CPR Coast Service. Many of the vessel's officers were also drawn from British Columbia operations, although most of the seamen were recruited in Glasgow. The 9,600 mile voyage was completed without difficulty. On her arrival at Esquimalt, on the morning of April 6, 1949, she was turned over to Yarrows, Ltd. for necessary repainting and minor repairs before being placed in operation at the end of the month. The *Marguerite* was followed in mid-June by the *Princess Patricia* and both vessels were fully operational for the 1949 summer season. The addition of the two new vessels made it possible to retire the *Charlotte* and the *Alice* and permitted a revision of scheduling and operating procedures that considerably increased the efficiency of the Princess fleet.

The direct summer night boat between Seattle and Vancouver was not resumed in 1949, and vessels were freed for other services. The *Princesses Patricia* and *Marguerite* operated on the Vancouver-Victoria-Seattle service which by that time was better termed the Tri-city Route rather than the Triangle Route since there were no direct Vancouver to Seattle connections. From this time on, all sailings proceeded by way of Victoria. In addition to operating as the Victoria-Vancouver night boats, the *Princesses Joan* and *Elizabeth* made one daylight sailing between the two cities so that once again, there was a twice-daily service between Victoria and Vancouver. At the same time, the *Princess Kathleen* was withdrawn from the Tri-city service and employed in summer luxury cruises to Alaska, operating out of Vancouver.

Declining business on the *Princess Adelaide*'s northern route and the age of the vessel made her continued use uneconomical, and the elderly *Princess* was withdrawn in 1948. This left only the *Princess Louise* and *Princess Norah* operating to northern ports in regular freight and passenger service and the *Princess Kathleen* running as a cruise ship.

The arrival of the *Patricia* and *Marguerite* also benefited the Nanaimo-Vancouver service, which was at this time dependent on the *Princess Elaine* and, during the summer, the *Princess Victoria.* Alternately, either the *Patricia* or the *Marguerite* made one sailing to Nanaimo each evening after arriving in Vancouver from Victoria. The vessel then laid over at Nanaimo for the night and made the return sailing to Vancouver the next morning. In this way, two extra sailings a day

The new *Princesses Marguerite* and *Patricia* were graceful and
beautiful ships. This scene shows the *Marguerite* steaming east
into Georgia Strait from Active Pass. — NICHOLAS MORANT, CPR

Active Pass is the narrow stretch of water
separating Galiano Island from Mayne Island to
the south, along the shortest water route between
Victoria and Vancouver. The steamships are the
Princess Marguerite, newly arrived from Scotland,
and the sturdy, nearly 40-year-old *Princess Mary*.
— NICHOLAS MORANT, CPR

Here, the *Princess Marguerite* has just overtaken the *Princess Mary* as both ships steam eastward. — NICHOLAS MORANT, CPR

The *Princess Victoria* was used for summer overload service at this time. — SKETCH, ROBERT D. TURNER

Here, the Princess Marguerite...

The Princess Victoria...

could be added to the service without the addition of extra vessels to the fleet.

No longer needed by the CPR, the *Princesses Alice* and *Adelaide* were put up for sale in 1949. Both vessels were acquired by the Typaldas Brothers Steamships Company of Piraeus, Greece, which renamed the old ships *Aegaeon* and *Angelika*. The two vessels were given an overhaul and a new coat of paint before sailing for the Mediterranean, where they were both to serve for nearly two more decades. Finally, in 1966, both ships were sold for scrapping. The *Alice* (*Aegaeon*) would not give up easily, however, and while under tow for the ship breaker's at Spezia, Italy, ran hard aground and was abandoned. The fact that both sisters had remained in service for over 55 years certainly demonstrated a quality of design and construction that would be hard to fault and difficult to equal.

The *Princess Charlotte* was last operated on the Tri-city Route on June 15, 1948. She followed the *Alice* and *Adelaide* to Greece in 1949 after being acquired by the same firm. In 1950, she was renamed the *Mediterranean*. While the *Alice* and *Adelaide* had been altered little for their new careers, the *Princess Charlotte* was refitted with a new bridge and had her three slender funnels trunked into a single large squat one. Her internal fittings were also modified to include a bar and cocktail lounge to better serve the luxury cruise market. She served her new owners well, but in 1965 she was finally removed from service; old age had finally caught up with her.

The freighter *Nootka*, like the *Charlotte*, left B.C. waters in 1950, when she was sold by the CPR to Peruvian interests. The *Princess Victoria* remained in service for a short while longer, providing overload capacity on the Nanaimo-Vancouver route during the summer months when tourist travel was at its peak.

The Princess of Nanaimo *and the* Chinook

With the new *Princess Marguerite* and *Princess Patricia* in operation between Vancouver, Victoria and Seattle, the CPR turned its attention to the Nanaimo-Vancouver service. The mainstay of the route was the 20-year-old *Princess Elaine*. Automobile traffic between Nanaimo and the mainland was growing steadily, doubling from 40,000 automobiles carried in 1939 to 80,000 in 1949. Increasingly, the *Elaine*'s design and capacity were proving inadequate to meet a large proportion of this growth. The ship was not engineered for rapid loading and unloading of vehicles and could accommodate only 60 automobiles on a sailing.

To alleviate the congestion developing on the route, the CPR needed a considerably larger vessel with a higher vehicle capacity. As usual, the Company turned to shipyards in Great Britain, placing an order with the Fairfield Company Limited's shipyards at Govan, Scotland for a 6,787 ton turbine-driven steamship whose design resembled ships then being built for cross-channel service between England and France.

The new vessel, christened *Princess of Nanaimo* at its launch-

With the arrival of . . .
By the late 1940's, the . . .

To accommodate ...

With the arrival of the *Princess Marguerite* the *Princess Kathleen* was freed for cruise service to Alaska. The tired old *Princess Charlotte* remained in service on the Triangle Route until the new *Princess Patricia* joined the fleet in June 1949. In this photo, the *Charlotte* steams past the new *Marguerite*. — CPR

By the late 1940's, the *Princess Elaine* was badly outdated for the auto-ferry service between Nanaimo and Vancouver.
— B.C. GOVERNMENT PHOTO

To accommodate increasing traffic and the *Princess of Nanaimo*, a new terminal was built at Nanaimo. In the distance, the *Princess Victoria* is departing for Vancouver in her last year of service. — B.C. GOVERNMENT PHOTOGRAPH

ing on September 14, 1949, was a dramatic change from the *Elaine* in both size and design. Sleek and rakish, with one funnel dominating her silhouette, the new ferry had nearly three times the displacement of the *Elaine*. Automobile doors were located forward and aft for side loading. By the use of ramps and elevators on the wharves, unloading time was reduced to 20 minutes. While this was an improvement over previous designs, it still required 45 minutes to one hour to prepare the vessel for departure. Two automobile decks were provided, giving the ship a capacity of between 130 and 150 vehicles and on the three passenger decks, 1,500 day passengers could be accommodated. The 18.5 knot vessel cost the CPR an estimated $4,500,000.

Few people would dispute the fact that the *Princess of Nanaimo* was an attractive, well-designed, modern vessel, but these characteristics notwithstanding, was she really suited to the Vancouver-Nanaimo run of the 1950's? A most revealing comparison can be made between the new CPR steamship and the new diesel-powered ferry M.V. *Chinook* of the Puget Sound Navigation Company, by then more commonly known as the Black Ball Line. The streamlined and attractive *Chinook* had been placed in service between Seattle, Port Angeles and Victoria in June 1947, fully two years before the *Princess of Nanaimo* was launched. The *Chinook* was designed by the naval architects Gibbs and Cox of New York and built by the Todd Shipyards of Seattle for operations on Puget Sound and across the Strait of Juan de Fuca — a more exposed, stormy stretch of water than the Strait of Georgia where the *Princess of Nanaimo* was to operate. The twin-screw, 18 knot ferry could carry 100 vehicles and 1,000 day passengers. Hence, her automobile capacity was about one third lower than the *Princess of Nanaimo*'s, but she had cost her owners only an estimated $2,000,000, which was less than half the price of the CPR vessel.

In short, for a one third increase in capacity — space often used only in peak traffic periods — the CPR purchased and was paying operating expenses on a vessel nearly half again as large and over twice the cost of the *Chinook*. Undoubtedly, had the CPR opted for the design of the simple, less elegant *Chinook*, there would have been charges that the Company was downgrading its service. The *Chinook*, however, was not exactly spartan. She had staterooms for more than 200 passengers, a dining salon with a capacity for 108 at a sitting, three lounges and a coffee shop.

It is highly probable that the CPR's commitment to follow a traditional, conservative approach to its ferry service in the late 1940's, when other options clearly existed, may well have been one of the most significant factors leading to the CPR's virtual withdrawal from the automobile ferry service on the Pacific coast just over ten years after the *Princess of Nanaimo* entered service. When the CPR needed an imaginative advance in its handling of the ferry service, perhaps equivalent to the boldness that prompted the construction of the *Princess*

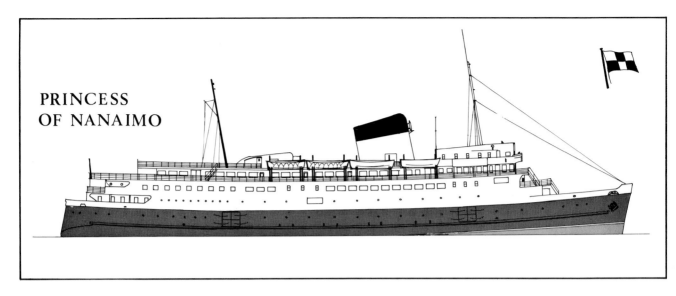

PRINCESS OF NANAIMO

The Princess of Nanaimo *was . . .*

The *Princess of Nanaimo* was a beautiful ship, but was poorly suited to handle the ferry service across the Strait of Georgia. These two Nicholas Morant photos show her off Vancouver's Stanley Park in August 1951. — BOTH CPR

The fast, streamlined,...
The Iroquois, *the same...*

The fast, streamlined, diesel-powered *Chinook* was built in 1947 for Black Ball's Seattle - Port Angeles - Victoria service. She was a modern vessel specially designed to permit fast handling of automobiles. In concept she was much more advanced than the CPR's *Princess of Nanaimo*. — JOE D. WILLIAMSON

The *Iroquois*, the same vessel used by the PSN during the rate war of 1907-1909, is hardly recognizable after being converted to an automobile ferry. She sailed between Seattle, Port Angeles and Victoria from 1928 to 1947, when she was relieved by the new *Chinook* and placed in freight service. — JOE D. WILLIAMSON

As the *Chinook* prepares to leave Victoria Harbour, she is met by the *Princess Kathleen*. The air photo shows the *Princess Maquinna, Nootka, Princess Charlotte*, Black Ball's *Iroquois*, and the *Princess Joan* in port. — BOTH PROVINCIAL ARCHIVES

As the Chinook *prepares ...*

191

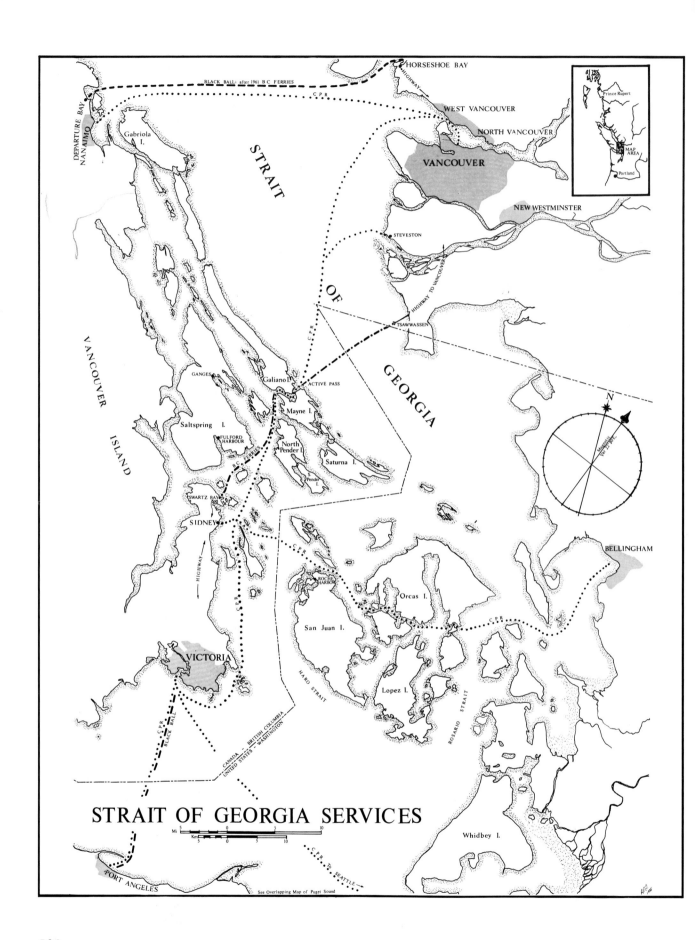

STRAIT OF GEORGIA SERVICES

Victoria years before, or the innovation in design that produced the *Motor Princess*, the Company chose a course that left it little flexibility for future action and opened a niche for a shrewd competitor to exploit.

Perhaps the near monopoly that the CPR had enjoyed on the Vancouver Island to Vancouver ferry services had led to complacency and had dulled the Company's competitive spirit. However, the situation on the Vancouver-Nanaimo run was not to remain static for very long. The old rival of the CPR, the Puget Sound Navigation Company, was about to move north to the Strait of Georgia to challenge the supremacy of the CPR's Princesses.

Meanwhile, time had caught up with the *Motor Princess*, the little diesel-powered automobile ferry. New federal government fire regulations, prompted by the tragic loss of the wooden steamship *Nordic* on the Great Lakes, prevented the continued use of the wooden vessel in passenger service without extensive alterations. The Company felt that the cost of these changes was not justified, and in 1950, she was withdrawn from the Sidney to Steveston run. After 1952, she was used as a freighter between Victoria and Vancouver. In 1955, she was sold to Gavin Mouat of the Gulf Islands Ferry Company, who had the vessel reconstructed with steel upperworks and an open car deck. In this configuration, the *Motor Princess*, subsequently renamed the *Pender Queen*, is still (as of 1975) in service for British Columbia Ferries, which purchased the Gulf Island Ferry Company in 1961.

In 1951, the CPR Coast Service acquired the 1,334 ton motor vessel *Island Connector* of the Clark Steamship Company and renamed her the *Yukon Princess*. This small freighter was to be used as a general cargo vessel and was also to carry asbestos concentrates from Skagway to Vancouver, a service that was maintained for just six years.

The overall outlook facing a number of the Company's coastal freighter operations was not bright. Losses were accumulating on several of the routes and it was only a matter of time before service cutbacks would be instituted. Typically, it was a problem of marginal services not justifying the high replacement cost of the aging vessels used on the routes. As if this was not a serious enough problem, one of the Company's most beautiful steamships, the *Princess Kathleen*, was heavily damaged in a collision with the CNR vessel *Prince Rupert*.

The Princess Kathleen *and the* Prince Rupert *Collide*

In the early morning hours of August 30, 1951, while on the Alaska cruise service, the *Kathleen* was steaming southbound from Ketchikan, Alaska to Prince Rupert at a leisurely speed of nine or ten knots. In addition to the crew of 120 officers and men, there were 294 passengers aboard. It was a peaceful night; the seas were calm, the winds light. There were only occasional patches of fog. While the *Kathleen* was making slow passage south, the CNR liner *Prince Rupert* was proceeding northbound towards Ketchikan from Prince Rupert at

In cruises to Alaska, the ...
CNR's new steamship ...

In cruises to Alaska, the *Princess Kathleen* provided effective competition for the CNR's new steamship, the second *Prince George*.
— CPR; MARK S. HORNE

approximately the same speed as the CPR vessel. As the two ships converged, heavy, dense fog closed in. On each vessel the officers on watch were aware of the presence of the other ship by radar contacts. On the *Princess Kathleen* the second officer was in charge of the watch, assisted by the fourth officer. The captain and first officer had retired for the night, having left, as was standard procedure, instructions in the night order book to be called in case of bad weather, fog or any other difficulty.

Realizing that there was a possibility of collision since the two ships were on converging courses, the second officer on the *Kathleen* altered course to starboard first by one half point on the compass, then by another half point, and finally by an additional full point. The officer felt these adjustments would give the approaching vessel adequate clearance. However, the radar bearing of the unseen steamship remained the same. At about 4:29 a.m., the officers on the bridge heard fog signals off the port bow and called Captain Hughes to the bridge. At the same time, speed was reduced to about six knots (slow ahead) as a further precaution. The captain had just reached the bridge and ordered the engines to be put full astern when the *Prince Rupert* suddenly appeared out of the fog. The CNR liner crashed into the *Princess Kathleen*'s port bow causing heavy damage, but fortunately no one was injured. The time of the impact was 4:33 a.m.

On the *Prince Rupert* a similar scene had occurred. The ship's second officer was in charge of the bridge, assisted by the extra third officer who, however, had gone below for breakfast at about 4:00 a.m. At approximately the same time, a distant visual contact was made with the *Princess Kathleen* shortly before fog closed in. At about 4:25, radar bearings confirmed the presence of the CPR steamship about two and a half miles distant, and nine degrees off the starboard bow. The second officer, still unassisted by the extra third officer, sounded fog signals, giving two short blasts to indicate his helm movement, and put the engines at stand-by.

He then altered course five degrees to port and three minutes later he ordered a further five degrees swing to port. At about 4:30, the second officer heard several long blasts from the *Kathleen* about four degrees off the starboard bow, almost dead ahead. Within minutes, the *Kathleen* loomed out of the fog, only 50 yards away, moving slowly across the bow. The second officer put the vessel hard-a-port and ordered the engines full astern, but it was too late. The crash was inevitable. The third officer still had not returned to the bridge, where he should have been monitoring the radar, and the captain had not been called from his cabin.

Fortunately, neither vessel was in danger of sinking, and once separated each was able to return to port under its own steam. However, the damage was extensive. Repairs to the *Kathleen* were estimated at $250,000, while the *Rupert*'s were nearly $100,000. In the subsequent Admiralty Court inquiry, the events leading up to the collision were reconstructed on the basis of the ships' logs and the testimony of the ships' duty officers, who replied candidly to the questioning. The court concluded that:

The faults of the *Prince Rupert* were singularly like those of the *Princess Kathleen*. This is not a case in which the fault of one led the other into a position in which her navigator could not avoid collision. On the contrary, it is a case in which the fault of both Second Officers, originating at substantially the same time and continuing until virtually the moment of collision, led inevitably to the disastrous event. The circumstances are not obscure. The collision would not have happened if either had taken steps to take off his vessel's way, or if either had stopped his engines (or better still reversed) upon hearing the fog-signal of the other, or if either had kept his course, or if either had appreciated the significance of the radar bearings, or if either had called the Master in proper time...In addition, the *Prince Rupert* improperly gave two short blasts helm signal; and her Second Officer failed altogether to call his Captain. Moreover, we think that in this vessel radar bearings were taken less frequently and with less accuracy due to the absence of the Extra Third Officer.

The court suspended the certificates of the two second officers for a period of three months and also suspended the extra third officer of the *Prince Rupert* for a similar period for failing to return to the bridge when it was apparent that the ship was once again in fog. Additionally, the court also censured the captain of the *Prince Rupert* for failing to keep a night order book in accordance with Company regulations. The court went on to commend the master of the *Princess Kathleen* "for the seamanlike manner in which he entered up and used his night order book."

It should be remembered that at this time radar was still new and unfamiliar to the merchant marine and most officers had not been thoroughly trained in its use. The court recommended that formal courses of instruction be given in radar navigation and also stressed the importance of using whatever means available to ensure adequate communication between vessels. Both ships carried radio telephones, albeit for commercial purposes, but had a radio telephone watch been maintained or communications established between the two vessels, the two-sided guessing game that led to the collision could have been avoided.

It may seem surprising that the two ships could collide, even in the rather confined waters of the Inside Passage, but it takes only a little carelessness or apparently minor infractions of orders at a critical time to lead to a tragedy.

Both the steamers were repaired and returned to service, but the bad luck of the *Princess Kathleen* was to continue. Just over a year later, not far from where the *Princess Sophia* had been lost years earlier, the *Kathleen* once again ran into difficulties.

It was the 7th of September, 1952. The *Kathleen* was steaming from Juneau to Skagway on the last cruise of the summer season. The voyage had been a peaceful one without incident

Lena Point, Alaska brought doom to the *Princess Kathleen*. She was stuck fast to the shore and the rising tide filled her from astern. The weight of the water finally dragged her off the reef and she sank into the channel. — T. DAVIES AND A. N. EIDE; PROVINCIAL ARCHIVES

The Loss of the Princess Kathleen

Lena Point, Alaska . . .

and all appeared in order as the watches changed at midnight. The chief officer was in charge, with a night watchman, a forward lookout and a quartermaster on the bridge. The weather was deteriorating with heavy intermittent rain squalls. Shortly after the Shelter Island light was passed, the chief officer, Mr. Savage, ordered a change in course to bring the vessel closer to mid-channel. He ordered simply "starboard," instead of the usual "starboard one-quarter point," which would have brought the ship onto the desired course. He then became preoccupied with the approaching squall and forgot to return the vessel to her original course once she had reached the position he wished. Thus, instead of coming to mid-channel, the *Princess Kathleen* continued across the channel at her cruising speed of ten knots. During this brief interval, as the chief officer was trying to make out the Sentinel Island light, the lookout reported land on the starboard bow and later ahead of the ship. However, the chief officer could not hear the report clearly. Belatedly the quartermaster told Savage that the ship was still bearing starboard. Assuming that the land sighted was Shelter Island, the chief officer ordered the ship hard-a-starboard, but it was too late. With a grinding crash, the liner ran hard aground on Lena Point. The time was 2:58 a.m.

Captain Graham Hughes came to the bridge immediately and began to assess the ship's position and damage. Juneau was contacted by wireless for assistance and soundings were taken inside and outside the ship. It was soon determined that the fore-peak bottom plating was torn open and No. 2 bottom tank leaking.

The lifeboats were lowered and the passengers mustered in preparation for abandoning the ship. At high tide, about three quarters of an hour after the grounding, Captain Hughes tried to back the ship off the rocks, but she was held fast and would not move. As the tide ebbed, the situation of the ship worsened. The wind had increased to a moderate gale from the northwest and it was driving the stern of the ship closer to the rock. Hughes tried to hold position with the ship's engines but was unsuccessful. The *Kathleen*'s list increased from five to 15 degrees. By 5:30 a.m., the list had worsened to 19 degrees and the captain ordered the passengers disembarked. Three and a half hours later all of the 307 passengers were safely landed.

Meanwhile, a United States Coast Guard cutter, the steamship *Alaska*, and several smaller craft had arrived on the scene. While the tide was on the ebb, the pumps had been able to contend with the flooding, but as it began to rise, the stern did not lift with it. The bow remained firmly stuck on the reef and the stern began to flood rapidly as water entered through the deck openings. Finally, by 11:30, the captain had no options left. Not wishing to endanger the crew, he was forced to give up his efforts to save the ship and ordered her abandoned. Two hours later the weight of the water in the ship finally overcame the hold of the rocks on the bow and the *Princess Kathleen* slipped free. She filled rapidly, standing almost vertically in the water with her entire bow exposed. A moment later she was gone, submerged under 130 feet of water.

The passengers were cared for to the best of the crew's ability. Fires were built and food prepared for the cold and uncomfortable travellers. The rain squalls of the previous night had turned to snow before dawn, and by daylight a heavy rain had set in. Meanwhile, crew members had cut their way through the underbrush to the nearest road. Buses eventually picked up the passengers and crew and took them to Juneau. "If ever a town was to be congratulated, it's Juneau," Captain Hughes later commented. "The people were wonderful. They even offered to move out of their houses to accommodate our passengers. Within an hour everyone was taken care of. I've never seen anything like it in my life."

The CPR immediately cancelled the midnight sailing of the *Princess Elizabeth* to Victoria and sent her north to Juneau to return the *Kathleen*'s passengers to Vancouver. So as not to leave the midnight boat passengers stranded, they were transported to Nanaimo by the *Princess Patricia*, then bussed to Victoria. Two Canso amphibious aircraft and a DC-3 airliner were also dispatched to Juneau to bring back some of the passengers who required immediate transportation to Vancouver.

Could the *Kathleen* be salvaged? That was the question pondered by all those who had become so attached to the ship. In 130 feet of water the vessel was not beyond reach and some thought it would be possible to raise the liner, then valued, according to the newspapers, at about $5,000,000. However, there were many complications. While it might have cost that much to replace the ship, her depreciated value was much less. The *Kathleen* was, after all, 27 years old. The salvage operations in exposed northern waters would have been both costly and hazardous.

After examination, the CPR decided against attempting to raise the ship and abandoned her to the insurance underwriters. An unidentified CPR official quoted in the *Vancouver Sun* remarked: "We all love the *Kathleen*, but we have to look facts in the face. If she lay in English Bay, it would be a different story." The *Sun* also reported that salvage experts estimated the costs of raising the *Kathleen* might be as high as $2,000,000. She was completely submerged, the stern in 130 feet of water and the bow in 60 feet. She was listing to 50 degrees to port with her propellers buried in the mud. To compound problems, tides were packing mud into the vessel.

Despite various proposals to salvage the *Kathleen*, the underwriters were no more optimistic than the CPR had been and refused to consider the matter. The *Kathleen* was left to join the remains of the *Sophia* and *Islander*.

The sinking of the *Princess Kathleen* resulted in 300 of the ship's passengers and crew pressing damage suits totalling $1,119,000 against the Company. However, with the approval of the U.S District Judge, John C. Bowen, the claims were settled for only $190,000 in May 1954.

By the early 1950's, the traffic had declined significantly on the *Princess Maquinna*'s route to Vancouver Island's west coast. She was withdrawn in 1952 to the sorrow of the many people who had come to know her well during her 40-year career. — JOHN NEWMAN

The *Princess Maquinna* was replaced by the small motor vessel *Princess of Alberni*, but she was not a success. — CPR

Service Cuts Along the Coast

By the early 1950's, the traffic . . .
The Princess Maquinna *was . . .*

Coincidental with the sinking of the *Princess Kathleen*, all steamship services to Alaska, other than luxury cruise operations, were facing a bleak economic future. Improvements in roads and in airline and barge services had cut signicantly into revenues, and moreover, fewer people were willing to live in the isolation of the small coastal communities served by the shipping industry. Gradually many of the families moved into the larger communities less dependent on shipping for communication with the outside world.

In November 1952, the CPR decided to withdraw the *Princess Louise* from the Alaska service and refit the vessel for cruise purposes to replace the *Kathleen*. Thus, only the *Princess Norah* remained available for the regular Alaska and North Coast passenger service. The *Yukon Princess* continued to be employed carrying freight, asbestos, and concentrates from Skagway to Vancouver until eventually she was replaced by the White Pass and Yukon Route's modern container ship *Clifford J. Rogers* in 1956.

In 1955, the CPR B.C. Coast Service and the Canadian National Railways reached an agreement to operate jointly the *Princess Norah* to the north coastal settlements. For this service, she was renamed *Queen of the North*. A weekly sailing provided calls at Westview, Ocean Falls, Kitimat, Prince Rupert and Ketchikan, Alaska. By this time, the CNR's steamship operations had been reduced to the summer only Alaska cruises of the new *Prince George*.

As with the Alaska services, declining traffic and revenues on the lightly travelled south coastal routes could not justify replacing the aging vessels in operation there. The service to the west coast of Vancouver Island was still handled by the *Princess Maquinna*, which by the early 1950's was entering her fourth decade of operation. The Gulf Islands and Powell River routes were maintained by the even more elderly *Princess Mary*.

The *Princess Mary* was the first of the two ships to be withdrawn from service. In May 1952, she was sold to the Union Steamship Company for use as a barge. Her superstructure was scrapped with the exception of the cafeteria and dining room, which is utilized as a restaurant in Victoria — the popular Princess Mary. In becoming the *Bulk Carrier No. 2*, the *Mary*'s hull shared the same fate as the *Princess Victoria*'s. The *Victoria* had been sold two months before the *Princess Mary* after having been laid up at Victoria since August 1950. The *Victoria*'s hull was acquired by Tahsis & Company for carrying bulk hog fuel. Neither of the former Princesses lasted long in this rather ignoble service. The *Victoria*'s hull was lost in Welcome Pass on March 10, 1953, while the *Mary*'s stripped-down hull sank in a storm on April 19, 1954 while under tow by the Union Steamship Company's tug *Chelan*, which, tragically, was also lost. The *Chelan* had been southbound from Skagway heading for Vancouver with the barge loaded with ore concentrates. Both vessels foundered in the storm, leaving no survivors from the tug's 14-man crew.

The *Princess Mary*, so well known to residents of the Gulf Islands, was withdrawn from service in 1951. — JOHN NEWMAN

Time also caught up with the *Motor Princess*, shown here at Ganges in the late 1940's. Her wooden superstructure was considered a fire hazard and the high cost of installing safety equipment was felt to be unjustified. She was relegated to carrying freight and eventually sold in 1955. However she was then completely rebuilt with a new steel superstructure and is still in service for B.C. Ferries.
— B.C. GOVERNMENT PHOTOGRAPH

During the mid-1950's, the *Princess Norah* was operated jointly by Canadian Pacific Railway and Canadian National Railways as the *Queen of the North*. Note the automobiles on the deck. — CPR

Time also caught up . . .
During the mid-1950's, the . . .

The *Princess Mary*'s Gulf Island route was taken over in April 1952 by the *Princess Elaine*, which had been relieved on the Vancouver-Nanaimo service at the end of the previous summer by the *Princess of Nanaimo*. However, the *Elaine* was not suited to the service. She could not manoeuver well in the confined harbours of the Gulf Island ports and she was too large to be economical on the inter-islands route. Nonetheless, she remained on the Gulf Islands and Powell River routes until the summer of 1953, when she was returned to the Vancouver-Nanaimo service, where traffic was increasing.

Thereafter, a reduced service on the Gulf Islands was provided by a newly acquired small coastal freighter, the *Princess of Alberni*, and by the *Princess Norah*. These two vessels sailed to the Georgia Strait ports in addition to their primary assignments on the coastal routes. The CPR Gulf Islands service was terminated in February 1954, and the following April the Powell River service was also ended.

Meanwhile, the *Princess Maquinna* had come to the end of her long career and was sold in November 1952, for use as a barge. As a fitting gesture to commemorate the long years of service she had provided, her bell was presented to the Mission to Seamen in Vancouver in October 1953, when her superstructure was scrapped. Her hull was used to carry ore concentrates from the Consolidated Mining and Smelting Company's works at Tulsequah, north of Juneau, Alaska. As the *Taku*, the hull remained in service for almost a decade, finally being scrapped in July 1962 at Vancouver.

Until a new vessel to replace the *Maquinna* could be purchased, the CPR chartered a small motor vessel, the *Veta C.*, to provide a limited freight and passenger service to the west coast of Vancouver Island. The *Princess of Alberni* was then purchased as a more permanent replacement by the CPR in April 1953. Originally the M.V. *Pomare*, she was acquired from Compania Naviera Ambas Costas S.A. of Mazatlan, Mexico. The 538 ton vessel was of wooden construction and measured just over 140 feet in length. Diesel-powered, she was capable of 12 knots.

The *Princess of Alberni* was turned over to the Victoria Machinery Depot for an overhaul, which included alterations to her cabins and the installation of cargo refrigeration facilities. These modifications were completed in late May and the *Princess* began her rather short, unsatisfactory career on the west coast of the Island. Her first skipper was Captain H. Murray, former first officer of the *Princess Maquinna*.

The *Princess*'s normal schedule called for a Thursday morning departure from Victoria with possible stops at 18 small ports of call before arriving in Port Alberni on Sunday. From Alberni, the little vessel returned to Victoria, arriving on Monday. For the people of the west coast villages, she represented quite a drop in service standards from the old but fondly remembered *Princess Maquinna*. She had cabin space for only six overnight passengers and only 24 day passengers could be

The Yukon Princess *was . . .*

The *Yukon Princess* was a post-war addition to the fleet, but her service was confined to hauling freight and asbestos concentrates.
— PROVINCIAL ARCHIVES

202

accommodated in the lounge, which also served as a dining room and lounge for the ship's officers.

Unfortunately, the *Princess of Alberni* was just not suited to the demanding requirements of the West Coast service. Her size limited her ability to operate in bad weather, and to make matters worse, her diesel engine was unreliable. Twice in her first year of operation the vessel was returned to port under tow, the second time necessitating the cancellation of her pre-Christmas sailing. Christmas mail, packages and produce bound for the West Coast spent the holiday season on the CPR dock in Victoria. It must have been a disappointing Christmas for the people of the isolated coastal communities.

If local people were distressed by the situation, the CPR was also unhappy. After the first five months of operation a loss of $45,000 had accumulated. The Company reported that the northbound sailings were consistently only two-thirds full, while the southbound runs carried practically no freight. Nevertheless, the service was continued by the CPR until the summer of 1958.

The Puget Sound Navigation Company Moves to Canada

Meanwhile, the Puget Sound Navigation Company, the CPR's rival in the coastal shipping and ferry trade from the days of the rate war, turned a perceptive eye to the Strait of Georgia service offered by the CPR and saw an opportunity to establish a fast, automobile-oriented ferry in direct competition with the CPR. There was, of course, the desire of any company to take advantage of an opening in the market, but also, the PSN was looking for a place to continue its operations. In Washington, the traditional home of the Company, the State had taken over nearly all of the important ferry services in Puget Sound in 1951 with the establishment of the Washington State Ferries, as a division of the State Toll Bridge Authority. The PSN retained its old steam ferries, the *Malahat* and the *City of Sacramento* (formerly known as *Asbury Park*), the smaller motor vessels *Bainbridge* and *Quillayute*, and the modern *Chinook*. All of these vessels except the *Malahat* were eventually transferred to Canadian registry and were to form the basis of the Company's move to Canadian waters.

In 1951, the Puget Sound Navigation Company established a Canadian subsidiary known as Black Ball Lines — Canada Limited, and announced that in August of that year the ferries *Quillayute* and *Bainbridge* would be placed in service on a route across Howe Sound connecting Horseshoe Bay, a fine sheltered anchorage, with Langdale on the Sechelt Peninsula. The establishment of this route marked only the beginning of the PSN's new operations in Canada.

In 1953, the *City of Sacramento* was also transferred to Canadian registry and towed to Victoria where the old vessel was stripped to the car deck at Capital Iron and Metals of Victoria and then turned over to Yarrows Ltd. of Esquimalt for a complete rebuilding. The conversion was completed that same year and under the name *Kahloke*, she emerged as a modern, streamlined, diesel-powered automobile ferry in many ways resembling the *Chinook*. The *Kahloke* had an automobile capacity of 100 vehicles and also provided accommodation for 1,000 day passengers.* The new diesel engines powered the ship at a speed of 19 knots.

Beginning on June 27, 1953, the *Kahloke* was assigned to a new service between Departure Bay, a sheltered harbour just north of Nanaimo on Vancouver Island, and Horseshoe Bay, Black Ball's already operational terminal about 20 miles northwest of Vancouver. For the first time, the CPR had direct, serious competition on the Nanaimo-Vancouver ferry route.

The CPR however, did not give up without a fight and initiated a new summer service on the Victoria-Port Angeles route which was heavily patronized by tourists. Using either the *Princess Joan* or the *Princess Elizabeth*, which would otherwise have laid over in Victoria between sailings on the Victoria-Vancouver night boat service, the CPR was able to schedule three round trips a day between Victoria and Port Angeles for the 1953 summer season. These were in direct competition to the service offered by Black Ball's *Chinook*, which was withdrawn in 1953 from the Seattle-Port Angeles segment of its operation to concentrate on the potentially more profitable Strait of Juan de Fuca crossing to Victoria. Up to four sailings a day were scheduled for the speedy vessel.

The operation by the CPR was a logical extension of its services and actually had been tried out briefly in 1934 and 1941 but without much success. It made better use of existing ships and offered high traffic volumes. During the winter, the CPR withdrew from the route and assigned the *Joan* and *Elizabeth* to the once a day service between Seattle and Victoria. The vessel arriving in Victoria after the night boat run from Vancouver made the Seattle trip while her sister ship made a sailing from Vancouver to Nanaimo.

While the *Chinook* was proving highly successful on the Victoria to Port Angeles service, the new Black Ball operations between Horseshoe Bay and Departure Bay were so promising that the Company felt it was better to move the *Chinook* to the new route. One more return trip a day could be scheduled than on the Port Angeles-Victoria run and consequently better use could be made of the vessel.

The proposal to withdraw the *Chinook* from the Victoria-Port Angeles service dismayed businessmen in both communities who feared the important tourist industry would suffer. However, Washington State Ferries agreed to place the ferry *Kalakala* on the route on a schedule comparable to that maintained by the *Chinook*. The *Kalakala* was eventually replaced on the run in 1960 by the M.V. *Coho*, a new vessel built for the route and operated by Black Ball Transport Incorporated.

*As operated by British Columbia Ferries in the 1970's the capacities of the *Kahloke* (now known as the *Langdale Queen*) and the *Chinook* (now *Sechelt Queen*) are considered to be about 80 vehicles and 600 passengers each.

Horseshoe Bay was . . .

Horseshoe Bay was Black Ball's mainland terminal. So successful was its operation that the *Chinook* was brought north to join the *Kahloke*, doubling the number of sailings on the run.
— B.C. GOVERNMENT PHOTOGRAPH

Black Ball's *Kahloke* was the most modern automobile ferry in British Columbia when she emerged from Yarrows in Victoria to compete with the CPR Princesses in 1953.
— B.C. GOVERNMENT PHOTOGRAPH

Few would guess that the *City of Sacramento*, shown at lower right, was actually the same ship.
— JOE D. WILLIAMSON

Black Ball's Kahloke *was . . .*
Few would guess . . .

The Kalakala, *undoubtedly . . .*
The small diesel ferry . . .

Battle for the Vancouver to Nanaimo Route

The *Kalakala*, undoubtedly the most distinctive ferry on the entire Pacific coast, replaced the *Chinook* on Black Ball's Victoria - Port Angeles service until the *Coho* was built for the route.
— JOE D. WILLIAMSON

The small diesel ferry *Bainbridge*, shown here in B.C. Ferries' colours is typical of the vessels Black Ball used to institute its service to Sechelt and Powell River, north of Horseshoe Bay.
— B.C. GOVERNMENT PHOTOGRAPH

The *Chinook* was transferred to Canadian registry and renamed *Chinook II*. Before being placed on the Horseshoe Bay-Departure Bay run with the *Kahloke*, she was rebuilt with doors in the bow to facilitate faster vehicle loading and unloading. With each ship making five return trips daily, a very efficient and modern service was provided. The Black Ball service was a major innovation in the operation of ferries in British Columbia and was potentially disastrous for the increasingly antiquated and inefficient service offered by the CPR. Interestingly, Captain Douglas Reynolds, formerly a master with the CPR, was marine superintendent for the Black Ball Lines' Canadian operations.

Black Ball further expanded its operations by chartering the ferry *George S. Pearson* from the Gulf Islands Ferry Company to operate on the Horseshoe Bay to Langdale route, permitting the *Quillayute* to be transferred for operations on Jervis Inlet to the north, connecting Earl's Cove with Saltery Bay. The Company also acquired the small steam ferry *Scotian*, out of service at Halifax, and renamed her *Smokwa* following her arrival on the West Coast. The addition of these small vessels in 1955 and 1956 marked a significant improvement in the ferry service operated to Powell River and Sechelt. The services made automobile travel and truck transport to Powell River from Vancouver practical and convenient and provided an efficient replacement for the direct steamship route from Vancouver abandoned by the CPR in 1954.

To improve and modernize the ferry service to Vancouver Island the CPR ordered, in 1953, a large, new diesel-powered vessel for the Vancouver-Nanaimo operation. This ship, the *Princess of Vancouver*, was the last addition to the Princess fleet acquired by the CPR with the primary function of carrying passengers and private automobiles on the Pacific coast. The handsome ship was similar in appearance to the *Princess of Nanaimo*, but was longer and had a lower funnel. The new Princess entered service on the Vancouver-Nanaimo route in the summer of 1955, and provided three round trips a day between the two cities.

The *Princess of Vancouver* had the added advantage of a high clearance cardeck which allowed railway freight cars to be transported as well as automobiles and highway trailer trucks. This feature enabled the ship to be used in a dual service capacity on the night and off-season sailings when there was less space required for private automobiles. Unlike the other Princesses, the *Princess of Vancouver* was equipped for stern loading and unloading.

The interior arrangements of the ship, though not as luxurious as those of her predecessors, were still elaborate for a vessel used in short cross-channel runs like that to Vancouver Island. They reflected the more modern, less decorative designs of the mid-1950's but were in keeping with the standards so long maintained by the coastal service of the CPR. Like so many of the other Princesses, she was constructed in Scotland. She was brought out to the Pacific coast from her builders, A. Stephen & Sons Ltd. of Glasgow, by Captain George A. Thompson of Victoria who had also been in command of the second *Princess Marguerite* on her delivery voyage.

With two modern vessels built especially for the Vancouver-Nanaimo service, the elderly *Princess Elaine*, and one or two of the Tri-city Route steamships available for part time service, the CPR should have been well able to compete with the Black Ball operation. However, a comparison of the services offered by the two rival companies indicates that this was not the case.

Black Ball had only the *Chinook II* and the *Kahloke* on the run. Each vessel offered five return trips a day between the terminals. Hence, with a total of 10 sailings in each direction a day, the Company could transport about 1,000 vehicles to and from Vancouver Island. In contrast, the CPR operated the *Princess of Vancouver*, the *Princess of Nanaimo* and the *Princess Elaine* each on three round trip sailings a day to the Island. In addition, either the *Princess Marguerite* or the *Princess Patricia* made one return trip. Based on the *Princess of Nanaimo* having a capacity of 130 vehicles, the *Princess of Vancouver* being able to carry 115, the *Princess Elaine* 60 and the *Princess Patricia* 50, the four vessels were able to transport a maximum of 965 vehicles to and from the Island. Thus, by committing three vessels full time as well as one vessel part time to the Vancouver-Nanaimo route, the CPR was unable to match the capacity of the Black Ball's two vessels. Obviously, Black Ball was making more efficient use of its ships and crews and would therefore incur significantly lower operating costs.

While the relative efficiency of the two companies' operations was a critical factor in their competitive struggle, the ability of the two services to attract the travelling public was equally important. The CPR offered reserved automobile space on a city to city service, with more luxurious vessels. Black Ball countered with shorter sailing and loading times from suburban terminals. The CPR had the advantage of being well established on the route, with a loyal clientele many of whom were almost personally attached to the Princesses. To some people the Black Ball ships, while modern and comfortable, appeared rather utilitarian and somehow lacking in personality.

For several years at least the situation appeared to have been a standoff, but the CPR was in reality losing ground. A general increase in traffic kept both lines busy and in 1957 the CPR handled a record 286,666 vehicles but did not make an overall profit on its operations. It is reasonable to assume that in time, because of increases in automobile traffic, the greater efficiency of the Black Ball operation would begin to shift the balance in favour of that service. However, before any conclusion could be reached, events unforeseen by either company were to intervene, making the ultimate outcome of the competition academic.

ISSUED BY
Canadian Pacific RY. CO. STEAMSHIP LINE
(BRITISH COLUMBIA COAST SERVICE)
PASSENGER'S PORTION
ONE WAY FIRST CLASS
Between
VANCOUVER, B.C.
&
NANAIMO B.C.
This portion of ticket is to be retained by passenger until asked for by purser or agent at termination of trip.
NOT GOOD FOR PASSAGE

BCS 5x4 Series 2 21356

Ticket. — AUTHOR'S COLLECTION

The multi-purpose *Princess of Vancouver*, designed to carry rail cars as well as highway vehicles, was not able to match the economy of the Black Ball vessels, although she out-performed all of the other Princesses on the Nanaimo - Vancouver route. — ROBERT D. TURNER

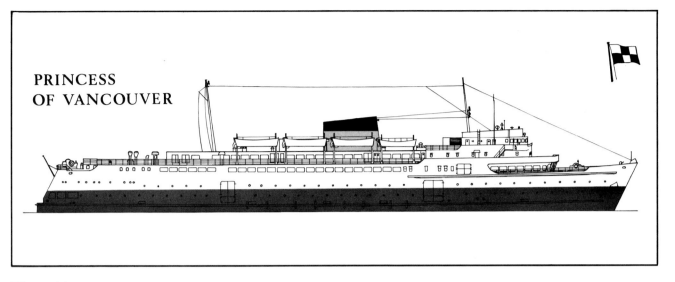

PRINCESS
OF VANCOUVER

The multi-purpose . . .

Sketch of *Princess Louise.* — AUTHOR

Retirement by the CPR was ...

Retirement by the CPR was not the end for the *Princess Louise*. She was eventually taken to Long Beach, California and permanently moored as a restaurant vessel. — ROBERT D. TURNER

Leaving the ferry slip at Vancouver, the CPR tug *Kyuquot* eases *Transfer No. 4* out into Burrard Inlet to begin the tow to Vancouver Island. The 1,042 ton barge was a product of the B.C. Marine Railway Company's yards at Esquimalt in 1913. The *Kyuquot* was sold in 1957 and the rail car ferry service was thereafter operated under charter by towing companies. — CPR

Her departing whistle made it final. The *Princess Elizabeth* would never return to Seattle. All but the CPR's summertime daylight service between the great port city on Elliott Bay and Victoria had come to an end. It was 4:00 p.m., February 25, 1959. — JOE D. WILLIAMSON

Leaving the ferry slip . . .
Her departing whistle . . .

Black Ball was right and the CPR was wrong. When the British
Columbia government went into the ferry business its vessels and
service were patterned after the CPR's old rivals. One of the first
two of B.C. Ferries' ships was the M.V. *Tsawwassen*, shown
above. She provided space for over 100 cars and could carry
1,000 passengers. — B.C. GOVERNMENT PHOTOGRAPH

Early in 1958, as Vancouver Island was preparing to celebrate the 100th anniversary of the Island becoming a British Crown Colony, prospects of a potentially crippling strike against both the CPR and Black Ball became serious. By the spring of that year both the Canadian Pacific Coast Service and Black Ball were without contracts for the majority of their employees. Conciliation boards recommended settlements in April for the three unions affected, but the proposals were not accepted.

On May 17th, the CPR was struck by the Seamen's International Union and all of the Company's Coast Service operations came to a halt. Without the CPR ferry services, the Island was not completely isolated, since there was still Washington State Ferries operating to and from Port Angeles and Anacortes and, Black Ball's Horseshoe Bay to Departure Bay (Vancouver-Nanaimo) services. However, if Black Ball employees also struck, the Washington State Ferries would be overwhelmed and traffic to and from Vancouver Island would grind to a virtual halt. This was the prospect that loomed on the horizon when on May 22nd, the Canada Merchant Service Guild and the National Association of Marine Engineers acknowledged the possibility of a strike against Black Ball Lines.

What followed was a summer of lengthy negotiations, political battles, disrupted family holidays and crippling losses to the tourist industry on Vancouver Island. On June 21, 1958, Black Ball was given 72 hours strike notice by the unions. In anticipation of increasing difficulties and the potentially calamitous effect of a protracted strike by Black Ball employees, the Premier of British Columbia, W. A. C. Bennett, after meetings with the unions, invoked the Civil Defence Act which gave the province the power to take over and operate the Black Ball ferries and prohibited a strike against the service. The provincial government had only limited powers relating to the strike against the CPR's service as it was under the jurisdiction of the federal government because the CPR was a federally chartered company. Black Ball's operations, however, were subject to provincial labour laws. Consequently, both federal and provincial governments became deeply involved in the developing crisis. A number of attempts at arbitration and negotiation were made without success and on July 18th, after the CPR ships had been inactive for two months, the Black Ball fleet was finally struck by the Canada Merchant Service Guild and the National Association of Marine Engineers.

This action, despite the proclamation of the Civil Defence Act prohibiting it, was not entirely unanticipated. The government had for some time been undertaking studies of the problems of transportation to and from Vancouver Island and was prepared for the worst. Both CPR and Black Ball had been queried to see if they were interested in expanding and modernizing their service and both had declined. Black Ball was a relatively small company with limited resources and had already been pursuing a slow but steady improvement and expansion

When the *Princess Patricia* was withdrawn from the intercity
routes she was rebuilt for cruises to Alaska, replacing the 40-year-
old *Princess Louise*. Painted a gleaming white, the *Patricia* makes
a beautiful sight in a setting highlighted by the mountains and
glaciers of the Alaska Panhandle. In the scene on the right she is
berthed at Skagway, Alaska. — BOTH NICHOLAS MORANT, CPR

PRINCESS
PATRICIA

of its services. A greater effort however, was beyond its financial capabilities.

The CPR was in a somewhat different position. The postwar decline in revenues on most of its ferry operations was continuing into the late 1950's and the inefficiency of even the newest ferries became more apparent. In addition, the Company was already deeply committtted to other programs which involved tremendous capital investments. Specifically, all CPR railroad operations in Canada were being dieselized and modernized, and the Company was also investing heavily in its fledgling airline operations. Consequently, the CPR was not prepared to invest further capital in the ferry services, particularly since four new ships had already been built since the war. The conservative decisions of the past two decades which left the CPR fleet ill prepared for operations in the 1950's and 1960's had only contributed to a situation that made the ultimate collapse of the Coast Service nearly inevitable.

Realizing both the urgency and necessity of stabilizing and improving the reliability of the ferry services to Vancouver Island, the provincial government announced on the day of the Black Ball strike that a new government-owned ferry service would be established between the Saanich Peninsula and the B.C. mainland. It was not until July 24th that Black Ball employees finally obeyed the back to work orders and on the same day the federal government enacted legislation ending the CPR strike. Within a few days both ferry services were in operation, but the decision to establish government ferry system was firm. Negotiations between the companies and the unions continued for months and it was not until early the following year and after two short strikes that agreements were finally reached.

Sale of the Princesses

While the strike against the CPR Coast Service was in progress, the Company announced the sale of three of its remaining vessels. The *Yukon Princess*, inactive since 1956, was sold to the Westley Shipping Company, placed in Liberian registry and renamed *West Princess* and eventually *Rosita*. The two remaining freighting vessels in the fleet, the *Princess of Alberni* and the *Princess Norah*, were both sold to the Northland Navigation Company, which renamed the vessels *Nootka Prince* and *Canadian Prince* respectively. With the sale of the three ships, the CPR ended over half a century of freight and passenger operations to the small coastal communities of Vancouver Island and the north coast. Northland Navigation maintained the routes with the help of government subsidies. However, after only ten months, the former *Princess of Alberni* was sold to the Canadian Tugboat Company and her service to the west coast of Vancouver Island was discontinued. The vessel was rebuilt into the tug *Ocean Crown* and is still in use. The former *Princess Norah* was to remain in Northland ownership until October 1964, when she was stripped of her machin-

The British Columbia Ferries fleet continued to expand after the virtual demise of the CPR Coast Service. Seven new vessels were added for the major routes to Vancouver Island from the mainland and a number of smaller ferries were built to serve the Gulf Islands. The scene above shows the *Queen of Vancouver* leaving Active Pass. To accommodate a steady growth in traffic, all seven of these ferries were lengthened to the configuration shown.
— ROBERT D. TURNER

ery and towed to Kodiak, Alaska to become the "Beach-comber," a restaurant and dance hall.

Thus, by the end of the 1958 strike, the Princess fleet had only eight active vessels, and was facing the imminent inauguration of the provincial government's new ferry service. The CPR wasted little time in withdrawing its other vessels. In February 1959, the affectionately remembered night boats, the *Princess Joan* and *Princess Elizabeth*, were withdrawn from the Victoria-Vancouver service and at the same time the daylight service between Victoria and Seattle was also suspended. By the time the service was cancelled, business had declined and become so uneconomical that passengers on the night boats were often outnumbered by the crew. At 11:59 p.m., on Tuesday, February 24th, the *Princess Elizabeth* sailed from Vancouver while simultaneously the *Princess Joan* slipped away from the CPR pier in Victoria to mark the final departures of the CPR's "midnight boats." On the *Elizabeth*'s last run a quiet ceremony was held on board. As she crossed the Strait of Georgia, the ashes of Charles M. Anderson, engineering officer with the Princesses since 1928, were scattered over the waves.

With the conclusion of the night boat service, the *Elizabeth* made one last sailing to Seattle. She departed from Elliott Bay at 4:00 p.m. on February 25th, receiving a sad parting salute from the Washington State Ferries' M.V. *Quinault*, the tugs *Carol Foss* and *Shannon Foss*, and maritime photographer Joe Williamson's launch *Susan Jane*.

The retirement of the *Princess Joan* and *Princess Elizabeth* meant that no vessels were available for the Victoria to Port Angeles summer service. Consequently, the run was dropped from the CPR schedule until 1962 when, with the termination of the Victoria-Vancouver service, the *Princess Marguerite* was able to make one sailing a day to and from Port Angeles.

The government acted with remarkable speed, and in May 1959, keels were laid for the first two of its ferries, the M.V. *Sidney* and M.V. *Tsawwassen*. Both were scheduled to begin operations the following spring. The two new ferries were built in British Columbia and were based on the designs of the recently completed *Coho*, which entered the Black Ball's service between Victoria, Port Angeles and Seattle on December 29, 1959. They were fast and designed to minimize terminal time while providing a comfortable and convenient service. For the Princess fleet, the new vessels would ultimately be a death blow.

After the retirement of the *Joan* and *Elizabeth*, the *Princesses Marguerite* and *Patricia* continued to provide a daytime service between Victoria and Vancouver throughout the spring and summer of 1960. For the summer months, the Victoria-Seattle day service was also reactivated. However, by the time the traffic was peaking, the B.C. government ferries were in full operation between Swartz Bay, a few miles north of Sidney on Vancouver Island, and Tsawwassen on the mainland, about 20 miles south of Vancouver. The two government

In reality little more than a self-propelled transfer barge, the *Trailer Princess* was nonetheless an important addition to the Princess fleet in the 1960's. — ROBERT D. TURNER

The concept of the *Trailer Princess* was carried forward in the design of the *Carrier Princess*, specially built for carrying trucks and rail cars. — ROBERT D. TURNER

In reality . . .
The concept of . . .

vessels combined to offer eight return trips every day. The sailing time was only one hour and forty minutes, but with allowance made for the driving time to the new terminals and for waiting prior to departure, the actual Victoria to Vancouver travel time was likely to vary from three and one half to four hours. Overcrowding could sometimes result in a wait of an additional two hours for the next sailing. Like Black Ball, the B.C. Ferries did not offer automobile reservations. It seems somehow fitting that the Captain of the *Sidney*, Thomas Parkinson was once master of the CPR's *Princess Elaine* and *Princess of Alberni*.

While the CPR's retirement from the steamship business had been rapid in the 1950's, in the early 1960's it was precipitous. After only one summer of competition with the B.C. Ferries for the Victoria to Vancouver business, the CPR announced the end of its historic service. By the end of September, for the first time since the turn of the century there were no CPR vessels operating on the famed Triangle Route. In future years only the Victoria to Seattle summer service would be maintained.

On the heels of this service cut, the two 30-year-old Princesses, *Joan* and *Elizabeth*, were put up for sale on November 8, 1960. Like their predecessors on the night service, the *Alice* and *Adelaide*, they were acquired by Greek shipping interests. They were both sold to the Epirotiki Line for operation in the Mediterranean between Venice, Piraeus and Haifa. Before entering this new service the steamers were overhauled and modified in Greece for cruise operation. Like the *Princess Charlotte*'s, the funnels of each vessel were trunked into a single exhaust stack. The *Elizabeth* became the *Pegasus* and *Joan* the *Hermes*. In 1971 both were sold for accommodation ships for oil exploration crews in the North Sea and in 1974 the former *Princess Joan* was scrapped.

In 1961, the CPR operated the *Princess of Nanaimo*, *Princess of Vancouver* and *Princess Patricia* on the Vancouver-Nanaimo route while the *Princess Marguerite* continued the summer only Victoria-Port Angeles and Victoria-Seattle service. The *Louise* was busy on cruises to Alaska and the *Elaine* was laid up in Victoria.

Meanwhile, the new British Columbia Ferries service was expanding. Two vessels, larger and with more lounge space than the *Sidney* or *Tsawwassen* were ordered for delivery by the spring of 1962. These two ferries were christened the *City of Victoria* and the *City of Vancouver*. As if to seal the demise of the CPR Coast Service, the government announced late in 1961 that it was purchasing Black Ball Lines — Canada Limited's fleet for $6,700,000 and was planning to build two more ferries (which were named the *Queen of Esquimalt* and *Queen of Saanich*) so that an hourly service could be provided on the Horseshoe Bay to Departure Bay route.

The next summer, in 1962, the CPR operated both the *Princess Patricia* and *Princess Marguerite* between Victoria and Seattle, handling capacity crowds of tourists visiting

Engine Telegraph and . . .

Engine Telegraph and ship's wheel from the *Princess Marguerite.* — BOTH ROBERT D. TURNER

Ship's Wheel . . .

Washington and British Columbia while attending the Century 21 Seattle World's Fair. During this short busy season, the two Princesses carried 548,737 passengers and 17,863 automobiles. In addition, while tied up at Seattle each night, they provided sleeping accommodations for 27,542 visitors to the World's Fair.

The *Princess Louise* continued on the Alaska cruise service while on the Nanaimo to Vancouver route the *Princess of Nanaimo* and *Princess of Vancouver* were assisted by the *Princess Elaine,* which was brought out of apparent retirement to handle the heavy summer tourist traffic. The 1962 season was only a brief reprieve for the *Elaine,* which had been offered for sale on April 17th.

By the summer's end the fate of the Princesses was sealed. The Company announced that after October 1, 1962 only one vessel, the *Princess of Vancouver,* would be maintained on the Vancouver-Nanaimo route. The CPR claimed that it could not compete with the new government ferry service.

It was subsequently disclosed that the *Princess Patricia* would undergo a major reconstruction to prepare her for the Alaska cruise service, replacing the *Princess Louise,* which was put up for disposal. That winter the *Princess of Vancouver* was the only Princess in service on the Pacific coast.

Captain Williams retired as manager of the Coast Service in 1962 and was succeeded by Harry Tyson, a CPR employee since age 14. He had worked his way up through various positions with the Company. Tyson is credited with modernizing the operation of the fleet by increasing the vehicle capacity of the remaining ships and subsequently developing trailer truck ferries. He retired from the CPR in June 1973. His position was taken over by H. L. Thompson, former CPR regional manager of planning and analysis. In late 1974, James Yates was promoted to manager after service as marine superintendent of the Coast Service.

In February 1962 the *Princess of Nanaimo* was transferred to the CPR's Bay of Fundy service on the Atlantic coast and renamed *Princess of Acadia.* The *Princess Helene,* in service on that run since 1930, was retired with the arrival of the *Princess of Nanaimo* in the Maritimes. The former *Princess of Nanaimo* sailed on the Bay of Fundy only until 1971, when a new diesel-powered vessel also named *Princess of Acadia* was placed in service. The older vessel reverted to her original name. Later she was renamed, *Henry Osborne,* and used as an automobile transport to Newfoundland. However, after being badly damaged in a grounding, she was scrapped in 1974.

Soon after the *Princess of Nanaimo* sailed to the east coast, both the *Elaine* and the *Louise* were sold to American interests for use as restaurant vessels. The *Louise* was eventually taken to Long Beach, California where she is now a popular attraction on the waterfront, and the *Elaine* was moved to Seattle. Various attempts to develop the *Elaine* into a restaurant failed and she was eventually scrapped.

Each winter during the 1960's and early 1970's the *Princess Patricia*, shown in the distance at her berth, and the *Princess Marguerite*, seen entering the harbour, were tied up at Victoria, the light traffic not justifying their use. In the summer tourist season, however, they were back in service.
— NICHOLAS MORANT, CPR

By the 1970's, fast intercity travel on the B.C. coast had become the domain of the B.C. Ferries fleet and the Twin Otter aircraft of Airwest Airlines Ltd. and the jet airliners of other airline companies. — ROBERT D. TURNER

The Passing of the Princesses

By the 1970's, fast ...

In this way, the fleet stabilized for the next decade. The *Princess of Vancouver* provided three sailings a day across the Strait of Georgia on a year-round schedule. In April 1963, she was overhauled by Yarrows Ltd. in Victoria and, with the removal of some of the lounge space, her automobile capacity was increased to 170 vehicles. She was back in service in time for the summer tourist season. The conversion was successful enough to prompt the Company to rebuild the *Marguerite* in 1970.

During the summer months the *Marguerite* sailed to Seattle and Port Angeles while the *Patricia*, repainted with a white hull and superstructure in the colour scheme of the CPR's Empress liners, sailed on the popular cruises to Alaska. Additionally, for two winters, the *Patricia* was chartered to Princess Cruises Limited for luxury cruises between Los Angeles and Acapulco, Mexico. This service proved so popular that the operators eventually purchased a new vessel, the *Princess Italia*, to replace the *Patricia*.

As if to fill the void left by the retirement of the majority of the remaining Princesses, in 1963 the new B.C. Ferries were renamed as "Queens." The *Sidney* and *Tsawwassen* became the *Queen of Sidney* and *Queen of Tsawwassen* and the *City of Victoria* and *City of Vancouver* became the *Queen of Victoria* and *Queen of Vancouver*. The government ferry fleet continued to expand until, as of 1975, 25 vessels were in service with two new "super ferries" and a truck ferry on order.

Despite the CPR's nearly total withdrawal from the passenger steamship trade, certain aspects of its operation on the Coast were actually prospering, notably the movement of trucks and freight to Vancouver Island from the mainland. The increasing volume of trailer truck traffic to the Island had created an opportunity for a new type of freight ferry service. To handle this traffic the CPR acquired what was perhaps its most unusual addition to the Princess fleet of the post-war period. The new vessel was named the M.V. *Trailer Princess* and was placed in service in the summer of 1966 carrying semi-trailers between Vancouver and Vancouver Island.

The features that made this ship stand apart from the other Princesses were apparent both in her history and the functional design required for her utilitarian role. The *Trailer Princess* was originally built in 1944 as a tank landing ship (LST) for the United States Navy at the U.S. Navy Yard in Boston, Massachusetts. However, less than one month after commissioning as *LST 1003*, the vessel was rebuilt by the Bethlehem Key Highway Shipyard in Baltimore, Maryland into an auxiliary repair shop for servicing other landing craft. *LST 1003* became the U.S.S. *Coronis* and was designated *ARL-10*.

Ready for war service, the *Coronis* sailed for the Pacific Theatre early in 1945 to take part in preparations for the invasion of Okinawa. While providing vital repair services to all classes of landing craft, the vessel was subjected to numerous attacks by the Japanese and in April she was credited with assisting in the destruction of three Kamikaze aircraft. At the

end of hostilities, the *Coronis* was stationed with the occupation forces at Wakayama, Japan. In 1946, she was decommissioned and placed in reserve at Portland, Oregon, where she remained until her acquisition by the CPR.

The *Trailer Princess*'s conversion was patterned after the design of the open-decked truck ferry M.V. *Greg Yorke*, which was built in Vancouver in 1964 and operated in freight service under charter by the CPR on the Nanaimo to Vancouver run. These vessels were really little more than self-propelled barges with a small bridge and superstructure built over an open deck where the truck trailers and railroad freight cars were carried.

The success of the *Trailer Princess* on the truck and trailer service to Vancouver Island prompted the CPR to retain Jackson, Talbot & Associates Ltd. of Vancouver to prepare designs for a second, larger vessel. In June 1972, the keel for the new ferry was laid at the Burrard Dry Dock Company's North Vancouver yard. The 380-foot, 6,000 ton vessel was designed with a service speed of 18 knots and a capacity for 50 trailers, 30 railcars, or 150 private automobiles. It was intended that the ship be able to provide a variety of services depending on seasonal requirements and also act as a relief vessel for the *Princess of Vancouver*. To allow for a limited passenger service that the Company planned to initiate between Swartz Bay and Vancouver Harbour, three large passenger lounges, five staterooms and a cafeteria were incorporated in the design. Her 18 knot speed would permit the ferry to make three round trips a day between Vancouver and Swartz Bay, significantly increasing the overall efficiency of this operation.

Interestingly, by providing a limited passenger service on this route, the CPR had re-entered the passenger business between southern Vancouver Island and Vancouver on the route that had so long been suggested for the CPR to adopt. However, the passenger service was only a secondary feature of this operation and it was discontinued in 1974. At her launch, the new ferry was named *Carrier Princess*, reflecting her very utilitarian function. As the CPR's newest vessel on the Pacific coast, she entered service in June 1973 and has proved a most satisfactory, if unglamourous, vessel in her daily operations.

By this time, both the *Princess Patricia* and the *Princess Marguerite* were nearing their twenty-fifth year in service on the Coast. While neither vessel had been in continuous use, due to winter layoffs, their age and design were becoming increasing handicaps. The "*Pat*," on luxury Alaska cruise service, was more immune to the passing of time than was the *Marguerite*. Throughout the early 1970's, both crew wages and fuel costs increased dramatically due to general inflation. In the late summer of 1974, the Company released figures indicating a loss of nearly $250,000 for the *Marguerite*'s last three summer seasons.

Ever anxious to cut operating losses, the CPR announced at the time that the *Princess Marguerite* would not resume the Victoria-Seattle and Victoria-Port Angeles service in the sum-

With a backdrop of the Olympic Mountains of Washington, the *Princess Marguerite* crosses the Strait of Juan de Fuca from Port Angeles to Victoria. — ROBERT D. TURNER

mer of 1975. On the morning of September 15th, the beautiful *Princess Marguerite* sailed from Elliott Bay in Seattle for Victoria to end over 70 years of CPR service between the two cities. The last remaining portion of the Triangle Route was finally abandoned by the CPR. The *Princess Marguerite* was offered for sale soon after and was sold early in 1975 to the British Columbia government. The service had become so vital to Victoria businesses that the government felt justified in continuing the service and, if necessary, underwriting any losses.

The *Princess Marguerite* was given an extensive overhaul and returned to service in 1975. Harry Tyson, retired manager of the CPR's Coast Service, was hired to head a new company known as British Columbia Steamships (1975) Ltd., to operate the *Marguerite*. The venture was a success and at the end of the first season, an operating profit of approximately $100,000 was reported. Encouraged by the success of this venture, the government also acquired the Canadian National steamship *Prince George* which was for sale in Vancouver following her retirement from Alaska cruise service. The *Prince George* was to operate on cruises along the coast to the smaller British Columbia communities which are often bypassed by the larger cruise vessels. However, following the December 1975 election, the new government cancelled the project in an austerity move and sold the *Prince George* for use as a restaurant vessel. The fate of the *Marguerite* was also briefly in question, but as no suitable private operator could be found the vessel was retained in service by the government.

As the CPR all but withdrew from its traditional services, it expanded briefly freight operations by chartering the rail car ferry *Incan St. Laurent* in 1975 to operate between New Westminster and Whittier, Alaska. This vessel is similar in concept to the *Carrier Princess* but features a fully enclosed car deck. She was built by Burrard Dry Dock of North Vancouver and had originally been intended for service in Quebec by Incan Marine Ltd. However, the planned service was temporarily cancelled and the vessel was placed in weekly service by the CPR for the Alaska Trainship Corporation of Seattle transporting materials for the trans-Alaska pipeline project.

After three-quarters of a century, the CPR's Coast Service is all but a memory to travellers. Neither the *Princess Patricia* nor the *Princess of Vancouver* can continue to operate indefinitely and any replacements that may be built someday would be far different ships from those traditionally associated with the CPR service.

Princesses still sail on the Coast, but with the passing of the *Marguerite* into government ownership, the era of the CPR's intercity steamships — the "pocket liners" of the Princess fleet — came to a close. Changing economics and lifestyles reflected in the demands of an impatient, automobile-oriented society made their passing inevitable.

It was the tourists that kept the *Princess Marguerite* in operation into the 1970's. Victoria, with its many attractions was an ideal destination for Americans wishing a one- or two-day vacation in Canada. — ROBERT D. TURNER

When the *Princess Marguerite* sailed for Seattle during the last weeks of September 1974 it seemed almost certain that the end had come at last as the CPR announced cancellation of all of her services. — ROBERT D. TURNER

It was the tourists . . .
When the Princess Marguerite *sailed . . .*

Fortunately the *Marguerite* was purchased and refitted for continued operation by the B.C. government under a Crown corporation, British Columbia Steamships (1975) Ltd. Her first sailing under new ownership took place on June 1, 1975, marking the beginning of a promising new career for the veteran coastal liner. — ROBERT D. TURNER

NOTES ON SOURCES
OF REFERENCE

A VARIETY of references, both general and specific, was consulted in the preparation of this book. In a general capacity, two volumes were of particular value: *Lewis and Dryden's Marine History of the Pacific Northwest* (1961) by E. W. Wright, and *The H. W. McCurdy Marine History of the Pacific Northwest* (1966) edited by Gordon Newell. These books, the first dealing with early shipping, before 1895, and the second covering the period from 1895 to 1965, contain a wealth of information on the personalities, vessels and historical events of the CPN and CPR and their competitors. Another book, *The Princess Story* (1974) by Norman Hacking and W. Kaye Lamb released in 1975 is a valuable reference, but was received too late to be a principal source for this account.

Other books useful for general reference include: *Personality Ships of British Columbia* (1969) by Ruth Greene; *The Night Boat* (1968) by George W. Hilton; *Canadian Pacific Afloat 1883-1968: A Short History* (1968) by George Musk; *Pacific Steamboats* (1958) and *Pacific Coastal Liners* (1959), both by Gordon Newell and Joe Williamson; *Vancouver Island's West Coast* (1962) by George Nicholson; *British Columbia; a History* (1958) by Margaret Ormsby; and *Whistle Up the Inlet, The Union Steamship Story* (1974) by Gerald Rushton. The journals *Harbour and Shipping, The Engineer, Engineering, Railway and Marine World*, and *Engineering News* were also helpful in yielding general information on the ships and technological developments they incorporated.

In providing statistical details on the vessels of the CPN and CPR and in compiling the fleet list at the end of the book, *Lloyd's Register of Shipping*, an annual listing of merchant ships, their builders, dimensions and engine types, was used as a primary source. Additional details were obtained from Musk's history of the Canadian Pacific's steamship services, and from Wright's and Newell's Pacific Northwest marine histories, all mentioned previously. Official records of the CPR were also consulted wherever possible.

Newspapers, including *The Daily Colonist* (Victoria), *The Province* (Vancouver), *The Vancouver Sun, The Victoria Daily Times, The Vancouver Daily World, The Vancouver News Herald, The Seattle Argus, The Seattle Times* and *The Seattle Post Intelligencer*, were extremely useful, particularly in chronicling specific events and incidents in CPN and CPR history, such as the disputes between Captain Irving and Vancouver's mayors, the sinking of the *Premier*, the rate war with the Puget Sound Navigation Company, and the *Islander* and *Princess Sophia* disasters. With their detailed, first-hand, often colourfully written accounts of such events, they add a personal quality to any history. The location of newspaper references was facilitated by use of the B.C. Newspaper Index, available on microfilm in the major B.C. libraries. Those wishing to obtain more detailed information on particular events mentioned in the book are referred to this source. However, it should be used only as a general guide, since it does not list every article on a given topic, and its coverage is sporadic.

Timetables, annual reports, brochures and advertising literature put out by the CPR and rival steamship companies were consulted throughout. These were obtained from the Provincial Archives and from private collections and many were reproduced in the newspapers.

The drawings appearing in this book were prepared by the author from original blueprints and plans. Exceptions are the drawings of the first *Princess Louise*, the *Islander*, the *Princess Elaine*, the *Princess Victoria* (as rebuilt) and the *Princess of Nanaimo*, which were prepared from photographs and known dimensions of the ships. Frequent reference was made to period photographs in researching each ship.

References of particular value in writing Chapter I on early shipping in the Pacific Northwest and the Canadian Pacific Navigation Company include the following books and articles: *The Steamboat Landing on Elliott Bay* (1962) and *The Sound of Steamers* (1965), both by Roland Carey; *Paddlewheels on the Frontier* (Vol. 1 — 1967 and Vol. 2 — 1971) by Art Downs; *Early Marine History of British Columbia* (1934) by Norman Hacking; *San Francisco Bay Ferryboats* (1967) by George H. Harlan; *Klondike* (1958) by Pierre Berton; *Gold Rush Narrow Gauge* (1969) by Cy Martin; and *S.S. Beaver: The Ship that Saved the West* (1970) by Derek Pethick. Of these, the first five were also used as references for Chapter II on the formation of the CPR's British Columbia Coast Service.

Other reference sources for Chapter II were: *Sternwheelers, Sandbars and Switchbacks* (1973) by E. L. Affleck; *The Empress of Victoria* (1968) by Godfrey Holloway; *Pacific Steamboats* (1958) by Gordon Newell and Joe Williamson; and *Vancouver Island Railroads* (1973) by Robert D. Turner.

For Chapter III, describing the "Great Rate War," M. McD. Duff's "Problems of Steamship Operation" (1937), Robert C. Leithead's "The Canadian Pacific Tri-City Route" (1967-68), Gordon Newell's *The Green Years* (a biography of Joshua Green) (1965), and *History of the Canadian National Railways* (1973) by G. R. Stevens were consulted. Leithead's article was particularly useful in chronicling the various schedule changes mentioned in Chapter II and succeeding chapters.

Sources of information for Chapter IV on the growth of the Princess fleet include, in addition to the articles by Duff and Leithead listed for the previous chapter: *The Land of Evangeline* (1947) produced by the Dominion Atlantic Railway; *Warships of World War I; No. 4 — Miscellaneous* (no date) by H. M. Le Fleming; and "B.C.'s Worst Marine Disaster" (about the sinking of the *Princess Sophia*) (1973) by Louise McFadden.

In writing Chapter V on the Princess ships from the 1920's to the end of World War II, the following books and articles were referred to: *Canadian Pacific Facts and Figures* (1937 and 1946) produced by the CPR; "The Race I Remember" (1971) by L. M. Stadum describing the *City of Victoria*; "A Princess Carries Royalty" (1968) by H. D. Halkatt; *Navies of the Second World War: German Submarines 1* (1965) by H. T. Lenton (for details on the submarine which sank the *Princess Marguerite*); "Princess Marguerite Went Down in Flames" (1965) and "Princess Kathleen . . . served bravely in war and peace" (1967) by T. W. Paterson; *History of the Canadian National Railways* (1973) by G. R. Stevens; and an unpublished address to a CPR Educational Group by Captain T. Rippon of the CPR on the "British Columbia Coast Steamship Service: Coastwise sailings, Steamers, Facilities etc." (December 12, 1939), made available by the Vancouver office of the CPR. Various CPR news releases on the *Princess Marguerite* and *Princess Kathleen* at war were also consulted. In his articles Paterson quotes the official CPR wartime history of these ships. Clippings from the CPR's Staff Bulletin provided details on the *Princess Norah*'s icebound winter sailing to Alaska.

References for Chapter VI on the fate of the CPR Coast Service in the post-war years include: The *Dogwood Fleet* (1967) by H. L. Cadieux and Garth Griffiths (on the B.C. Ferries); *The Evergreen Fleet* (1971) by Harre Demoro (on the Washington State Ferries); and *The Queens of British Columbia* (1974) by Peter Favalle (on the B.C. Ferries).

It is hoped that those interested in delving deeper into the history of shipping on the Pacific coast or in exploring particular aspects of the CPR Coast Service and its history will find this source discussion and the bibliography which follows helpful.

BIBLIOGRAPHY

Affleck, E. L. 1973. *Sternwheelers, Sandbars and Switchbacks.* (Revised Edition). The Alexander Nicolls Press, Vancouver, B.C.

Berton, Pierre. 1958. *Klondike.* McClelland and Stewart Limited, Toronto, Ont.

Cadieux, H. L. & Griffiths, Garth. 1967. *Dogwood Fleet.* Cadieux and Griffiths Ltd., Nanaimo, B.C.

Canadian Pacific Railway, General Publicity Department. (Editors). 1937. *Canadian Pacific Facts and Figures.* Canadian Pacific Foundation. CPR, Montreal, P.Q.

Canadian Pacific Railway, Department of Public Relations. (Editors). 1946. *Canadian Pacific Facts and Figures.* (Revised Edition). Canadian Pacific Foundation Library. CPR, Montreal, P.Q.

Carey, Roland. 1962. *The Steamboat Landing on Elliott Bay.* Alderbrook Publishing Company, Seattle, Wash.

Carey, Roland. 1965. *The Sound of Steamers.* Alderbrook Publishing Company, Seattle, Wash.

Demoro, Harre. 1971. *The Evergreen Fleet.* Golden West Books, San Marino, Calif.

Dominion Atlantic Railway. 1947. *The Land of Evangeline.* Dominion Atlantic Railway Company, Halifax, N.S.

Downs, Art. 1967. *Paddlewheels on the Frontier.* Volume 1. B.C. Outdoors Magazine, Cloverdale, B.C.

Downs, Art. 1971. *Paddlewheels on the Frontier.* Volume 2. B.C. Outdoors Magazine, Cloverdale, B.C.

Duff, M. McD. 1937. "Problems of Steamship Operation." In: CPR General Publicity Department (Editors). *Factors in Railway and Steamship Operations.* Canadian Pacific Foundation Library. CPR, Montreal, P.Q.

Favalle, Peter. 1974. *The Queens of British Columbia.* Discovery Magazine Ltd., Vancouver, B.C.

Greene, Ruth. 1969. *Personality Ships of British Columbia.* Marine Tapestry Publications Limited, West Vancouver, B.C.

Hacking, Norman. 1934. *Early Marine History of British Columbia.* Unpublished Graduating Essay. University of British Columbia, Vancouver, B.C.

Hacking, Norman R. and Lamb, W. K. 1974. *The Princess Story, A Century of West Coast Shipping.* Mitchell Press Ltd., Vancouver, B.C.

Halkatt, Capt. H. D. 1968. "A Princess Carries Royalty." *The Daily Colonist (Islander)*, July 21, 1968: p. 2, Victoria, B.C.

Harlan, George H. 1967. *San Francisco Bay Ferryboats.* Howell-North Books, Berkeley, Calif.

Hearn, George and Wilkie, David. 1966. *"The Cordwood Limited" A History of the Victoria & Sidney Railway.* B.C. Railway Historical Assoc., Victoria, B.C.

Hilton, George W. 1968. *The Night Boat.* Howell-North Books, Berkeley, Calif.

Holloway, Godfrey. 1968. *The Empress of Victoria.* Pacifica Productions Ltd., Victoria, B.C.

Le Fleming, H. M. (no date). *Warships of World War 1: No. 4 — Miscellaneous.* Ian Allan Ltd., London, U.K.

Leithead, Robert C. 1967-68. "The Canadian Pacific Tri-City Route." *The Sea Chest,* Vol. 1 (Nos. 1-3).

Lenton, H. T. 1965. *Navies of the Second World War: German Submarines 1.* Macdonald & Co., London, U.K.

McFadden, Louise. 1973. "B.C.'s Worst Marine Disaster." In: Downs, Art (Editor). *Pioneer Days in British Columbia.* Foremost Publishing Company Ltd., Surrey, B.C., pp. 104-111.

Martin, Cy. 1969. *Gold Rush Narrow Gauge.* Trans-Anglo Books, Los Angeles, Calif.

Musk, George. 1957. *A Short History and Fleet List of the Canadian Pacific Ocean Steamships 1891-1957.* Canadian Pacific Railway and the World Ship Society, London, U.K.

Musk, George. 1968. *Canadian Pacific Afloat 1883-1958. A Short History.* Canadian Pacific Railway, London, U.K.

Newell, Gordon. 1965. *The Green Years.* Superior Publishing Company, Seattle, Wash. (A bibliography of Joshua Green).

Newell, Gordon (Editor). 1966. *The H. W. McCurdy Marine History of the Pacific Northwest.* Superior Publishing Company, Seattle, Wash.

Newell, Gordon and Williamson, Joe. 1958. *Pacific Steamboats.* Superior Publishing Company, Seattle, Wash.

Newell, Gordon and Williamson, Joe. 1959. *Pacific Coastal Liners.* Superior Publishing Company, Seattle, Wash.

Nicholson, George. 1962. *Vancouver Island's West Coast.* Published by the author, Victoria, B.C.

Ormsby, Margaret. 1958. *British Columbia; a History.* Macmillan Company of Vancouver Ltd., Vancouver, B.C.

Paterson, T. W. 1965. "Princess Marguerite Went Down in Flames." *The Daily Colonist (Islander),* October 31, 1965: pp. 4-5, Victoria, B.C.

Paterson, T. W. 1967. "Princess Kathleen ... served bravely in war and peace." *The Daily Colonist (Islander),* October 8, 1967: pp. 10-11, Victoria, B.C.

Pethick, Derek. 1970. *S.S. Beaver: The Ship that Saved the West.* Mitchell Press Limited, Vancouver, B.C.

Rushton, Gerald. 1969. "Union Steamship Company of British Columbia, A Short History." In: Greene, Ruth. *Personality Ships of British Columbia.* Marine Tapestry Publications Limited, West Vancouver, B.C.

Rushton, Gerald. 1974. *Whistle Up the Inlet, The Union Steamship Story.* J. J. Douglas Ltd., North Vancouver, B.C.

Stadum, Lloyd M. 1971. "The Race I Remember." *The Sea Chest,* Vol. 4 (No. 3).

Stevens, G. R. 1973. *History of the Canadian National Railways.* Collier-Macmillan Canada Ltd., Toronto, Ont.

Turner, Robert D. 1973. *Vancouver Island Railroads.* Golden West Books, San Marino, Calif.

Wright, E. W. 1961. *Lewis and Dryden's Marine History of the Pacific Northwest.* Antiquarian Press, Ltd., New York, N.Y.

APPENDIX I

SHIPS OF
THE PRINCESS FLEET

1. Vessels taken over by the Canadian Pacific Railway from the Canadian Pacific Navigation Company in 1901.

NOTE: Ships are listed in order of acquisition.

*REGISTERED DIMENSIONS: Reported in Lloyd's Register of Shipping or where indicated (B.P.) the between perpendiculars dimensions as tabulated in Lloyds.

**KEY TO ABBREVIATIONS: Cy., cylinder(s); Tr. Exp., Triple Expansion; Quad Exp., Quadruple Expansion; Sc., screw(s).

NAME	YEAR BUILT	BUILDER	LENGTH/ BREADTH/ DEPTH*	GROSS TONS	ENGINES/TYPE OR NO. SCREWS/ BORE/STROKE**	YEARS OF CPN/CPR SERVICE; DISPOSITION
Princess Louise (I) (ex Olympia)	1869	J. Inglis, New York, N.Y.	180/30/13	932	1 Cy./Sidewheeler/ 46/132	1879 (HBC), 1883-1906 1906 Marpole MacDonald 1908 Vancouver Dredging & Salvage Co. (barge)
R. P. Rithet	1882	A. Watson, Victoria, B.C.	117/33/8	817	Two 1 Cy./ Sternwheeler	1882 (Irving), 1883-1909 1909 Terminal Steam Navigation Co. as Baramba
Maude	1872	Burr & Smith San Juan I., Wash.	113/21/9	175	Compound/1 Sc./ 9, 18/20	1883-1903 (orig. a sidewheeler) 1903 B.C. Salvage Co. 1914 scrapped
Yosemite	1862	J. W. North, San Francisco, Calif.	282/35/13	1525	1 Cy./Sidewheeler/ 57/132	1883-1906 1906 T. Grant (U.S.A.) 1909 wrecked
Charmer	1887	Union Iron Works, San Francisco, Calif.	200/42/13	1044	Tr. Exp./1 Sc./ 23,34,56/36	1887-1935 1935 sold for scrap
Islander	1888	Napier, Shanks & Bell, Glasgow, Scotland	240/42/14	1495	Two Tr. Exp./ 2 Sc./20,31,52/36	1888-1901 1901 sank
Danube	1869	J. Elder & Co., Glasgow, Scotland	216/28/21	887	Compound/1 Sc./ 28,50/30	1890-1905 1905 B.C. Salvage Co. as Salvor 1918 J. P. Davies 1920 A. Menchaca as Nervion

NAME	YEAR BUILT	BUILDER	LENGTH/ BREADTH/ DEPTH*	GROSS TONS	ENGINES/TYPE OR NO. SCREWS/ BORE/STROKE**	YEARS OF CPN/CPR SERVICE; DISPOSITION
Transfer	1893	A. Watson, New Westminster, B.C.	122/24/5	264	Two 1 Cy./Stern-wheeler	1893-1909 1909 R. Jardine, scrapped
Tees	1893	Richardson, Duck & Co., Stockton, England	165/26/11	679	Tr. Exp./1 Sc./ 16.5,27,44/30	1897-1923 1923 Pacific Salvage Co. as *Salvage Queen* 1933 Island Tug & Barge Co. as *Island Queen* 1937 scrapped
Queen City	1894	R. Brown, Vancouver, B.C.	116/27/10	391	Compound/1 Sc./ 11,30/22	1897-1916 1916 scrapped
Beaver	1898	Victoria, B.C.	140/28/5	545	Two 1 Cy./Stern-wheeler	1898-1919 1919 B.C. Provincial Govt.
Willapa (ex *General Miles*)	1891	Astoria, Oregon	136/22/10	373	Compound/1 Sc./ 26,32/28	1898-1902 1902 Bellingham Bay Transportation Co. – *Bellingham* 1912 Puget Sound Nav. Co. 1919 laid up 1950 burnt out
Amur	1890	Strand Slipway Co., Sunderland, England	216/28/11	907	Tr. Exp./1 Sc./ 20,33,54/33	1900-1911 1911 Coastwise S.S. & Barge Co. 1924 A. Berquist as *Famous* 1926 wrecked 1929 scrapped
Otter	1900	CPN Co. Ltd., Victoria, B.C.	128/24/11	366	Compound/1 Sc./ 12,24/18	1900-1931 1931 Gibson Bros. Ltd. 1937 lost by fire

2. Vessels built for or purchased by the CPR after 1901.

   (A) *Passenger Vessels*

NAME	YEAR BUILT	BUILDER	LENGTH/ BREADTH/ DEPTH*	GROSS TONS	ENGINES/TYPE OR NO. SCREWS/ BORE/STROKE**	YEARS OF CPN/CPR SERVICE; DISPOSITION
Princess May (ex *Cass, Arthur, Ningchow, Hating*)	1888	Hawthorn, Leslie & Co. Ltd., Newcastle, England	249/33/18	1394 *1717*	Two Tr. Exp./ 2 Sc./19,30,50/33	1901-1919 1906 superstructure *rebuilt* 1919 *Princess May* S.S. Co. early 1930's scuttled
Princess Victoria	1902	C. S. Swan & Hunter, Ltd., Newcastle, England	300/40/15 *300/58/15*	1943 *3167*	Two Tr. Exp./ 2 Sc./26,40,43 & 43/33	1903-1952 1929 *rebuilt* as auto ferry 1952 Tahsis & Co. (barge) 1953 sank

NAME	YEAR BUILT	BUILDER	LENGTH/ BREADTH/ DEPTH*	GROSS TONS	ENGINES/TYPE OR NO. SCREWS/ BORE/STROKE**	YEARS OF CPN/CPR SERVICE; DISPOSITION
Princess Beatrice	1903	B.C. Marine Rwy Co., Ltd., Esquimalt, B.C.	193/37/15	1290	Tr. Exp./1 Sc./ 18,30 & 50/36	1903-1928 1928 sold for scrap
Joan	1892	Albion Iron Works Co., Ltd., Victoria, B.C.	177/30/11	821	Compound, 4 Cy./ 2 Sc./16,32,24	1905-1914 1892 E&N Rwy 1905 CPR 1914 Terminal Steam Navigation Co. as *Ballena* 1920 scrapped
City of Nanaimo	1891	McAlpin & Allen, Vancouver, B.C.	159/32/9	761	Compound, 2 Cy./ 1 Sc./14,28/18	1905-1912 1897 E&N Rwy 1905 CPR 1912 Terminal Steam Navigation Co. as *Bowena* 1922 Union Steamship Co. as *Cheam* 1926 scrapped
Princess Royal	1907	B.C. Marine Rwy Co., Ltd., Esquimalt, B.C.	228/40/17	1997	Tr. Exp./1 Sc./ 22,35,60/36	1907-1933 1933 scrapped
Princess Charlotte	1908	Fairfield Co., Ltd., Glasgow, Scotland	330/47/24	3926	Two Tr. Exp./2 Sc./24,38,43 & 43/ 33	1908-1949 1949 Typaldas Bros. 1950 named *Mediterranean* 1965 scrapped
Princess Adelaide	1910	Fairfield Co., Ltd., Glasgow, Scotland	290/46/15	3061	Tr. Exp./1 Sc./ 27,42,48 & 48/39	1910-1949 1949 Typaldas Bros. as *Angelika* 1967 scrapped
Princess Mary	1910	Bow, McLachlan & Co., Ltd., Paisley, Scotland	210/40/14 *248/40/14*	1697 2155	Two Tr. Exp. / 2 Sc./16,27,44/30	1910-1952 1912 *lengthened* at Esquimalt 1952 Union Steamship Co. as *Bulk Carrier No. 2* (barge) 1954 sank – but part of superstructure still exists as a restaurant in Victoria
Princess Alice	1911	Swan, Hunter & Wigham Richardson, Ltd., Newcastle, England	291/46/14	3099	Tr. Exp./1 Sc./ 27,42,48 & 48/39	1911-1949 1949 Typaldas Bros. as *Aegaeon* 1966 wrecked

NAME	YEAR BUILT	BUILDER	LENGTH/ BREADTH/ DEPTH*	GROSS TONS	ENGINES/TYPE OR NO. SCREWS/ BORE/STROKE**	YEARS OF CPN/CPR SERVICE; DISPOSITION
Princess Patricia (I) (ex *Queen Alexandra*)	1902	W. Denny & Bros., Dumbarton, Scotland	270/32/12	1158 orig. 665	Three Steam Turbines/3 Sc.	1912-1937 1937 scrapped
Princess Sophia	1911	Bow, Mc-Lachlan & Co., Ltd., Paisley, Scotland	245/44/24	2320	Tr. Exp./1 Sc./ 22,37 & 60/36	1911-1918 1918 sank
Princess Maquinna	1912	B.C. Marine Rwy Co., Ltd., Esquimalt, B.C.	233/38/14	1777	Tr. Exp./1 Sc./ 20,33,54/36	1912-1953 1953 Union Steamship Co. as *Taku* (barge) 1962 scrapped
Princess Irene	1914	W. Denny & Bros., Dumbarton, Scotland	395/54/28	5900	Four Steam Turbines/2 Sc.	1914-1915 1915 destroyed by explosion at Sheerness, U.K.; never reached Pacific coast
Princess Margaret	1914	W. Denny & Bros., Dumbarton, Scotland	395/54/28	5934	Four Steam Turbines/2 Sc.	1914-1919 1919 British Admiralty 1929 scrapped; never reached Pacific coast
Island Princess (ex *Daily*)	1913	Macdowell, Tacoma, Wash.	116/25/8	339	Tr. Exp./1 Sc./ 12,18 & 29/18	1918-1930 1930 Gulf Islands Ferry Co. as *Cy Peck* 1961 B.C. Ferries 1966 J. H. Todd & Sons, Ltd. as floating fishing camp 1975 private use, Saltspring Island
Princess Louise (II)	1921	Wallace Shipbuilding & Dry Dock Co., Ltd., N. Vancouver, B.C.	317/48/35	4032	Tr. Exp./1 Sc./ 28,43,50 & 50/39	1921-1965 laid up Fall 1962-65 1965 sold for restaurant at Long Beach, Calif.
Motor Princess	1923	Yarrows, Ltd., Esquimalt, B.C.	165/44/9	1243	12 Cy. Diesel/ 2 Sc.	1923-1955 1955 Gulf Islands Ferry Co. 1961 B.C. Ferries, later renamed *Pender Queen* (still in service)
Princess Kathleen	1925	John Brown & Co., Ltd., Clydebank, Scotland	350/60/17	5875	Four Steam Turbines/2 Sc.	1925-1952 1952 sank

NAME	YEAR BUILT	BUILDER	LENGTH/ BREADTH/ DEPTH*	GROSS TONS	ENGINES/TYPE OR NO. SCREWS/ BORE/STROKE**	YEARS OF CPN/CPR SERVICE; DISPOSITION
Princess Marguerite (I)	1925	John Brown & Co., Ltd., Clydebank, Scotland	350/60/17	5875	Four Steam Turbines/2 Sc.	1925-1942 1942 torpedoed, sunk
Princess Elaine	1928	John Brown & Co., Ltd., Clydebank, Scotland	291/48/13	2027	Three Steam Turbines/3 Sc.	1927-1963 1963 sold for restaurant vessel 1976 scrapped in Seattle
Princess Norah	1929	Fairfield Co., Ltd., Glasgow, Scotland	250/48/23	2731	Tr. Exp./1 Sc./ 24,38,45 & 45/36	1928-1958 1955-57 operated jointly with CNR as *Queen of the North* 1958 Northland Navigation Co. as *Canadian Prince* 1964 *Beachcomber* – restaurant at Kodiak, Alaska
Princess Elizabeth	1930	Fairfield Co., Ltd., Glasgow, Scotland	353/52/25	5251	Two Quad. Exp./2 Sc./16,23,33,48/33	1930-1960 1960 Epirotiki Line as *Pegasus* 1971 L. Dupes & Assoc. as *Highland Queen*
Princess Joan	1930	Fairfield Co., Ltd., Glasgow, Scotland	353/52/25	5251	Two Quad. Exp./2 Sc./16,23,33,48/33	1930-1960 1960 Epirotiki Line as *Hermes* 1971 L. Dupes & Assoc. 1974 scrapped
Princess Helene	1930	W. Denny & Bros., Ltd., Dumbarton, Scotland	320/51/24	4055	Six Steam Turbines/2 Sc.	1930-1963 Bay of Fundy service, Atlantic coast 1963 Marvic Navigation Inc. as *Helene, Carina II,* and *Carina*
Princess Marguerite (II)	1948	Fairfield Co., Ltd., Glasgow, Scotland	356/56/16	5911	Two Steam Turbines, turbo-electric/2 Sc.	1948-1975 1975 B.C. Government B.C. Steamships (1975) Ltd. (still in service)
Princess Patricia (II)	1948	Fairfield Co., Ltd., Glasgow, Scotland	356/56/16	5911 later *6062*	Two Steam Turbines, turbo-electric/2 Sc.	1948-1976 (still in service) 1962 *rebuilt*
Princess of Nanaimo	1951	Fairfield Co., Ltd., Glasgow, Scotland	358/62/14	6787	Four Steam Turbines/2 Sc.	1951-1974 1963-71 *Princess of Acadia*, Bay of Fundy service 1972 *Henry Osborne* 1974 scrapped
Princess of Alberni (ex *Pomare*)	1945	Martinolich Ship Building Co., San Francisco, Calif.	139/33/16	601	Two Diesel/2 Sc.	1953-1958 1958 Northland Navigation Co. as *Nootka Prince* 1959 Crown Zellerbach Canada Ltd. as *Ocean Crown* (still in service)

NAME	YEAR BUILT	BUILDER	LENGTH/ BREADTH/ DEPTH*	GROSS TONS	ENGINES/TYPE OR NO. SCREWS/ BORE/STROKE**	YEARS OF CPN/CPR SERVICE; DISPOSITION
Princess of Vancouver	1955	A. Stephen & Sons, Ltd., Glasgow, Scotland	416/66/15	5554	Two Diesel/2 Sc.	1955-1976 (still in service)
Princess of Acadia	1971	St. John Ship Building & Dry Dock Co. Ltd., St. John, New Brunswick	440/66/40 (B.P.)	10109	Four Diesel/2 Sc.	1971-1976 Bay of Fundy, Atlantic coast (still in service)
(B) *Freight Only Vessels*						
Princess Ena	1907	Garston Graving Dock & Ship Building Co., Ltd., Garston, England	195/38/15	1368	Compound/1 Sc./20,43/30	1907-1931 1931 F. Millerd 1938 scrapped
Nootka (ex *Canadian Adventurer, Emperor of Port McNicoll*)	1919	Port Arthur Shipbuilding Co., Port Arthur, Ont.	251/44/20	2069	Tr. Exp./1 Sc./ 20,33 & 50/40	1926-1950 1950 Enrique Echecopar (Peru) as *Iquitos* 1957 Comercio Amazonas (Peru) as *Nootka*
Yukon Princess (ex *Ottawa Parapet, Island Connector*)	1946	Pacific Dry Dock Co., Vancouver, B.C.	214/37/20 (B.P.)	1334	Tr. Exp./1 Sc./ 14,23, & 38/27	1950-1958 1958 Westly Shipping Co., as *West Princess, Rosita*
(C) *Truck/Trailer Ferry Vessels*						
Trailer Princess (ex *LST 1003, USS Coronis*)	1944	U.S. Navy Yard, Baltimore, Md.	308/57/19	2689	Two Diesel/2 Sc.	1966-1976 (still in service)
Carrier Princess	1973	Burrard Drydock Co., N. Van- couver, B.C.	365/66/24 (B.P.)	4353	Two Diesel/2 Sc.	1973-1976 (still in service)
(D) *Tugs*						
Czar	1897	T. H. Trahey, Victoria, B.C.	101/22/11	152	Quad. Exp./1 Sc./ 11,14,20,31/24	1905-1914 1902 E&N Rwy 1914 G. F. Payne 1918 Imperial Munition Board 1919 Pacific Construction Co. – scrapped

NAME	YEAR BUILT	BUILDER	LENGTH/ BREADTH/ DEPTH*	GROSS TONS	ENGINES/TYPE OR NO. SCREWS/ BORE/STROKE**	YEARS OF CPN/CPR SERVICE; DISPOSITION
Nanoose	1908	B.C. Marine Rwy Co., Ltd., Esquimalt, B.C.	115/24/15	305	Compound/1 Sc./ 17,40/27	1908-1946 1946 sold for breakwater
Qualicum (ex *Colima*)	1904	Heafie & Levy, Philadelphia, Pa.	96/22/12	200	Compound/1 Sc./ 16,32/24	1911-1946 1946 sold for breakwater
Nitinat (ex *William Jolliffe*)	1885	J. Readhead & Co. S. Shields, England	149/26/14	332	Compound/1 Sc./ 30,60/30	1914-1924 1924 Pacific Salvage Co. as *Salvage Chief* 1925 wrecked
Dola	1907	Wallace Shipbuilding & Drydock Co., Ltd. N. Vancouver, B.C.	96/22/11	176	Tr. Exp./1 Sc./ 10,17 & 28/20	1917-1933 1933 *Dola* Tug Co. 1953 sank
Kyuquot (ex. *St. Florence*)	1919	J. Crichton & Co., Chester, England	135/29/14	419	Tr. Exp./1 Sc./ 18,28 & 48/28	1924-1962 1962 sold for scrap

APPENDIX II

SHIPS OF THE PUGET SOUND NAVIGATION COMPANY INVOLVED IN THE 1907-09 RATE WAR

NOTE: All vessels registered at Port Townsend, Washington.

*REGISTERED DIMENSIONS: Reported in Lloyd's Register of Shipping.

**KEY TO ABBREVIATIONS: Cy., cylinder(s) ; Tr. Exp., Triple Expansion; Sc., screw(s).

NAME	YEAR BUILT	BUILDER	LENGTH/ BREADTH/ DEPTH*	GROSS TONS	ENGINES/TYPE OR NO. SCREWS/ BORE/STROKE**	NOTES AND DISPOSITION
Rosalie	1893	Hay & Wright, Alameda, Calif.	137/27/10	319	Compound/1 Sc./ 15, 34/24	Wooden construction. Operated by Nickel Ferry Co. (San Francisco Bay) ; sold to Alaska Steamship Co.; then to PSN, burned at Seattle, 1918.
Chippewa	1900	Craig Ship Building Co., Toledo, Ohio	200/34/20	996	Tr. Exp./1 Sc./ 20,32.5,55/30	Steel construction. Built for Arnold Transportation Co. (Great Lakes) as coal burner; to PSN 1907, converted to oil, rebuilt to auto ferry 1926, dieselized 1932; to Washington State Ferries, condemned, 1964; burned at Oakland, 1968.
Iroquois	1901	Craig Ship Building Co., Toledo, Ohio	214/34/21	1169	Tr. Exp./1 Sc./ 21,34,58/30	Steel construction. Built for Arnold Transportation Co. (Great Lakes) as a coal burner; to PSN 1907, converted to oil; sold 1920 to Chicago & South Haven SS Co. (Great Lakes) ; repurchased by PSN 1928 and rebuilt as ferry, 1952 rebuilt to diesel freight vessel, scrapped 196?.

NAME	YEAR BUILT	BUILDER	LENGTH/ BREADTH/ DEPTH*	GROSS TONS	ENGINES/TYPE OR NO. SCREWS/ BORE/STROKE**	NOTES AND DISPOSITION
Whatcom (ex *Majestic*)	1901	E. W. Heath, Everett, Wash.	169/30/14	657	Tr. Exp./1 Sc./ 18,30.5,51/24	Wooden construction. Built for Thompson Steamboat Co. to PSN, sponsored, widened and renamed in 1903, rebuilt to ferry 1921 and renamed *City of Bremerton*, scrapped 1939.
Indianapolis	1904	Craig Ship Building Co., Toledo, Ohio	180/32/19	765	Tr. Exp./1 Sc./ 18,30,50/30	Steel construction. Built for Arnold Transportation Co. (Great Lakes) as a coal burner, to PSN 1905 and converted to burn oil, 1933 rebuilt to ferry, 1938 scrapped.

APPENDIX III

SHIPS OF THE GRAND TRUNK PACIFIC RAILWAY (1910-1920) & CANADIAN NATIONAL RAILWAYS (1920-1975)

*REGISTERED DIMENSIONS: Reported in Lloyd's Register of Shipping.

**KEY TO ABBREVIATIONS: Cy., cylinder(s); Tr. Exp., Triple Expansion; Sc., screw(s).

NAME	YEAR BUILT	BUILDER	LENGTH/ BREADTH/ DEPTH*	GROSS TONS	ENGINES/TYPE OR NO. SCREWS/ BORE/STROKE**	NOTES AND DISPOSITION
Prince Albert (ex *Bruno*)	1892	Earle's Co. Ltd., Hull, England	232/30/14	1015	Tr. Exp./1 Sc./ 23.5,35,57/33	Bought from Wilson Line 1910, sold 1929; used in rum running. Rebuilt as tug *J. R. Morgan*, scrapped 1949.
Prince John (ex *Amethyst*)	1910	Scott & Sons, Bowling, England	185/30/11	905	Tr. Exp./1 Sc./ 17,28,45/33	Bought by GTP 1910; sold to Union Steamship Co. 1940 and renamed *Cassiar II*, scrapped 1950-51.
Prince George (I)	1910	Swan, Hunter & Wigham Richardson Ltd., Newcastle, England	307/42/24	3372	Two Tr. Exp./2 Sc./23.5,37,41,41/ 33	Built for Seattle-Victoria-Vancouver-Prince Rupert service; destroyed by fire at Ketchikan 1945, scrapped 1949 at Seattle.
Prince Rupert	1910	Swan, Hunter & Wigham Richardson Ltd., Newcastle, England	307/42/24	3379	Two Tr. Exp./2 Sc./23.5,37,41,41/ 33	Built for Seattle-Victoria-Vancouver-Prince Rupert service; sold 1956 and scrapped in Japan as *Prince Maru*.
Prince Charles (ex *St. Margaret*, ex *Chieftain*)	1907	Ailsa Ship Building Co., Ayr	242/33/11	1344	Tr. Exp./1 Sc./ 21.5,35,58/36	Purchased 1925 from Orkney & Shetland Steam Navig. Co.; 1940 to Union Steamship Co. as *Camosun II*; sold 1945.

NAME	YEAR BUILT	BUILDER	LENGTH/ BREADTH/ DEPTH*	GROSS TONS	ENGINES/TYPE OR NO. SCREWS/ BORE/STROKE**	NOTES AND DISPOSITION
Prince William (ex *Aktion*, ex *M10*)	1915	A. G. Neptun Rostock, Germany	177/24/10	409	Two Tr. Exp./2 Sc./13,21,33/18	Operated briefly on West Coast during early 1930's.
Prince Henry	1930	Cammell Laird & Co. Ltd., Birkenhead, England	366/57/27	6893	Six Steam Turbines/2 Sc.	Withdrawn from West Coast service 1931; chartered as *North Star*; 1939 to RCN as *Prince Henry*; 1947 became transport *Empire Parkeston*, scrapped 1962.
Prince David	1930	Cammell Laird & Co. Ltd., Birkenhead, England	366/57/27	6892	Six Steam Turbines/2 Sc.	Withdrawn from West Coast service in 1931; to RCN 1939; 1947 to Charlton Steam Shipping Co. as *Charlton Monarch*, scrapped 1951.
Prince Robert	1930	Cammell Laird & Co. Ltd., Birkenhead, England	366/57/27	6892	Six Steam Turbines/2 Sc.	To RCN 1939; 1947 to Charlton Shipping Co. as *Charlton Sovereign*; 1952 to Italian reg. as *Lucania*, scrapped 1962.
Prince George (II)	1948	Yarrows Ltd., Esquimalt, B.C.	350/52/18	5812	Two 6 Cylinder Uniflow/2 Sc./ 23/26	Declared surplus 1975 after fire at Vancouver; purchased 1975 by B.C. Government for B.C. Steamships (1975) Ltd.; 1976 sold for restaurant vessel, Nanaimo, B.C.

APPENDIX IV

PRINCIPAL BLACK BALL LINES' FERRIES OPERATED IN COMPETITION WITH THE CPR (1952-1961)

*REGISTERED DIMENSIONS: Reported in Lloyd's Register of Shipping.

**KEY TO ABBREVIATIONS: Cy., cylinder(s); Tr. Exp., Triple Expansion; Sc., screw(s).

NAME	YEAR BUILT	BUILDER	LENGTH/ BREADTH/ DEPTH*	GROSS TONS	ENGINES/TYPE OR NO. SCREWS/ BORE/STROKE**	NOTES AND DISPOSITION
Kahloke (ex *Asbury Park* ex *City of Sacramento*, see below)	rebuilt 1953	converted by Yarrows Ltd., Esquimalt, B.C.	288/58/13	3911	Four Diesel/2 Sc.	Rebuilt to carry 100 automobiles and 1,000 passengers, 19 knots; 1961 to B.C. Ferries, renamed *Langdale Queen* in 1964, in service 1975 but due for retirement 1976.
City of Sacramento (prior to 1953 rebuilding)	1903	William Cramp & Sons, Philadelphia, Pa.	297/50/15	3016	Two Tr. Exp./2 Sc./23,37.5,43, 43/30	Operated by Monticello Steamship Co.; Southern Pacific-Golden Gate Ferries, Ltd. (San Francisco Bay); 1942 to War Shipping Administration; to PSN (Puget Sound); 1952 to Canadian Registry and rebuilt.
Chinook	1947	Todd Shipyards Corp., Seattle, Wash.	318/53/13	4106	Four Diesel/2 Sc.	Built for Seattle-Port Angeles-Victoria service. Transferred to Canadian registry in 1954, rebuilt with bow doors on car deck and renamed *Chinook II* for Horseshoe Bay-Departure Bay service; to B.C. Ferries 1961 and renamed *Sechelt Queen*, in service 1976.

APPENDIX V

REPRESENTATIVE BRITISH COLUMBIA FERRIES' SHIPS

*REGISTERED DIMENSIONS.

NAME	YEAR BUILT	BUILDER	LENGTH/ BREADTH/ DEPTH*	GROSS TONS	ENGINES/NO. OF SCREWS	NOTES
Queen of Sidney (ex *Sidney*)	1960	VMD, Victoria, B.C.	310/74/17	3128	Diesel/2 Sc.	Space for 106 cars when built. In service 1976. *Queen of Tsawwassen* identical.
Queen of Vancouver (ex *City of Vancouver*)	1962	Burrard Drydock, North Vancouver	310/74/17	3341	Diesel/2 Sc.	Space for 106 cars. Rebuilt with ramps (1968) to carry 145 cars.
	rebuilt 1972	Vancouver Shipyards, North Vancouver	394/76/17	4901	Unchanged	Lengthened to carry 192 cars. In service 1976. 6 other ships nearly identical.

— PROVINCIAL ARCHIVES

INDEX

Page references in italics indicate photographs or illustrations. The following index is limited to the narrative and illustrations in *The Pacific Princesses*. Readers are referred to the accompanying appendices for details of the ships, their name changes, and dispositions.